THE

PENNSYLVANIA ASSOCIATORS,

1747–1777

Joseph Seymour

WESTHOLME

Yardley

Frontispiece: *Battle of Princeton* by William Mercer, c. 1787. (*Courtesy of the Philadelphia History Museum at the Atwater Kent, The Historical Society of Pennsylvania Collection*)

First Westholme Paperback 2024

Westholme Publishing, LLC
904 Edgewood Road
Yardley, Pennsylvania 19067
Visit our Web site at www.westholmepublishing.com

ISBN: 978-1-59416-420-0

Also available as an eBook.

Printed in the United States of America.

THE PENNSYLVANIA ASSOCIATORS

To volunteer soldiers, past and present, whose service went unrecorded, and whose deeds went unheralded.

Contents

List of Illustrations

Introduction

A painting hangs in the collection of the Atwater Kent Museum of Philadelphia (*see frontispiece*). Executed by William Mercer (1773-1850) around the year 1787, it depicts the Battle of Princeton, fought January 3, 1777. In the painting, General George Washington, astride a bay charger, salutes an arriving officer with his sword while an artillery crew fires to support the infantry. Orderly platoons of troops advance against a distant enemy while clouds of billowy black smoke obscure a dazzling sunrise. At first glance, the painting appears as little more than a curious work of early American folk art–the figures doll-like and with faces as impassive as angels on a New England headstone. To the casual observer, the painting comes across as the crude product of an uninformed amateur, an allegorical, inaccurate, and unrealistic portrayal of an eighteenth century battle. The opposite characterization is in fact true.

William Mercer studied under the famous Philadelphia artists James and Charles Willson Peale. Both served as officers during the Revolutionary War. Charles Willson Peale, who had recently moved from the family home in Chestertown, Maryland, in 1774, was a captain in a Pennsylvania battalion at the time of the battle. James Peale served his native state as an ensign in Colonel William Smallwood's Maryland Battalion. Both were veterans of the campaign.

The painting, actually a close copy of an original by James Peale, has been proven to be accurate in many details.[1] Mercer's rendering is in fact a multiple portrait. It is first and foremost a compelling image of the battle at its critical juncture, the counterattack following the meeting engagement at the Clark orchard. Second, it is a heroic depiction of General Washington. Third, and perhaps most important, it is an artistic tribute honoring Pennsylvania's contribution to the Revolutionary War.

Of the American units identified, all but one is from Pennsylvania.[2] Conspicuous in their brown coats and round hats, the men of Philadelphia's infantry battalions advance in support of blue-coated state regiments. Troopers of the Light Horse of Philadelphia guard the artillery and Washington. The violence of battle has subsumed the barren winter landscape, and the death of General Hugh Mercer, the artist's father and the centermost figure in the painting, is relegated to insignificance. The viewer's eye is instead compelled to linger on the gun crew in the foreground as it calmly pours deadly fire into the British line (fig 1.). Who are these well-dressed soldiers? How is it that, at this early stage of the war, such disciplined artillerists, who could only have learned their art in the local militia, stand their ground in the face of British regulars?

The figures in Mercer's painting are neither the product of artistic license nor historical myth. They belonged to crack battalions fielded by the city of Philadelphia. Known at various times as the Military Association of Philadelphia, the Philadelphia Association, or simply Associators, this long-neglected organization represented a new constituency in Pennsylvania politics. Organized December 7, 1747, at Philadelphia through a resolution passed on November 21, the Military Association was an all-volunteer enterprise pledged to defend Pennsylvania. Associators served as the de facto defense force for the colony, whose leadership—a loose coalition of pacifists and land barons—foreswore military preparedness on religious and ideological grounds and yet whose political legitimacy hinged, in part, on a chartered mandate to defend the colony.

In the course of their thirty years' service, the Associators achieved increasing levels of importance within Pennsylvania's military infrastructure, reaching their peak through participation in Revolutionary committees. Associators shared the drive to resist and the means to execute that resistance. Associator participation in the Revolutionary committees of 1775 and 1776

Fig. 1. Detail from William Mercer's *Battle of Princeton* showing several Pennsylvania units, including the Philadelphia infantry with their round hats and brown coats to the left of center (and below a depiction of the artist's father General Hugh Mercer mortally wounded beside his injured white charger), troopers of the Light Horse of Philadelphia with their sabers raised at center, and the smartly dressed members of the Philadelphia Artillery in the foreground. (*Courtesy of the Philadelphia History Museum at the Atwater Kent, The Historical Society of Pennsylvania Collection*)

enabled Pennsylvania to be among the first and most successful at bringing troops to the field. By organizing, the Association helped bring the legitimacy of Pennsylvania's leadership into question in the decades preceding the Revolutionary War, so that by 1775, the Association found itself as the only legitimate military leadership in the colony. Its very standing projected the Associators, themselves a loose coalition of artisans and merchants, into unprecedented positions of power and authority.

The history of the Military Association must necessarily focus on the Philadelphia Artillery, to date the only organization known to have existed continuously from the founding of the Association in 1747 to its transition into the militia in 1777. The Philadelphia Artillery therefore serves as the model against which other Associations within and outside of Philadelphia can be measured.

Much like Mercer's *Battle of Princeton*, the story of the Philadelphia Artillery that follows presents a multiple portrait. First and foremost, it depicts a colonial military organization. Like artillery in other localities, the Philadelphia Artillery drew its leadership from artisans such as house carpenters, joiners, and shipwrights, as well as merchants, mariners, and tradesmen who earned their living from the port. Artillerists trained Pennsylvania men in the school of the soldier, or basic military instruction, served as a temporary defense, and provided a pool of skilled technicians from which the army could draw during wartime. Second, the artillerists' story shows how a small group of men used Philadelphia's Military Association to resist what they considered arbitrary rule before and during the American Revolution.

Two typical Associations emerge from the sources. The Philadelphia Association focused primarily on harbor defense and maintaining the train of artillery (consisting of all of the ordnance and attached stores, gun crews, and administrative and support staff) prior to the organization of the city battalions in 1775. Associations organized outside of Philadelphia are harder to reconstruct because of a relative dearth of official or even private correspondence from regions west of the Schuylkill River. Western Associators tended to organize as light infantry or ranger companies, had less money with which to work, and were less successful when it came to pressuring the governor and Pennsylvania Assembly for funding.

The structures of the artillery's sister branches, horse and foot, are harder to re-create because of their relatively unsophisticated organization and use of weapons and equipment that could be privately purchased, or stored in or near the home. Indeed, even contemporary observers disagreed on their level of proficiency or even their existence. Governor John Evans apparently organized a Governor's Guard in 1706 at Philadelphia, with a reputed strength of ten companies, that critics argued numbered no more than "forty bedraggled men."[3] Benjamin Franklin's 1732 report of Proprietor Thomas Penn's visit noted that a mounted escort accompanied him through town, but failed to state whether this cavalcade represented the Governor's Guard, a military unit from outside the colony, or, less likely in a place like Philadelphia, a consortium of affluent martinets. Whoever these armed riders were, they or men like them performed a similar office in 1741.[4]

Associators organized over a dozen regiments in 1747 and 1748, some of which may have survived into the 1750s or 1760s. Lynford Lardner, for one, drilled a troop of light horse in northwestern Philadelphia County in 1756 and again in 1764. Printer William Bradford held commissions in the Association in 1748, 1756, and 1775. Merchant John Nixon did the same in 1756 and again in 1775.

During its final phase, the Military Association mobilized a staggering array of resources, expanding to include battalions of foot, rifle, light infantry, rangers, troops of light horse, and artificers, to name a few. Associators also supplied expertise, material, and services such as publishing, shipbuilding, gun founding, and small-arms manufacture to the Revolutionary cause. Because Pennsylvania lacked a permanent militia law prior to 1777, the official record falls silent regarding many of these organizations. Few muster rolls, notices of fines, regulations, or other records that would enable historians to trace the continuous existence of foot or mounted units have survived.

Artillery, on the other hand, was common in the American colonies, and its presence is easier to trace due to its size and the fortifications it required. Armaments had arrived with the first settlers at Jamestown and at Salem, Massachusetts Bay Colony, in 1629. In port cities and large coastal towns, sizable populations of seafarers and carpenters convened to finance, man, and maintain ordnance that was often publicly owned and carefully inventoried. Trains of artillery, consisting of guns, mortars, and howitzers, fitted on carriages with all the accoutrements and ammunition necessary for service in the field, soon augmented volunteer trainbands that perfected the latest tactics using the most sophisticated weapons available. Artillery units engaged in comprehensive military training. In 1638, Bostonians organized the Ancient and Honourable Artillery Company along the lines of London's Honourable

Artillery Company–a school of the soldier where young volunteers could receive a course of basic military instruction in how to handle cannons, firelocks, swords, pikes, and other weapons before moving on to the complex tasks of gunnery, the science of munitions manufacture, gun founding, and fortification.[5]

Other port cities followed suit. Outside of New England, New Amsterdam on the Hudson River, and the Swedish Fort Christina on the Delaware River, boasted trains of artillery. Guns overlooked the Philadelphia waterfront as early as 1729 (center left in fig. 2).[6] New York and Newport, Rhode Island, fielded trains of artillery as early as the 1740s. Benjamin Franklin borrowed cannon for Philadelphia's train of artillery from Governor George Clinton of New York in 1747. In 1756, approximately sixty members of the Charleston militia organized an artillery company.[7] In spring that year, Rhode Island organized existing elements into the United Company of the Train of Artillery of the Town of Providence. Colonial artillerists turned captured guns on French defenders during the Siege of Louisbourg, on Cape Breton Island, in what is now Nova Scotia, in 1745, and provincial artillery saw limited action during the American campaigns of the Seven Years' War. But despite the known perpetuation of some of these trains, the narrative falls relatively silent prior to the beginning of the Revolutionary War, when Americans fielded well-served, well-maintained trains of artillery that stood toe to toe with their Royal Artillery opposite numbers at Boston, at Trenton, at Princeton, and elsewhere.[8]

Trains of artillery performed a special function above and beyond their specific mission of destroying the enemy with overwhelming firepower, and that was to provide training and support for soldiers of all branches. Artillerists therefore represented a unique culture within the military structure. Membership in the artillery, as in all militia companies, reflected one's social status and occupational background. To the tradesmen and mariners who organized, trained, and equipped the artillery, this membership posed no deep mystery. The records that they left reflect their familiarity with the institution and one another; but the jargon, shorthand, or even outright omissions in those records continue to challenge and frustrate historians tasked with expanding their history.

Fig. 2. "The Prospect of Philadelphia From Wickacove, exactly delineated by G. Wood," 1735. Note the battery of cannon overlooking the waterfront. (*Courtesy Winterthur Museum, bequest of Henry Francis du Pont*)

As publisher of the *Pennsylvania Gazette* before 1748, Franklin reported on the artillery in Philadelphia in 1729, 1731, 1732, 1734, 1740, and 1741.[9] Clearly, there was an active artillery presence in Philadelphia, even in peacetime. Franklin later contradicted himself. In part 3 of his *Autobiography*, written between August 1788 and May 1789, Franklin recalled that, in 1747, "Spain having been several Years at War against Britain, and being at length join'd by France, which brought us into great Danger, and the laboured and long-continued Endeavours of our Governor Thomas to prevail with our Quaker Assembly to pass a Militia Law, and make other Provisions for the Security of the Province having proved abortive, I determined to try what might be done by a voluntary Association of the People."[10] While few Philadelphians did more to publicize the artillery, Franklin's motives may have been less than altruistic and more self-serving. Franklin took credit for the formation of a volunteer defense force out of nothing, although a fort had been standing on Society Hill since at least 1729. Franklin later recounted that the governor accepted the Pennsylvania Assembly's appropriation of "bread, flour, wheat or *other grain*" for New England troops with the understanding that "other grain" referred to grains of gunpowder. Still later, Franklin recalled how his fund-raising efforts brought about the purchase of a cannon, euphemistically categorized as a "fire-engine."[11]

The Associators at times "provided Franklin with political leverage" and "additional organized allies to contest control of the Quaker elite who had for so long dominated the legislative process in the Commonwealth."[12] But to accept the Associators merely as Franklin's private army is to ignore the inconsistencies between Franklin's newspaper accounts and his *Autobiography*. The Associator Artillery served Pennsylvania continuously between 1747 and 1777, and other Associations formed as contingencies required, often as well-trained, well-organized units. But the train of artillery was more than one man's political muscle.

Less self-serving Philadelphians also left written records. One month after Franklin finished part 3 of his *Autobiography*, Benjamin Loxley wrote an account of his own time in the military, documenting four decades of service in Philadelphia, from the early 1740s until 1776.[13]

Alexander Graydon's *Memoirs of a Life, Chiefly Passed in Pennsylvania, Within the Last Sixty Years*, first published in 1811, contributes an additional anecdote of Loxley's leadership of the Associator Artillery during the Paxton Boys' march on Philadelphia in 1764.[14] Noted antiquarian and founder of the Pennsylvania Historical Society, John Fanning Watson, compiled these accounts in the 1830s, which he published in his three-volume chronicle *Annals of Philadelphia and Pennsylvania, In the Olden Time; Being a Collection of Memoirs, Anecdotes, and Incidents of the City and its Inhabitants, and of the Earliest Settlements of the Inland Part of Pennsylvania, From the Days of the Founders*. Franklin, Graydon, and Watson portray the Association as a temporary military solution and ignore the evidence provided by narratives such as Loxley's, which portray a continuously existing organization. These accounts suggest that the Philadelphia Artillery was neither a temporary military solution nor the brainchild of any one individual, but the continuation of a military practice common in the English-speaking world that was overlooked or even shunned by many Pennsylvania leaders.

Subsequent histories perpetuate Watson's portrayal of the Philadelphia Artillery, granting that the Associators were born out of military necessity but arguing that William Penn's "Holy Experiment"–the administration of government according to the values of love, charity, and toleration–fell prey to external enemies rather than to internal pressure.[15] Philadelphians turned to military solutions only under pressure from an immediate hostile threat, then stored their arms and returned to workbench and plow once that threat had been met and overcome. Indeed, by the 1740s, Spanish privateers and *guarda costas*, or coast guard, Spanish ships commissioned to interdict smugglers, preyed on Philadelphia merchantmen on the Delaware River and Bay, while tribes allied to the French threatened the colony from the west. In short, the enemies of peace conspired to rip Pennsylvania asunder.

Identifying the subjects of Mercer's portrait is all well and good, but what of their apparent discipline? Surely such troops were only found in the ranks of professional European armies, the only soldiers capable of standing up in ordered ranks to fight. Indeed, proponents of military professionalism and advocates of military economy alike have long perceived the colonial militias as little more than rustics with pitted muskets in their hands who ran at the first sight of European professionals.[16] Career soldiers have long dismissed the provincials as undisciplined, untrustworthy, and uneconomical, relying instead on regulars and full-time provincial soldiers to fight their campaigns, while their defenders extolled the patriotic virtue of the early American militia. We are left with the impression that the militia was known to have existed, and that its members served with valor during wartime but, as old soldiers will, faded away during peacetime.

Contrary to traditional assumptions, militias were often well organized and well trained, but they also were often misunderstood and misused. Indeed, when in Crown service and gauged against the professional soldiers with whom they served, militia soldiers often failed to meet the expectations of the regular officers who commanded them; while those same officers often failed to understand the beliefs and attitudes that motivated the militia in the first place.[17] Rather than considering the colonial militia a collection of "bedraggled men," we should view them as a pool of trained soldiers constituted to meet a recognized threat, though neither organized nor trained to fight the sort of war anticipated by their regular comrades. More recent histories show that the colonial militia often fielded forces that, if not up to the standards of their regular counterparts, were at the very least adequate for local defense and provided soldiers with the rudimentary training and equipment necessary for expeditions outside of their localities or home colonies.

In the years before the American Revolution, Pennsylvania lacked a militia law, but not an organized defense.[18] The forces the colony managed to muster were often commensurate with the needs and the resources of the province at the time and answered specific military threats that were unique to the region. The Pennsylvania militia was an enduring force throughout the colonial period, was highly competent, and was tasked not with imperial conquest but with defending a critical region of the British Empire.

This assessment of the Pennsylvania militia during the colonial era is indeed accurate, but it points to another problem inherent in accounting for the Military Association. That problem arises from the very use of the word "militia." The Associators were militia in only the most general sense of the word, and Philadelphia's train of artillery was something else entirely. A militia is the result of a legal mandate that requires every franchised adult to render military service. In England and its possessions, the legal mandate for military service has existed for over one thousand years and is codified in hundreds of statutes and upheld as common law. Pennsylvania had no militia law before 1777, but Pennsylvania's leaders, their affirmations to the contrary, were still required to field soldiers in defense of the realm, if not in the maintenance of public order. For Pennsylvania's proprietary government, the Associators provided a convenient alternative to universal service and may have acted on occasion as a de facto militia, but that was only one facet of their service.

Historians have gone far in illuminating our image of the Associators and militia during the Revolutionary War, but they leave the reader to infer that they somehow sprang up almost overnight and had no prewar antecedents. These histories usually begin the story not far from Lexington, Massachusetts, sometime after daybreak on April 19, 1775, and not without justification. The Continental Army was, after all, founded shortly after that, when George Washington assumed command of the forces that surrounded the British Army in Boston, and it is from that point that the lineage of the regular army descends. Indeed, the sheer complexity and sophistication of the Continental Army is reason enough to begin an organizational history with its founding and not with the founding of various state militias.[19] The Associators were likewise so complex, so decentralized, and organized over such a long time span as to impede a comprehensive analysis. Their history must necessarily be anecdotal and impressionistic in many places.

With few exceptions, British and American armies tended to organize around the regiment of foot, or infantry. Throughout the period of this study, regiments usually consisted of a single battalion, the battalion being the maneuver unit and the regiment being the administrative unit. Each battalion consisted of two or more companies. The company tended to consist of one or more platoons, the platoon being the basic maneuver element, and the company being the administrative unit. While companies and platoons occasionally fought as independent units, they tended to fight as part of a battalion or regiment, their soldiers executing fire and maneuver commands from a captain or a lieutenant. Because horse and artillery units fought differently, they also organized a little differently, but under similar echelons of command. Army unit histories, therefore, are frequently limited to commanding officers or to units organized at the battalion level or above. Battalions were commanded by a field-grade officer such as a major (originally, the officer who commanded a majority of companies), or a lieutenant colonel, since that is the level at which units fought, from which reports were submitted, and to which honors were conferred.[20]

Commanders imparted their own personality to the units they led. Because commanders were responsible for recruiting, the soldiers they procured inevitably reflected the social and economic networks within which those commanders functioned.[21] Commanders were also responsible for training their units, and within the constraints of military discipline they imparted their unique style on a unit.[22] Associator units were not only led by men with shared interests but in many cases comprised men pursuing remarkably similar occupations.[23]

Franklin's "voluntary Association of the People" may well have tapped a vein more vital than marginalized tradesmen could have articulated. To understand the level of sentiment, it is necessary to consider the Philadelphia Artillery and the organization to which it belonged as both a colonial and a Revolutionary War unit. As a military is an instrument of policy, the question of how and for whom that military served becomes a prime consideration. Not only did the Military Association serve through four decades, but it served four governments (the Pennsylvania Assembly, the Crown of England, Pennsylvania's Committee of Safety, and the Continental Congress) and fought in two imperial wars, several border wars, and a war of national liberation without changing leadership. The governments it served were sometimes inimical, and the enemies it fought may have been erstwhile comrades. The actions and the attitudes demonstrated by other Associations outside of Philadelphia often echoed or even mimicked those of the Philadelphia Artillery. Given so much variation in policy, ideology, and military function, the motivations that guided the members of the Association must be assessed. Who were the Associators, and what motivated so many of them, after years of service to the Crown, to cast their lot with the Revolution?

Knowing which units William Mercer portrayed in his painting provides insight into only part of the story. The Philadelphia Artillery was part of a military organization with significant political and social overtones that waxed and waned according to the immediacy of the military threat or the intensity of the domestic political battle. It comprised Philadelphians who aspired to inclusion in the Pennsylvania dominated by a landed and mostly pacifist oligarchy. Before the mid-1750s, the province pursued a unique external policy that was dramatically different from the policies pursued by its colonial neighbors. Chapter 1 will discuss how most of Pennsylvania's defense requirements were fulfilled through diplomacy and alliances with powerful groups such as the

Haudenosaunee, or the League of Six Nations. Consisting of the Seneca, Cayuga, Onondaga, Oneida, and Mohawk, the Five Nations (which became the Six Nations after the Tuscaroras joined the League in 1733) were known to outsiders as Iroquois.

Pennsylvania's policy of nonviolent diplomacy with neighboring nations, known as the Long Peace, reflected the religious convictions of the colony's ruling Quaker elite and as such constituted an externalization of the Holy Experiment. It by no means represented the beliefs of the entire population. The Long Peace furthermore conflicted with Pennsylvania's obligation to help defend the British Empire. Chapter 2 will show how two military expeditions brought this conflict to the forefront of Pennsylvania politics and resulted in the formation of Pennsylvania's Military Association. The Military Association served as a political vehicle for defense-minded Philadelphians and for those with an imperial, rather than Quaker, vision.

Chapter 3 will trace the evolution of the Associator's independent political role during the Seven Years' War. Chapter 4 will show how Philadelphia nearly went to war with western frontiersmen during the March of the Paxton Boys in 1764, despite shared views on colonial defense and antipathy for the colonial leadership. Chapter 5 will trace the involvement of the Associators' leadership during the Stamp Act crisis, the Non-Importation resolves, and in early Whig committees. Chapter 6 will detail Associator participation in the Revolutionary War, the creation of Continental units from some of its force structure, and service on the field of battle. An appendix outlines a number of Associator organizations, some of their officers, and the few enlisted Associators that have come to light. Given the size and complexity of the Military Association, it is by no means an exhaustive list, but hopefully it will help readers place the many Associator companies, troops, battalions, and regiments mentioned in the body of the history within their proper context and timeline.

For over two hundred years, the story of the Military Association has been neglected. Because the Associators often stood at odds with the government they served, official documentation of their existence is incomplete or misleading. In its day, the Association was such an accepted part of the fabric of Philadelphia life that it rarely elicited comment, except when some emergency called it into service, or some state occasion merited its loud stamp of approval, or when it served a purpose for some prominent politician. The train of artillery and the forts that it called home were Philadelphia's military show-piece. It is therefore natural that William Mercer gave the artillery such prominence in his painting.

In Pennsylvania, the militia mandate took the form of a voluntary organization, known as the Military Association, with a two-fold political mission: to defend the colony and to exert pressure on the pacifist elements within it. A look at the organization and the composition of the Associators, told from their perspective, will help illustrate Pennsylvania's transformation from a uniquely pacifist enclave to a cockpit in a war for empire, and finally to a hotbed of revolution.

ONE

PENNSYLVANIA
BEFORE THE
MILITARY ASSOCIATION

Nearly one hundred miles from where it emptied into the Atlantic Ocean, the Delaware River cut a mile-wide path, separating low, cretaceous seabed to the east and high, clay banks, gravel, and springy topsoil to the west, land containing, William Penn thought, "in Some places a fast fatt earth."[1] Here he crossed out a word, then continued, "Like to our best Vales in England especially by inland . . . Rivers, God"–here Penn crossed out more words before continuing–"in his wisdom have order it so that the . . . advantages of the country are divided."[2] Penn then scribbled out "the navigable Rivers have by much the poorest Soyle."[3]

In late summer 1683, the thirty-eight-year-old Penn had been in the colony that bore his name, or more properly, that bore his father's name, less than a year. In that time, Pennsylvania had grown from a few paper transactions to a colony that he reckoned numbered about four thousand inhabitants.[4] Numerous plantations already lined the banks of the Delaware and Schuylkill rivers, to say nothing of the creeks and inlets above and below the two great rivers, taking the best land. New arrivals from Ireland, Wales, Germany, and the Netherlands joined the Lenni Lenape Indians, Swedes, and English who were already there, adding active hands and backs to the new venture. Those who had followed the English moreover seemed amenable to his colony. Pennsylvania showed every sign of success, yet Penn fretted over his draft of a lengthy tract addressed to his patrons, the Free Society of Traders.[5]

The letter, which the society published later that year in London, stood as a defense of Penn's faith and a testament to the commercial venture on which he had embarked two years earlier.[6] One of Penn's most ardent detractors, the Baptist Thomas Hicks, had recently alleged that Penn was a Jesuit, a serious offense in Protestant England.[7] Penn could brush off Hicks's claims. He had, after all, weathered jail and the judgment of the English legal system, but his financial backers were another matter altogether. The Free Society of Traders had purchased twenty thousand acres of Pennsylvania real estate, more than any single investor, with the exception of Penn himself.[8] Other English colonies had foundered, or come to the brink of extinction in their first year. For his colony to succeed, Penn had to persuade his investors to sell shares in a commercial venture that faced stiff competition from established colonies in New England, New York, the Jerseys, Maryland, Virginia, the Carolinas, and the Caribbean. Equally pressing for Penn was the future of the recently planned city of Philadelphia.

Religious schisms had long fueled bitter civil war across England, Scotland, and Ireland, most recently in a series of conflicts known as the Wars of the Three Kingdoms. On the continent, the Thirty Years' War killed one in every three people and left much of the land in ruins. Most of London burned in the Great Fire in late summer 1666. In terms of human suffering, the seventeenth century had been the worst in modern memory, a fact with which Penn was well acquainted. As dutiful son of Admiral William Penn, the conqueror of Jamaica, he hand delivered dispatches from the fleet to the restored King Charles II. The last great outbreak of bubonic plague in London disrupted Penn's law studies at King's Inn, in 1665. A year later, as a junior officer in the British Army serving in Ireland, he took an active role in quelling a soldiers' mutiny at Carrickfergus Castle outside Belfast. Penn had experienced human brutality firsthand—under arms in the service of the king and in jail in the service of his faith—but life in Pennsylvania would be different, he hoped.

Prior to Penn's departure in late summer 1682, economist Sir William Petty warned him that

> not only Pennsilvania but all ye habitable Land upon the face of ye Earth will (within ye next 1500 years) bee as fully Peopled as England is now, That is to say, That there will be a head for Four Acres of Land." Petty cautioned the new proprietor to "sett out a peece of Land conteyning 7 times that number in acres, wch Land out to bee chosen for its situation, healthfulness, and fertilitiy, and to bee defenceable by nature as much as may bee.[9]

That October, shortly after he arrived in Pennsylvania, Penn directed agents William Crispin, John Bezar, and Nathaniel Allen to select a site on springy ground with ample drainage that would enable colonists and adventurers—the self-employed entrepreneurs who took huge personal and financial risks in the hopes of huge profits—ready access to the millions of acres deeded to him under his charter.[10] Penn had promised a city lot to any investor who purchased at least five hundred acres, envisioning his colony as an agrarian utopia and Philadelphia as "a greene Countrie Towne, wch will never be burnt, and always wholesome."[11]

The health, safety, and spiritual serenity of its inhabitants lay foremost in the proprietor's thoughts even before he set sail, and they likely pressed on his mind as he labored over the draft of his letter to the Free Society, but circumstances, mainly monetary in nature, forced Penn to locate his city on less than optimal ground. In addition to the Free Society of Traders, over three hundred separate interests had purchased the requisite acreage that entitled them to a city lot.[12] Recent arrivals from England had already staked claims on whatever choice land remained, or land with the best water access. Moreover, Penn honored existing Swedish and Dutch deeds, such as that held by Peter Cock, whose family owned several hundred acres around Shackamaxon. Penn's agents turned to the three Swanson brothers, who lived at Wiccacoe, another Swedish settlement on the Delaware. This parcel being too small, Penn purchased a parallel tract along the Schuylkill from Cock and

Peter Rambo. Within this tract of land, Surveyor General Thomas Holme laid out the new city.

Although the city was larger by far than any other in North America, its size fell far short of Penn's hopes for a worldly paradise, and far short of the promises he had made to his creditors. One visitor described the site of the city "extended on a bay in the river, in the shape of a crescent."[13] Dock Creek, which flowed into the Delaware River near the city center north of Society Hill (named, incidentally, for the Free Society of Traders), formed a small but substantial harbor for oceangoing vessels. At its mouth sat the Blue Anchor Tavern, where tradition has it that Penn made his first landfall. Smaller watercraft transferred cargoes and used Dock Creek and its many tributaries to deliver goods to and from ships anchored in the harbor.[14] As much as it facilitated maritime commerce, Dock Creek posed a considerable barrier to land travel and urban development, as did numerous other creeks and springs around the new city.[15] Few church spires rose to meet arriving ships. Natural features and not man-made structures dominated the cityscape, unless one counted the masts of the hundreds of ships that visited the city annually. In Penn's time, and for several decades after its founding, Philadelphia consisted of a few muddy streets, two- and three-story buildings (some of brick, but most of wood), a warehouse here or there, and a shipyard or two to break up the low silhouette. Far from the "greene Countrie Towne" of his dreams, Philadelphia in its first years grew into a grubby commercial hub, a small town of "four score houses," rising above a sandy bluff surrounded by swamps and virtually landlocked when winter storms stilled river shipping. Mother Nature and human nature appeared to converge to threaten Penn's vision.

In terms of character, Philadelphia was also a small town, the realm of Penn as Lord Proprietor. Born of the idealism of its founder, a mere idea quickly grew into a city as settlers poured off the ships that braved the Delaware's fickle winds and sandy shoals to tap the vast forests, oyster beds, and fisheries they found there, at Penn's pleasure. King Charles II delegated almost unlimited powers to William Penn. Indeed, the charter literally left no stone unturned, granting the proprietor and his assignees the unfettered use of all natural resources, including

> the free and undisturbed use and continuance in, and passage into and out of all and singuler Ports, Harbours, Bays, Waters, Rivers, Isles, and Inletts, belonging unto, or leading to and from the Countrey or Islands aforesaid, And all the Soyle, lands, fields, woods, underwoods, mountaines, hills, fenns, Isles, Lakes, Rivers, waters, Rivuletts, Bays, and Inletts, scituate or being within, or belonging unto the Limitts and Bounds aforesaid, togeather with the fishing of all sortes of fish, whales, Sturgeons, and all Royall and other Fishes, in the Sea, Bayes, Inletts, waters, or Rivers within the premisses, and the Fish therein taken; And also all Veines, Mines, and Quarries as well discovered as not discovered, of Gold, Silver, Gemms, and Pretious Stones, and all other whatsoever, be it Stones, Mettals, or of any other thing or matter whatsoever, found or to bee found within the Countrey, Isles, or Limitts.[16]

The Crown authorized Pennsylvania to levy taxes on goods leaving and entering the colony.[17] Most important, the royal charter empowered Penn to raise an army and make war.[18]

The proprietor served not only as the king's representative in Pennsylvania; he was also its chief magistrate and captain general, or commander in chief, of the militia. Defense remained the proprietor's responsibility, as an assignee from King Charles II, as it had been for all English subjects since 1181. That year, King Henry II issued an edict known as the Assize of Arms that required all freemen to bear arms in defense of the realm. In 1285, King Edward I enacted the Statute of Winchester, which required all enfranchised freemen eligible for military service to help the king maintain law and order in lands between England's cities and towns, where constables and justices of the peace had no jurisdiction.

The statutes of Queen Elizabeth I established standards for compulsory military service, regular training, and standardized equipment.[19] In 1581, William Lambard summarized all of these acts in his comprehensive description of the duties of Crown officers, *Eirenarcha: Or of the Office of the Justices of Peace.* The law prescribed penalties for noncompliance for specific obligations. Any subject (clergymen, judges, attorneys, and other civil officers excepted) sixteen to sixty years old who failed to keep a longbow and arrows in his house could be fined, as could heads of households who failed to keep a bow and two arrows for every male child six to seventeen, or who had "not brought them uppe in Shooting."[20] Freemen were to muster under arms. To ensure that modern weapons were available to all who needed them, regardless of their economic status, justices were to ensure that bowyers sold bows to all ages and made four bow staves of "suitable wood" for every bow stave made of the more costly and less prolific yew.[21] Captains were forbidden to take bribes and could not excuse anyone from service in exchange for a reward. They were likewise required to pay soldiers a decent wage.[22] While the queen expected her subjects to defend the realm with the longbow, separate requirements permitted the ownership and possession of more advanced weapons, such as crossbows and matchlock muskets. The law required towns to store arms and armor, and to maintain arsenals, as well as butts, or archery ranges, on which to train. Trainees had to demonstrate a minimum level of proficiency.[23] Any person owning lands valued at from two hundred to four hundred pounds per year was required to keep horses and armor in readiness.[24]

The introduction of firearms as infantry weapons soon rendered the longbow obsolete and altered the specific requirements, but not the spirit of the law. Subsequent amendments accommodated the new technology and tactics coming into use. By the 1630s, laws required freemen to report to muster with matchlocks or snaphaunces, and a minimum load, which usually consisted of about twelve prepared charges.[25] Foot companies included soldiers wielding pikes and half-pikes to protect musketeers.

Passed in 1676, the Duke of York's Laws effectively governed the English colonies in North America during William Penn's lifetime. These laws established ages of eligibility, mandated warehouses or arsenals in every town, required that small arms be owned and supplied at public expense to those who could not afford them, and set training schedules, officers' commissions, rudimentary articles of war, and a schedule of fines for noncompliance.[26]

Penn had been brought up as an accomplished swordsman and a soldier. He had accompanied his father in the king's service with the Duke of York's fleet, and he had served as a junior officer in Ireland. Penn had also read law at the King's Inn and, as a Friend, often used his extensive knowledge of jurisprudence to defend himself against such high crimes as heresy and treason. Penn should have been well aware of all statutes, Crown edicts, and common laws regarding all aspects of military preparedness that were still on the books at the time of Pennsylvania's founding. While these laws were not always enforced, they were enforceable. Yet Pennsylvania's inhabitants were not required to arm themselves, organize into companies, or train in the martial arts. Instead, Penn urged his lawmakers to conduct their business graciously and lovingly. "Heat," Penn advised the Provincial Council in 1685, "is no where commendable, but in Government dangerous.... If faults are committed, lett them be mended without noise & animosity."27

Fortunately for the proprietor, defense remained a relatively moot point in his lifetime. The Delaware River that brought Pennsylvania's first settlers yielded all "sortes of fish, whales, Sturgeons, and all Royall and other Fishes" to benefit the proprietor and other inhabitants. The river also served as a barrier to any invader contemplating an attack from the sea. The Allegheny Mountains protected Pennsylvania to the north and west, the French did not consider the Ohio River valley strategically important in Penn's lifetime, and Pennsylvania at any rate lay too far south and east to tempt Canadian war parties.28 Any attacker would have a hard time reaching most of Pennsylvania's population. Had those enemies been able to penetrate the forests and Pennsylvania's mountain ranges, they may have met stiff opposition from Philadelphia's native allies, local clans of the Lenni Lenape.

In his letter to the Free Society of Traders, Penn described the Lenni Lenape, also known as the Delaware Indians, in considerable detail.29 As individuals, the natives appeared to Penn to be "tall straight," and well built. "They tread strong & cleaver, & . . . walk with a lofty chin." 30 To the erudite Penn, their language, an Algonquin dialect, seemed "lofty, yet narrow . . . like short hand in writing, one word serves in place of three, & the rest is supplyed by the understanding of the hearer."31

Penn studied their language in order to speak directly to them, admiring such "words of sweetness" as *anna*, meaning mother, *issimus*, brother, and *netap*, friend.[32] When a European came to visit, Penn described how they would offer him a place in their wigwam and the best cut of meat.[33] Penn noted their generosity as well as the importance of ritual gift-giving.[34]

As the royal charter empowered Penn "to reduce the savage Natives by gentle and just manners to the Love of Civil Societie and Christian Religion," Penn noted that "the Poor people are under a dark night," but cited their belief in a supreme being and their understanding of metaphysics with some optimism.[35] The principles of nonviolence, cordiality, and toleration of other cultures served as the foundation for the Society of Friends. Penn envisioned Christianized Indians living alongside Friends and other refugees from war-torn Europe sharing in the colony's rich natural resources and engaging in commerce that would allow it to prosper and grow. Establishing a sound Indian policy was as critical to Penn as establishing a good harbor, laying out a safe and healthful city, and encouraging the sale of land to speculators and all other comers.

To speak of a colony pursuing a foreign policy appears at first paradoxical. Yet from the time of Pennsylvania's founding in 1682, William Penn did just that. Though part of an empire, Pennsylvania could and did function as a sovereign state capable of enacting its own foreign policy.[36]

Even when reacting to Maryland's claims against Pennsylvania's territory, Penn proved both charitable and conciliatory toward his neighbor to the south. In 1683, Charles Calvert, Lord Baltimore, claimed "all ye land from Upland [Chester] to ye falls of Delaware," encompassing not only the new city of Philadelphia but nearly all of the lands that Penn had worked so hard to acquire from the Lenni Lenape.[37] Even worse, Maryland's claim left Pennsylvania "no place where ship or boat could come . . . thereby discouraging hundreds ready to purchase, and to come, and provoking others [that] have purchased and not paid to fling up their deeds," a transgression that Penn allowed would provoke "men to seek ye utmost Revenge, and all [that] will and force could accomplish." [38] Penn's reaction to Baltimore's alleged wrongdoing would not be his last. The Pennsylvania-Maryland border dispute would remain a bone of contention during Penn's lifetime and for many decades thereafter, until finally settled in 1767 by a team of surveyors led by Charles Mason and Jeremiah Dixon, resulting in the establishment of the Mason and Dixon Line. Although visibly provoked by Baltimore's alleged trespass, Penn insisted in his letter, which he wrote to Governor Samuel Jennings of West Jersey and not to Lord Baltimore, "I am of a better spirit and more heavenly policy."[39]

Penn had the luxury of pursuing a nonviolent "foreign policy." He was, after all, a subject of one of the world's ascending powers. The force of English arms had subjugated Pennsylvania's nearest European neighbor, New Amsterdam, as well as its satellites on the Delaware River more than eight years before Penn's arrival. Penn held outright title to one of the former Dutch settlements, New Castle, and the twelve-mile compass arc around it, as well as lands in West Jersey. By grant of charter, King Charles II had conferred some of his royal prerogative upon Penn. By accepting that charter, Penn and his successors tacitly took responsibility for propagating Crown interests within the province, thereby dividing sovereignty between king and assignee.[40]

The province of Pennsylvania therefore functioned as an individual actor within the framework of the English realm, pursuing a pacifist external policy based on the values of the Society of Friends. Pennsylvania was not the only colony to pursue its own external policy. English holdings in North America were so vast as to preclude a single colonial administration. The other English colonies served their own needs first and foremost. Each colonial governor was also the captain general of his colony's militia.[41] Though bound to assist each other in time of war, the colonies pursued independent defensive policies even when pursuing territorial issues in support of the empire.[42]

Virginia battled local tribes intermittently from the time of its founding in 1607. Trainbands, led by experienced soldiers such as Captain John Smith and consisting of local conscripts and volunteers, defended a network of fortified villages around a cluster of houses. This generally met Virginia's defensive needs through the end of the First Powhatan War in 1614.[43]

Virginia enacted a rudimentary militia law on March 5, 1624, during the war with Powhatan's successor, Opechancanough. That same year, King James I dissolved the Virginia Company, established Crown rule, and appointed a royal commission to assess the state of Virginia's military affairs.[44] The commission's members recommended four reforms: the populating of Virginia's hinterland, construction of a palisade across the York Peninsula, the arming and training of eligible settlers under a regular drill schedule; and a permanent provincial garrison, in addition to the enrolled militia. Virginia settlers acted on all but the fourth recommendation, that of organizing a full-time provincial force.[45]

In 1625, a rudimentary military obligation developed, but not as the royal commission envisioned, as once again Virginia's burgesses factored economic growth into their considerations. Male colonists ages seventeen to sixty were required to serve in time of war. Established colonists, known as "old planters," and those with less than one year's residency were exempt from service. Old planters conceivably supported the economy, while newcomers needed time to recuperate their strength from the transatlantic voyage, as well as to establish a livelihood that would enable them to purchase arms, armor, accoutrements, and most important, the free time that military instruction required. Service and training languished during economic booms, as Virginia's labor force turned to other pursuits.

A tentative ceasefire was reached in 1632 with two of the tribes in Opechancanough's confederacy. In 1633, Virginia completed the York Peninsula wall, a palisade that protected the tidewater settlements from landward attacks, using conscripted labor, and the men in each county were organized into a company under the county lieutenant. But county companies were little more than manpower pools from which military commanders created trainbands in time of need.[46]

The Powhatan truce deteriorated in the early 1640s, while Sir William Berkeley was governor. County companies reached a new level of sophistication in 1642, when Berkeley improved command, control, and readiness by directing every commander to provide his company with a drum, flags, headquarters tent, and monthly training.[47]

Berkeley's preparations were hardly premature. The Powhatan Confederation renewed hostilities on April 18, 1644, with coordinated attacks on several Virginia locales. Opechancanough's strategy nearly succeeded in breaking Virginia's defenses, but his small number of warriors made a sustained offensive impossible, forcing a lull in the fighting.[48] When the shock of the initial attacks subsided, Virginia colonists were able to regroup, communicate, and counterattack under Berkeley's leadership.

In 1652, Virginia's legislative assembly, the House of Burgesses, moved with the times to authorize county regiments, consisting of every eligible male. By this time, regiments were better organized. They typically consisted of a headquarters, including a colonel, lieutenant colonel, major, captains, and junior officers; eight to ten companies of foot; and a mounted company.[49] Regimental officers were subject to evaluation and review. Virginia continued to maintain the county regiments into the 1670s, but relied on mounted rangers for local security.

As in Virginia, veteran soldiers such as Myles Standish, Daniel Patrick, and John Underhill trained Plymouth and Massachusetts Bay colonists in the latest tactics almost from the outset, using weapons and other warlike equipment imported from England.[50] The weapons that Massachusetts Governor John Endicott ordered for the defense of Salem in 1629 included one hundred snaphaunces and matchlocks, sixty pikes that were about sixteen feet long, twenty half-pikes, and one hundred swords.[51] In addition to public arms, all adult males, except clergymen and magistrates, were required to own and maintain arms, and keep a basic load of ammunition ready at all times.[52] Those who could not afford arms were to be supplied them at public expense.

Town companies soon replaced trainbands, with the General Court, Massachusetts's legislative body, tightly controlling officers' commissions as well as the development of new communities.[53] Having obtained a permit from the General Court, a group of colonists established a plantation by clearing land. Once that plantation had a large enough population, the General Court granted it the status of a township. Adult males within the company were organized first under noncommissioned officers, and later, as the settlement grew to town status, under the command of a captain.

New Englanders warred against Pequots in 1634, allied with local tribes and fighting in militia companies organized from the several towns of the New England colonies. The General Court organized three county regiments in December 1636. During King Philip's War in 1675 and 1676, town councils conscripted soldiers out of the town companies for service in the county regiments. In Massachusetts, military organizations mirrored civil government and the religious mores and social values of its population. Massachusetts Bay even supplied key personnel to serve in Cromwell's army and navy.[54] By the 1670s, Massachusetts had abandoned conscription in favor of volunteer companies or troops of horse organized out of the general militia. Town companies and county regiments were retained for administration, training, and local defense.

Maryland also placed great weight on military service, initially relying on trainbands, as Virginia, Massachusetts, and Plymouth had done. Like Pennsylvania, and unlike Virginia, Plymouth, and Massachusetts, Maryland organized under a proprietor, Cecil Calvert, Lord Baltimore. As in Massachusetts Bay, military organization conformed to civil government. Every manor, as an assignee of the lord proprietor, was required to organize a trainband of fifteen men and provide it with ammunition. As in Massachusetts, the Maryland Assembly recognized a manor when it registered a minimum number of male residents; in Maryland's case, twenty.[55] In 1638, the assembly passed an Act for Military Discipline.[56] Maryland had by this time organized military districts, known as hundreds. Commanders of each hundred were to see to it that householders mobilized no less than one-third of their eligible manpower during emergencies.[57] The act required every head of household, whether male or female, to maintain a bastard musket of either match or flint ignition, a pair of bandoliers, four pounds of shot, one pound of powder, and a sword.[58] Although still used at sea or in the defense of fortifications, pikes were by this time obsolete as infantry arms. Bastard muskets were an innovation better suited for newer, more fluid infantry tactics. They were shorter, of smaller caliber, and did not require the use of a rest.[59] As elsewhere, commanders were to furnish arms to those who could not afford them. The act required monthly inspections and fines for non-compliance.

In alliance with the Susquehannocks until 1674, Maryland's lord proprietor authorized a fort on the Susquehanna in the 1660s, which the colony equipped with cannon.[60] In 1674, Maryland's proprietary government betrayed the Susquehannock when it made peace with the Senecas and declared war on its former ally. In 1675, the Susquehannock were defeated by the Senecas and massacred in Virginia by John Bacon's rebels. Maryland subsequently dispersed the Susquehannocks and relied on mounted patrols in the last quarter of the seventeenth century. Three other forts were authorized, one in Charles County, one in Anne Arundel County, and one in Baltimore County near the falls of the Patapsco River. A captain, nine soldiers, and four Indians would garrison each of the forts and patrol supply routes and lines of communication.[61]

The conflicts that sent Virginia and Maryland to war raged across Penn's lands. In accordance with its charter and following the latest military doctrine, Pennsylvania should at the very least have organized a defense similar to Maryland's. Paradoxically, Pennsylvanians enjoyed the "Long Peace."[62] Pennsylvania, like New England, had been founded as a religious haven, and like other European colonies, it relied on commerce and territorial expansion to survive. But in contrast with Puritan New England or commercial ventures elsewhere, William Penn envisioned a "greene Countrie Towne," populated by diverse European Christian sects living in harmony with Christianized natives. Pennsylvania's peaceful half-century was the product of unnumbered and largely unnamed translators and negotiators who traveled the forest paths between the great political centers of Pennsylvania at Conestoga and the Five Nations council at Onondaga. Theirs was no easy task. Interpreters and traders learned the language, culture, and customs of the other side. Native and European interpreters alike learned the nuances and minutiae of diplomatic protocol. They risked life and limb on the journey itself. It was the interpreters who kept the dialogue between cultures open.[63]

Pennsylvania consequently took diplomacy quite seriously. The governor and assembly spent a great deal of money on gifts to the friendly tribes. Not surprisingly, these gifts were often military hardware or intelligence. The first treaty, concluded July 15, 1682, between Penn's deputy, William Markham, and several local Lenni Lenape leaders headed by Kowyockhickon and Attoireham, included "Twenty Gunns," two barrels of powder, two hundred bars of lead, and forty pounds of shot.[64] Two weeks later, three Lenni Lenape leaders–Peperappamand, Pyterhay, and Eytepamatpetts–"Indian Sachamakers, who were the first owners of ye Land called Soepassincks, & of ye island of ye same name," and who had not been present at the original transaction, demanded an additional ten firearms, which Lieutenant Governor Markham signed over.[65]

Pennsylvania's policy of relying on its native allies for defense continued unchallenged for decades. As late as 1745, "the Governor . . . asked the Opinion of the Board whether Mr. Conrad Weiser shou'd not be directed to employ some Young Indians as Scouts to procure Intelligence."[66] Other tribes, including refugee Susquehannocks and Conoys from Maryland, and Shawnees from west of the Ohio River, came to settle on vacant land in Pennsylvania.[67] Pennsylvania in turn relied heavily on those tribes for its security. As the son of a prominent naval officer, William Penn had been brought up in the martial arts. So had his agent William Crispin, who purchased the land that became the site of Philadelphia. Pennsylvania's rulers were not opposed to defense. They merely chose to defend their colony by means other than force.

If Pennsylvania's collective pacifism mandated the absence of a militia, Penn's skillful land acquisition enabled it. Unlike Maryland, Pennsylvania was willing to pay for land in a medium of exchange that would benefit the Lenni Lenape militarily and financially. The gifts in turn encouraged them to open the land to European settlement. In addition to weapons, Kowyockhickon and the other assembled headmen received cloth, blankets, wampum, kettles, clothing, tools, tobacco, rum, cider, beer, and three hundred Dutch guilders. Its leaders were even willing to bargain: Peperappamand, Pyterhay, and Eytepamatpetts insisted that the wampum contain equal amounts of white and black beads—black beads being reckoned at twice the worth of white beads.

The Long Peace was more than just a mutual desire for good relations between cultures. Just as it had with the development of the Delaware River plantations and the founding of the city of Philadelphia, an underlying economic agenda guided the proprietor. Moreover, local natives were receptive to the newcomers. The Lenni Lenape had had previous contact with the Swedes and the Dutch, and in some instances had sided with the Susquehannocks during the Beaver Wars, a series of devastating conflicts in the latter half of the seventeenth century initiated by the Five Nations to win control of the fur trade.

The Five Nations, strengthened by the entry of the Tuscaroras after 1733, were no less a threat to the Lenni Lenape, despite decades of war. Only a few years before Penn's arrival, the powerful confederation consolidated its power over the lands west of the Lenni Lenape in the Susquehanna River valley by defeating the Susquehannock nation.

Most important of all to Pennsylvania's unfettered expansion, war and epidemic disease had depopulated the Lenni Lenape and other tribes. Relocation gave the survivors an alternative to war in the face of European and native expansion.[68] Had they been without access to open land, the Lenni Lenape reception of Pennsylvania's emissaries might have been much different. Lenni Lenape compliance, as much as geography, diplomacy, and domestic politics, tended to favor the Quaker policy of nonviolence.

The safety of the colony nonetheless remained the governor's responsibility, one that William Markham, in tolerating and even harboring pirates, famously failed to meet prior to his removal in 1699.[69] Indeed, the freebooters who walked freely on the streets of Philadelphia at the close of the century did so most likely because Pennsylvania lacked the means to apprehend them.[70] After 1701, the governor was often a non-Quaker, which gave him the moral freedom to attend to requirements of defense. William Penn organized the Governor's Guard, most likely a volunteer trainband, in 1706. Other colonial governors used their position as captains general of the militia to wield great power through appropriation bills, contracts, and the patronage of military commissions, but Pennsylvania's constitution prohibited such patronage. If Pennsylvania pursued a foreign policy that was unique in North America, it was the assembly, Pennsylvania's unicameral legislative body, and not the proprietor, who directed those diplomats.

Penn's original frame of government, enacted February 2, 1683, established the Provincial Council and the Pennsylvania Assembly under the proprietor and lieutenant governor. Three men from each county, elected by popular ballot on a rotating basis, made up the council, whose powers included judicial and fiscal review, execution of the colony's laws, appointment of justices of the peace, and maintenance of public order. Each county elected representatives to the assembly. Due in part to Markham's previous mismanagement of colonial affairs, Penn dissolved the council as a branch of government, under the Charter of Privileges, in 1701, although it lived on as an ad hoc advisory group to the governor or lieutenant governor. Justices of the peace were thereafter chosen by direct ballot, and while Penn continued to appoint the Provincial Council on an ad hoc basis, as well as provincial judges and county sheriffs, the abolition of the council left the governor with no power base from which to check the assembly. The assembly's control of Pennsylvania's finances left its governor relatively impotent to use those offices as a form of patronage.[71]

For several decades, beginning with the founding of the colony in 1681, relations between the colonists and the various Indian tribes of the region were notably peaceful. The Long Peace reflected Quaker ideology, and Quaker control of the assembly was fundamental to its perpetuation. But here again the religious factor merely underscored more worldly issues.

The proprietor was the largest landowner in the colony.[72] He was also the colony's titular chief executive. William Penn's son Thomas, who succeeded him as proprietor, frequently made financial decisions that threatened his father's dream of an enlightened social order.[73] The royal charter, for example, granted the collection of certain revenue for the Penn family known as quit rents.[74] When a settler or land agent bought an acre of proprietary land, he paid a flat rate for it, plus a yearly rate known as a quit rent. Land acquisition, a cornerstone of Pennsylvania's foreign policy, thus became a vested interest of the Penns as businessmen, in addition to an important foreign policy matter for the Penns as proprietors. The proprietor's status as the colony's largest landowner also affected commerce. The balance of trade favored Great Britain.[75] Pennsylvania merchants therefore made up the difference in specie, causing currency to flow out of the colony. In 1724, Pennsylvania printed a small issue of inflated paper money to correct this deficit.[76] The currency would help settlers pay their quit rents and would stimulate trade. The land-rich but cash-poor Penns accepted only pounds sterling, or its equivalent in Pennsylvania currency.[77] The Penn family therefore jeopardized Pennsylvania's economic welfare in the pursuit of personal gain.

The Pennsylvania Assembly thereafter battled to limit the Penns' fiscal and financial independence.[78] Quaker leaders in turn fought to ensure that the assembly would remain a Quaker bastion. The three eastern and most heavily Quaker counties of Philadelphia, Bucks, and Chester each held eight of the thirty-six seats in the assembly. The city of Philadelphia elected two seats. The rest of the counties had from one to four representatives apiece.[79] Thus the Quakers (although increasingly in the minority in the coming decades of the eighteenth century) automatically held a majority on any vote, provided they stuck together. The nature of Pennsylvania's factional politics—maintained through ties of marriage, business, and religion—meant that the Quaker representatives would do just that, especially on votes that would threaten their control of the assembly.[80]

Calling themselves the Old Party, the Quakers maintained this status quo for the first fifty years of the colony's existence.[81] Allocation of assembly seats, coupled with the proprietor's inability to grant patronage positions, enabled a convenient perpetuation of pacifist policy until the middle of the eighteenth century. The Pennsylvania Assembly had by that time become a virtual Quaker stronghold.[82]

During the Long Peace, Pennsylvania relied on alliances to meet external security concerns. Prior to 1700, the most important alliance was with local clans of the Lenni Lenape, with councils generally held at Philadelphia. Penn confirmed the first land transaction concluded between William Markham and Lenni Lenape representatives, led by Kowyockhickon and

Attoireham in October 1682, for a tract of land in what is now lower Bucks County:

> Beginning at a certaine white oake in the Land now in the tenure of John Wood, and by him called the Gray Stones over against the ffalls of the Dellaware River, And soe from thence up by the River side to a corner marked Spruce Tree with the letter P at the ffoot of a mountayne, And from the sayd corner marked Spruce Tree along by the Ledge or ffoot of the mountaines west north west to a Corner white oake, marked with the letter P, standing by the Indyan Path that Leads to an Idyan Towne called Playwickey, and near the head of a Creek called Towsissinck, And from thence westward to the Creek called Neshammonys Creek, And along by the said Neshammonyes Creek unto the River Dellaware, alias Makeriskhickon; And soe bounded by the sayd mayne River to the sayd ffirst mentioned white oake in John Wood's Land; And all those Islands called or knowne by the severall names of Mattinicunk Island, Sepassincks Island, and Orecktons Island, lying or being in the sayd River Dellaware.[83]

Local clans soon ceded most of southeastern Pennsylvania to the Penns.[84]

Treaties outside of Pennsylvania also affected the colony's course. In 1701, the Treaty of Montreal effectively ended the last of the Beaver Wars. The focal venue for negotiations thereafter shifted from Philadelphia to the town of Conestoga, where a few Susquehannock refugees, known thereafter as Conestogas, established themselves among Lenni Lenape, Conoys (Potomacs), and Shawnees, under a protectorate of the Five Nations known collectively as the Tree of Peace.[85]

Conestoga lay an easy journey from both Philadelphia and the Five Nations Council at Onondaga. The latter would gradually rise to prominence in Pennsylvania's foreign affairs through the first half of the eighteenth century. The Five Nations Council, also known as the Longhouse of the Five Nations, maintained a somewhat nebulous hegemony that stretched from the Hudson River to the Great Lakes. For the keepers of the Longhouse, suzerainty in Pennsylvania was assured through two treaties. The first, concluded at Albany,

New York, in 1677, loosely bound the English colonies and the Five Nations.[86] The second treaty was negotiated between the Five Nations and the Lenni Lenape (by this time also known as the Delawares) on the one hand, and an envoy representing Maryland and Virginia on the other, to make peace between those colonies and the Susquehannocks and Five Nations.[87] A series of land cessions by the Lenni Lenape further eroded their influence with the proprietors of Pennsylvania.

By the 1730s, the always fragile Long Peace tottered. Nothing did more to tear it apart than the infamous Walking Purchase. In 1686, William Penn negotiated with the Lenni Lenape for a tract of land in eastern Pennsylvania measured by the distance a man could walk in a day and a half. When he died in 1718, Penn left his estate in a shambles and the execution of the terms of the purchase to his son Thomas. Seeking some much-needed revenue, Thomas Penn, in September 1737, directed Pennsylvania agents to clear a path and select three representatives to run rather than walk the course dictated in the terms of the purchase. One of the runners gave up, the other fell into a creek and drowned, but the third, Edward Marshall, completed it, a distance of sixty-five miles, giving the Penns approximately seven hundred fifty thousand acres, or about one thousand two hundred square miles. Lenni Lenape representatives immediately cried foul, claiming that the Pennsylvania agents had violated the spirit of the treaty by running a nonstop course rather than walking a path and stopping regularly to rest and eat. Over time, factions within the Lenni Lenape sought to make up for their lost lands at the hands of the Penns and their lost prestige following their defeat in the Beaver Wars by retreating west to the tribes of the Ohio River valley, and ultimately, forging alliances with the French.[88]

The founders of Pennsylvania were at the center of a vast and shifting Indian polity; the colony eventually came to rival New York as the now-Six Nations' closest ally. After a council was held at Onondaga in summer 1743, two Iroquois headmen, Shickelamy of the Oneida and Canasatego of the Onondaga, invited Pennsylvania diplomat Conrad Weiser to mediate a dispute between Virginia and the Six Nations. The power dynamic between Philadelphia and its native allies, which had originally revolved around local clans in the Delaware Valley, and

later at Conestoga, shifted once again, this time to communities at Shamokin, a town of about eight cabins located in a
large stand of oak near the mouth of the West Branch of the
Susquehanna River. This was home to Lenni Lenape emigrants; their overlords, the Six Nations; and Tutelos, a Siouan-
speaking nation displaced during the Beaver Wars that had
migrated into Pennsylvania as wards of the Six Nations.[89] The
native inhabitants of Shamokin spoke different languages
(Algonquin, Siouan, and Iroquois) and were often rocked by
political discord, but they represented the constituent tribes of
Pennsylvania and lived considerably closer to the Six Nations
council at Onondaga, where they could provide the growing
colony with intelligence from that quarter and serve as a proxy
for its interest.[90] The shift in power and population from
Philadelphia, to Conestoga, to the forks of the Susquehanna
marked a shift in power from the Lenni Lenape–by now more
or less divided between an eastern faction centered on the
headwaters of the Schuylkill River and a western faction centered on the West Branch of the Susquehanna at Allegheny–to
the Six Nations. The shift also represented Pennsylvania's
realignment toward the Six Nations, the region's true power
brokers, and away from the alliance established between local
clans of the Lenni Lenape and William Penn in 1682. The
Lenni Lenape and their confederates would continue to appeal
to the bond of friendship first brokered by Penn. But wars, disease, alcoholism, and relocation had dispersed the Lenni
Lenape clans and left them disunited and subjects of the Six
Nations, who relegated them to the status of "women," unable
to sell the land they lived on.

Likewise, the Shawnee, defeated in the Beaver Wars, had for
many years watched their land in the upper Susquehanna and
upper Delaware valleys fall to European settlement and the
Five Nations, who claimed that land as a spoil of war. In June
1732, a Shawnee delegation voiced its concern to Governor
Patrick Gordon. Some years before,

> the 5 nations Came and Said our Land is goeing to bee
> taken from us, Come brothers assistt us Lett us fall upon and
> fightt with the English, we answered them no, wee Came
> here for peace and have Leave to Setle here, and wee are In

League with them and Canott break itt. About a year after they, ye 5 nations, Told the Delawares and us, Since you have nott hearkened to us nor Regarded whatt we have said, now wee will [put] pettycoatts on you, and Look upon you as women for the future, and nott as men. Therefore, you Shawanese Look back toward the Ohioh, The place from whence you Came, and Return thitherward, for now wee Shall Take pitty on the English and Lett them have all this Land.[91]

The Shawnee retreated west into land north of the Ohio River. They were joined by some elements of dispossessed Lenni Lenape.[92]

The Treaty of Lancaster, concluded in June 1744 between representatives of the Six Nations and Maryland, Virginia, and Pennsylvania, ceded almost five hundred thousand acres of land to Pennsylvania that had previously been controlled by the Lenni Lenape, this time without the acquiescence of all interested parties, most importantly, the Lenni Lenape themselves.[93] Henceforth, the Six Nations, whose lands lay beyond Pennsylvania's territorial desires, would help oust the Lenni Lenape from Pennsylvania in return for a free hand in the region of the upper Susquehanna, leading some Lenni Lenape to seek an independent course in the coming decades.[94]

Pennsylvania negotiators formed new treaties with the Shawnee and the Lenni Lenape because of the Penn family's vested interest in land acquisition, imperial concerns over the possibility of French incursions into the Ohio River valley, and Pennsylvania traders' concerns over competition from Virginia. The Six Nations became an increasingly vocal opponent of this alliance throughout the late 1740s.[95] The Albany Congress of 1754 aimed to unify colonial Indian policy and coordinate defense. The congress failed in part because the colonies, "especially Pennsylvania," proved "unwilling to surrender their ties to the [western] tribes."[96] French expansion into the Ohio and pressure from the Six Nations would soon end the Long Peace. Internal pressures likewise threatened it.

At the same time, many settlers on the Pennsylvania frontier were not pacifists. Also, new arrivals from Europe, redeemed servants, and an increasingly affluent group of allied tradesmen and merchants in Philadelphia imposed change on Pennsylvania's collective core values. Those who traveled in the wake of the first religious refugees and those who lacked the status or the wherewithal of the mercantile sort looked to the river for their living, or looked inward to the lands beyond the Schuylkill. Pennsylvania became a house divided in ambition and in character, with one vision tied to new land and new wealth, and another tied by commerce to the old.

Protestant frontier inhabitants caused a change in Pennsylvania's domestic affairs, a change that in turn modified Pennsylvania's external politics. The arrival of large numbers of non-Quakers during the first quarter of the eighteenth century disrupted the political balance, concurrently pushing the frontier west and north. Increased contact between cultures modified relations between Pennsylvania's diverse ethnic groups, sometimes irrevocably. The changing power dynamic wrought by these newcomers led to calls by factions such as that led by Benjamin Franklin for an increasingly aggressive territorial policy. Others, whether motivated by patriotism, occupational affinity, or mere necessity, formed informal defensive associations.

The immigrants who came to Pennsylvania before the 1740s followed English farming practices, which emphasized small, easily managed fields centered on a town or village.[97] Early German settlements profited from this pattern of settlement. In 1684, Willem Streypers, one of the original purchasers of the tract about six miles from Philadelphia that became known as Germantown, kept "a shop of many kinds of goods, and edibles. Sometimes I ride out with merchandise, and sometimes bring something back, mostly from the Indians, and deal with them in many things."[98] Dense forests, proprietary proscription of farms larger than five hundred acres, and organized townships kept farms small and the frontier east of the Susquehanna River, where industry, such as weaving in Germantown, vied with homesteading as an occupational pursuit.[99] For many years, numbers of indentured servants had come into the colony to serve as a labor base. Pennsylvania afforded poor emigrants a greater opportunity to work off their passage than New England, with its poor soil and established population, or the South, with its slave economy.

After a period of service, usually seven years, servants gained their freedom and joined an increasingly non-Quaker, nonpacifist constituency. Wars in Europe, particularly in the Rhineland Palatinate, stimulated further immigration from German-speaking countries, though many of those who now came were from more established Protestant sects. Their opposition was to a particular war, not to war in general. In contrast to the relatively unskilled population of indentured servants, these so-called "Palatine boors" constituted a skilled population of farmers (hence the term *boor,* an archaic term for a farmer or peasant) who brought superior land-use and land-clearance techniques to Pennsylvania.[100] Farms began to grow in size and productivity.

Beginning about 1740, Scots-Irish migrants settled in the limestone valley regions beyond the lands contained within the first purchases, traveling over steep stony ridges covered by mature stands of "white Pine, very lofty and so close, that the Sun could hardly shine through," chestnut, white oak, and huckleberry, crossing the wide but shallow Susquehanna River, and on into the Cumberland Valley, Sherman's Valley, and the Juniata, an area known as the Conolloway tracts.[101] In the wake of the Jacobite Rebellion of 1745, and also as a result of the systematic eviction of tenant farmers and tradesmen from the Scottish Highlands known as the Highland Clearances then coming into force, large numbers of their compatriots followed.[102] There, one or more cooperating households could, in a matter of days, erect a cabin for themselves and a shed for their livestock. Using hatchets or felling axes, homesteaders hacked bark a hand's breadth wide from nearby trees, a practice known as girdling, which soon killed the tree without felling it. Without leaves, sunlight could reach the forest floor, where the squatters planted corn, while their livestock could feed on grasses or shoots that grew in the marginal land. In the fall, the corn yielded a crop that could sustain a family through its first winter.

Together with the Palatine Germans and indentured servants, the Scots-Irish helped to accelerate the westward push of the Pennsylvania frontier. These squatters occupied land and established their own councils to regulate disputes, creating a divide between the Quaker-dominated east and the frontier settlements.[103]

Much like the Scots-Irish themselves, the lands beyond Penn's original purchase were products of dispute. Land deals conducted within Penn's lifetime were executed under terms that were amenable to all parties. When one party disputed the terms of the agreement, or the quantity of goods exchanged, as Peperappamand, Pyterhay, and Eytepamatpetts had done at one of the very first purchases, Pennsylvania officials strove to make amends. When it became apparent to the Philadelphia government that alcohol had deleterious effects on tribal negotiators, Governor Patrick Gordon strove to ban its sale. When that proved problematic for a number of reasons, Gordon at least worked to limit the supply to a few gallons at a time, and its dispersal to the end of the negotiating process.

In May 1750, a posse led by Provincial Secretary Richard Peters, Lancaster County Sheriff James Galbraith, explorer, land speculator, and Indian agent George Croghan, and noted frontier diplomat Conrad Weiser forcibly removed the squatters from Sherman's Valley and the Conolloway tracts, in some cases burning their houses, under orders from Governor Andrew Hamilton and with the approbation of the Six Nations, upon whom Pennsylvania relied for much of its frontier security.[104] Just as their experience in Scotland and Ireland had charted their journey across the Atlantic Ocean and into the Pennsylvania forest, this latest clearance and eviction, this time at the hands of elected officials of the proprietary government, helped to shape the course the western counties would take.

Pennsylvania established five counties from 1729 to 1752. Lancaster County, bordering Philadelphia and Chester counties to the east and the Susquehanna River to the west, was incorporated in 1729. York County was incorporated in 1749, and Cumberland County in 1750, both on the western bank of the Susquehanna. Berks and Northampton counties were incorporated in 1752, hemming in Lancaster County on the north and west, and in turn cutting off the old political center of Conestoga from the frontier. Pennsylvania's population, which had stood at about twenty thousand in 1701, grew to almost a quarter of a million by the middle of the century.[105]

The new arrivals and the commerce they brought turned Philadelphia into a crowded city. The banks of Dock Creek teemed with workshops, lumber yards, and the homes of those who could not afford the high rents of High and Walnut streets. Comprising the area between Walnut Street to the north and South Street at the city's edge, Dock Ward stretched from the marshy mouth of the creek from which it took its name and a good deal of its character to the vacant lots at the western edge of the city around Fourth or Fifth Street. By 1775, crowded Dock Ward was the second-most-populous neighborhood in the city, behind only Mulberry Ward, home to a similar populace.[106]

The emigrants soon made Dock Ward one of the prime business districts of Philadelphia, a place where mechanics were able to accumulate some wealth.[107] In a city where trades tended to cluster geographically, Dock Ward became known for its concentration of merchants, shipwrights, carpenters, and practitioners of related trades.[108] Immigrants from Scotland, Ireland, Germany, and the Low Countries needed a place to live. Oceangoing vessels had to be built and repaired. Population growth translated into increased business for those who followed a trade in carpentry and shipbuilding.

Artisans represented a large and affluent segment of the city's population. Light winds during the winter and summer months made maritime trade a seasonal profession. Sailmakers, merchants, mariners, and shipwrights mingled with carpenters and joiners at work during different seasons of the year.[109] By 1750, one in every ten Philadelphians was engaged in the house-building trade, and a little over 2 percent were either shipwrights or carpenters.[110] Throughout the 1740s and 1750s, in a city obsessed with status, those who worked in trades held relatively low social rank.[111]

The wars that caused so much displacement in the American wilderness and in Europe had another effect on Philadelphia's waterfront: privateering grew dramatically. From 1739 to 1748, 4,646 privateers–civilians licensed to attack enemy shipping in wartime–sailed out of Philadelphia in forty-seven ships as Great Britain pursued a maritime offensive against Spain during the War of Jenkins' Ear.[112] Those who worked in Philadelphia's maritime trades had as much of a vested interest in maintaining the Delaware River port as the German and Scots-Irish homesteaders had in maintaining their farms and fields.

Sometime before March 1729, a private consortium built a thirteen-gun battery on Society Hill between Pine and South streets in the heart of Dock Ward (fig. 3).[113] The fort stood for several years until it was replaced by an improved fortification nearby.[114] The Society Hill fort defended the Philadelphia waterfront. But the fort's existence, coupled with the presence of so many privateers, belied the fact that there was little or no enemy threat to Philadelphia. The threat of a seaborne invasion was so remote that the Penns recalled Governor John Evans in 1704, in part for fabricating the rumor that a French fleet had put into Delaware Bay.[115]

William Penn founded Philadelphia on a spot nearly one hundred miles up the Delaware River yet far enough away from sea lanes to avoid the depredations of pirates and enemy warships. From the time of the founding of Pennsylvania in 1682 until the War of Jenkins' Ear in the 1740s, a war that effectively and irrevocably forced the colony's leadership to acknowledge its role in the British Empire, Pennsylvania pursued an independent course according to the interests of the established ruling elite. By 1748, the changing relationship between the proprietary interests championed by the Quakers and their allies, and non-Quaker aspirations represented by tradesmen and their allies and supported by mainstream Protestant ideology, threatened to change the face of Penn's "greene Countrie Towne."

For most of its early history, Pennsylvania had little or no need for a colonial militia. Enabled by a substantial Quaker majority, the Pennsylvania Assembly in Philadelphia pursued an expansionist foreign policy based on tribal diplomacy and a

Fig. 3, opposite. "A survey of the city of Philadelphia and its environs shewing the several works constructed by His Majesty's troops, under the command of Sir William Howe, since their possession of that city 26th. September 1777, comprehending likewise the attacks against Fort Mifflin on Mud Island, and until its reduction, 16th November 1777. Surveyed & drawn by P. Nicole." For several decades, the City of Philadelphia extended a few blocks west of the Delaware River, with open space to the west, north, and south. The narrow waterway between the mouth of Dock Creek and Windmill Island at right formed a harbor for oceangoing ships and local watercraft. (*Library of Congress*)

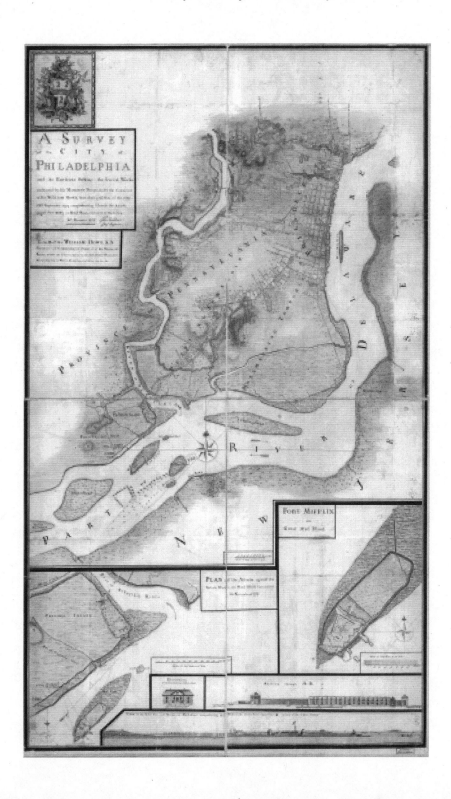

complex network of alliances known at the time as the Long
Peace.[116] Natural barriers deterred external enemies and facilitated trade. Robust relations, first with the Lenape and later
with the Six Nations, facilitated rapid territorial growth without recourse to war.

But during the early eighteenth century, Pennsylvania's
defensive needs changed. Native and European population
shifts realigned the frontier and threatened the Long Peace. By
the 1740s, Pennsylvania's longstanding pacifist policy teetered
on the brink of extinction. Westward expansion nevertheless
remained the principal aim of Penn and his heirs, for only
through the sale of proprietary lands could they hope to square
their family's debts and ensure the survival of his "Holy
Experiment": a colony established under the tenets of a faith
that eschewed worldly goods and shunned military service.

The sale of proprietary lands remained the primary interest
of his heirs throughout the colonial era. Ironically, the first formal challenge to Quaker policy manifested itself not on the
frontier, but on the banks of the Delaware River, where a rising
constituency of affluent tradesmen and merchants made their
home. Protected by geography and allied tribes, Pennsylvania
followed a pacifist policy. The Society Hill fort nonetheless
fired no fewer than eight official salutes between 1729 and
1741. On March 3, 1729, the *Pennsylvania Gazette* recorded the
city's observance of St. David's Day. Cannon fired while
Philadelphians drank toasts to King George II and the Church
of England. Two years later, the newspaper recorded a similar
observance of St. David's Day.[117] On August 12, 1732, proprietor John Penn arrived in Philadelphia.[118] Several hundred riders escorted him through town. The parade stopped at
Lieutenant Governor Patrick Gordon's house, where Penn was
saluted by the Society Hill fort. Two years later, Philadelphians
again celebrated St. David's Day in style.[119] This time, the proprietor, the governor, and several dignitaries attended a Welsh-
language sermon at Christ Church. Gordon then entertained
them at his house, where the guests drank a series of toasts to
the accompaniment of cannon on Society Hill. Later that year,
a large mounted contingent escorted John Penn from New
Castle, in the Three Lower Counties (Delaware), to
Philadelphia.[120] Again, artillerists on Society Hill fired a

salute.[121] On April 17, 1740, the *Pennsylvania Gazette* recorded a similar demonstration. In July, a cannonade from the hill welcomed Governor William Gooch of Virginia.[122] In 1741, a military contingent paraded through town to the continuous firing of the guns of the Society Hill fort.[123] Philadelphia may have been a Quaker stronghold, but some in the city were willing to salute the king, the Anglican Church, and visiting dignitaries, even the proprietors, who had by this time abandoned the faith of their father, with military pomp.

The maintenance of a fort on Society Hill, on the Philadelphia waterfront one hundred miles from the Delaware Capes, represented Pennsylvania's shifting demographics. Coupled with population shifts in the west, it signaled at least some Pennsylvanians' disaffection with the political order. As the century wore on, war and the threat of war crept slowly closer to the province as a pacifist faction continued to rule over an increasingly nonpacifist and underrepresented population that included fragmented groups of Shawnee, Lenni Lenape, Conestogas, indentured servants from Europe known as redemptioners, homesteaders, artisans, and mariners. From 1745 to 1754, as the Long Peace unraveled, Pennsylvania's landed proprietor battled a Quaker assembly for control of a population that was neither landed nor Quaker.

TWO

FOUNDING THE ASSOCIATION, 1740–1748

If the Society Hill fort was a sign of Pennsylvania's shifting demographics, two military campaigns in the 1740s demonstrated the need for a trained military cadre in Philadelphia. The first, an expedition in 1740 to Cartagena, Colombia, on the Spanish Main, involved hundreds of Pennsylvanians. The second, to New York in 1746, as part of a projected invasion of Canada, enlisted fewer numbers but involved several influential men who publicized the disastrous effects of sending untrained, ill-equipped recruits into battle. The two expeditions preceded the founding of Philadelphia's Military Association on November 21, 1747. While serving as Associators, hundreds of Philadelphians met on common ground and developed a collective identity.

Benjamin Loxley was one of those men. He was born in Wakefield, Yorkshire, England, on December 20, 1720. He sailed to Philadelphia in 1734, where he lived at his uncle's farm in nearby Darby Township before taking up a trade.[1] In 1737, he apprenticed to Joseph Watkins to learn carpentry and joinery, worked hard, and prospered early. Ambitious, educated, and affluent, with family waiting for him upon his arrival and the prospect of taking up a lucrative trade, he stood apart from the urban poor who made up a majority of Philadelphia's population at this time.[2] Nevertheless, his life should have passed without comment, but for one exception. In 1740, he became interested in cannons and enlisted as one of the levies being raised for an expedition against Cartagena. That decision started his military career: over the next thirty-seven years, Loxley's life as a soldier would come to define him as much as his trade of carpentry.

The Pennsylvania that young Benjamin found was more suited to an energetic apprentice than a prospective soldier. Penn's concessions all but invested the Society of Friends as the established church of Pennsylvania. Careful districting of Pennsylvania's counties in the years before Loxley's arrival guaranteed that wealthy Quakers would enjoy a majority in the assembly. On the frontier, the Long Peace ensured nonviolent territorial expansion, which in turn increased the wealth of the Penn family by opening new land to settlement. Military opportunity was mostly limited to nongovernmental concerns such as privateering, the somewhat obscure Governor's Guard, and the earthen fortification that stood near Society Hill, not far from the neighborhood where Loxley would make his home.

The arrival of thousands of non-Quakers like Benjamin Loxley in Philadelphia throughout the early eighteenth century nevertheless signaled change. Privateering provided a brisk business for hundreds of Philadelphia mariners and fortune seekers. Artillerists at the Society Hill fort fired regular salutes to the king, proprietor, and governor. Philadelphians were conspicuous in military-style parades and ceremonies. Benjamin Franklin, himself a relative newcomer to Philadelphia, having run away from his brother's printing office in Boston in 1723, publicized these demonstrations in the *Pennsylvania Gazette* from 1729.

This new breed of Pennsylvanian, typified in part by men like Franklin and Loxley, strove for a greater say in Pennsylvania's political affairs throughout the first half of the eighteenth century, but lacked the organization to obtain it.[3] In other colonies, the body politic often consisted of the same individuals who made up the militia.[4] Upon discharge from service following a major war, provincial veterans could look to their old commanders or the local community for patronage or other support.[5] The commander of the local militia company or regiment was likewise often an important official who could turn to his former soldiers as available labor, or a source of votes.

The creation of an organized militia in Pennsylvania should have given the governor extra leverage when dealing with the assembly, Pennsylvania's only legislative body. But in 1740, Pennsylvania had no law requiring military service. Many patronage positions, such as justice of the peace, coroner, or sheriff, were directly elected. The governor and his assignees therefore had little to say regarding their assumption of power. The Pennsylvania Assembly, made up mostly of Quakers, in turn held enormous power in relation to the governor. It chose a defense policy based on diplomacy and alliances with powerful tribes such as the Six Nations, and nonintervention in the border conflicts and imperial disputes of its colonial neighbors. As events would soon show, Pennsylvania's lack of a militia proved disastrous for many of the colony's residents as they answered the call to arms during the War of Austrian Succession.

On April 14, 1740, Governor George Thomas announced that Great Britain had formally declared war on Spain, turning the War of Jenkins' Ear from a series of naval skirmishes into a full-blown imperial conflict. News of the declaration found Pennsylvanians eager to fight. On April 17, the *Pennsylvania Gazette* reported that "the people express'd their Joy in loud Huzzas," as ships in the harbor fired their guns and the cannon at the Society Hill fort boomed in rapid celebration.[6] Liquor flowed freely throughout the day as revelers toasted King George II and the military leaders of the expedition. In the evening, flames from a bonfire on Society Hill rose into the April sky.[7] In May, the Crown asked for three thousand five hundred troops from eleven colonies for an expedition against Cartagena.[8]

Defended by extensive fortifications, Cartagena represented an important base for the paramilitary *guarda costas* that prowled North American waters in search of English and American skippers illegally involved in trade with Spain's New World colonies.[9] Moreover, Cartagena served as a center for the trade fairs conducted annually between Spanish and colonial merchants.[10] Admiral Edward Vernon's raid there on

March 24, 1740, spurred widespread speculation in Great Britain and America that Cartagena waited like a plum ripe for picking.

Lieutenant Governor William Gooch of Virginia would command the levies, originally designated as Major General Alexander Spotswood's 43rd Regiment of Foot, collectively as His Majesty's American Regiment of Foot, and later Gooch's Regiment, or simply as the American Regiment.[11] Because of Pennsylvania's relatively large population, the Crown determined its quota at four hundred men, consisting of natural-born subjects and longtime residents "inur'd to the Climate," organized into eight companies of fifty men each.[12] Pennsylvania exceeded this mark and raised an additional three hundred recruits. With the exception of the costs of food and transport, the Crown would fund the expedition. Governor Thomas therefore expected little opposition on the part of the ruling Quaker factions and their political allies, who would make no warlike allocations.

Thomas appointed the company commanders.[13] The eight captains were William Thinn (or Thynne), Thomas Freame, Robert Bishop, Thomas Clark, Robert Farmar, Thomas Lawrie, William McNight, and Archibald Gordon.[14] Of the eight, Clark, a Royal Navy veteran; Thinn, who had held a commission with the Royal Welch Fusiliers; and possibly Gordon, had known military experience.

By early August, the companies were organized but still untrained. In any other colony, they may have come with some modicum of military instruction behind them. But this was Pennsylvania, where no machinery existed to educate young men in military exercises, no quarterly or even annual musters summoned the yeomanry to be counted, and no training assemblies instructed them in the basics of how to clean, load, shoulder, present, and fire their arms, much less to face about, march from column into line, and touch hands to an officer when he walked by. To bridge the deficiency, Colonel William Blakeney of the British Army arrived with several lieutenants, also regulars, to assist in turning civilians into soldiers.[15] Blakeney, a military specialist whose forte was drill, had been appointed adjutant general of the levies. He soon set to work writing a manual of arms for the new recruits.[16]

Understanding that most of the recruits were untrained, Blakeney designed his new manual to be easier to learn. The final product, Blakeney's *Exercise*, a drill manual widely published in Great Britain and the American colonies, simplified Humphrey Bland's *Treatise of Military Discipline*, the British Army tactical manual of the period.[17]

Loxley recalled that he received his training in 1742.[18] Even as an old man writing long after the Revolutionary War had ended, Loxley's pride in his status as a drill master shone through when he remembered how, "at our Fort all through the Spanish War until 1747 I taught the exercise to a great many in this province."[19] In military service, hundreds of young men like Benjamin Loxley grew as a breed apart; technically adept and militarily authoritative. As a soldier, he was able to achieve a rank and status he could never hope to attain as a journeyman carpenter. Over time, Loxley's military identity so permeated his being that he claimed descent "from an old and warlike lineage," no doubt a double reference to his own military prowess and to the legendary Robert Loxley, alias Robin Hood, held by some to have lived in Benjamin Loxley's hometown of Wakefield.[20]

In contrast, the American Regiment's rank and file came from "the lower sort." Uniforms, consisting of red regimental coats trimmed with green, red waistcoats, brown fustian breeches, grey ribbed stockings and "English shoes" were provided as an inducement to enlist, as were linen waistcoats and trousers for the tropical climate of South America.[21] The uniform provision suggests that many of the recruits were just the sort of young men who typically filled the ranks of an eighteenth century army.[22] Desertion notices appearing in the *Pennsylvania Gazette*, which describe the clothes worn by deserters and their trades (or lack thereof), bear witness to the low social status of many.[23] In other colonies, such as Massachusetts, organized militias guaranteed a degree of participation from all levels of society.[24] Pennsylvania, on the other hand, sent runaway apprentices, the unemployed, or the impoverished to sweat in the trenches before Cartagena or worse, to rot in the holds of Royal Navy transports as reserves.

Colonial militia laws generally required members to arm and equip themselves. Because Pennsylvania had no such law, the Crown also supplied weapons to the recruits. The muskets were the same basic type as those used by regulars, but provincial levies were often issued secondhand and obsolete muskets, deemed unfit for service by the royal armorers at the Tower of London, and auctioned by lot, which were then packed in straw and exported to the colonies by the thousands.[25] A notice about a deserter in the *Pennsylvania Gazette* describes one of these muskets. It bore an inscribed crown over "GR" (Georgius Rex) on the lock, or firing mechanism, indicating government issue.[26]

The Pennsylvania Assembly forced the recruits to spend their own money as well. Because there were no barracks in Philadelphia, the companies were quartered in outlying villages to take the burden off the city.[27] Innkeepers charged the recruits the usurious rate of twelve pence per day for lodging. Such gouging quickly ate up the men's pay, underscoring the motives that put them in their red coats in the first place.[28] Had this been England and not Pennsylvania, and they king's troops and not provincials, the law would have prevented innkeepers from charging more than four pence per day.[29] No such abuse would have occurred if Pennsylvania had possessed a militia law.

Haste and poor planning hampered the entire training process. On September 8, 1740, the *Pennsylvania Gazette* reported that "the seven Companies in this Province, were all embark'd: and 'tis said the Transports will sail down in a few Days. The Companies are all full, and the men chearful and in good Heart. They were reviewed by his Honour the Governor before they went on board, and performed their Exercise to Admiration. The Company rais'd in the Lower Counties will embark at New Castle."[30] The *Pennsylvania Gazette*'s report was overly optimistic, and the training hollow. The levies sailed to the West Indies with less than a month's training. Blakeney's *Exercise* consisted of a little over twenty pages of written instruction in the school of the soldier. The seven Pennsylvania companies, in their new red coats and service muskets, could make a fine show of the manual of arms, but that was about all they could do. With no militia law to mandate proper training, no higher headquarters to support them, and little or no knowledge of regimental staff work, camp discipline, or tactics, the recruits were little better than uniformed laborers.

The expedition itself was a disaster. More than eight hundred men from Pennsylvania served on it from 1740 to 1742.[31] Some of those who survived the heat and disease of the Caribbean were later pressed for service as sailors aboard British men-of-war. Only about six hundred from the entire expedition of three thousand five hundred survived.[32] A few eventually made it home to Pennsylvania.[33] The American Regiment remained in the West Indies until 1744, providing the British Army and the Royal Navy with a cheap source of manpower.[34]

Veterans of the expedition who found their way back to Pennsylvania carried an uneasy memory with them. As stories of disease, malnutrition, and mistreatment of provincial soldiers circulated among the taverns and tap houses of eastern Pennsylvania, the enthusiasm of the expedition's early days died away. Cartagena lingered as a persistent memory, an event that set its veterans apart.[35] A notice in the *Pennsylvania Gazette* reporting a deserter from the New York expedition noted that the man in question had "enlisted before upon the Cartagena Expedition, and deserted."[36] As an old man writing of his service to the province, Benjamin Loxley recalled Cartagena as a seminal event in his early life, despite the fact that he never left Philadelphia.[37] Cartagena cast a dark shadow across the middle colonies. When the Provincial Council called for volunteers for an invasion of Canada in 1746, the *Pennsylvania Gazette* announced no fanfare, no "joy in loud huzzas," no bonfire, and no cannon booming from Society Hill.

The Cartagena expedition showed that Pennsylvania needed some sort of military institution, despite its independent external policy. Armed expeditions outside the colony were inevitable. Before long, the Crown again asked Pennsylvania to provide troops for an expedition against one of its enemies. This time, the target was New France.

In a letter dated April 9, 1746, Prime Minister Thomas Pelham Holles, Duke of Newcastle, announced plans for a two-pronged assault on Canada.[38] The plan was actually the brainchild of the Massachusetts governor, Sir William Shirley, who had the year before orchestrated the capture of the French fortress Louisbourg on Cape Breton Island, in the Gulf of Saint Lawrence.[39] Shirley planned the invasion as a coordinated effort on the part of New England and the middle colonies. New England troops were to assemble at Louisbourg. Those of New York, New Jersey, Pennsylvania, the Three Lower Counties (Delaware), Maryland, and Virginia would advance up the Champlain Valley from Albany. William Gooch, now a brigadier general, commanded the southern force. This expedition did not benefit Pennsylvania strategically or territorially. Indeed, there was some risk that it could incur the wrath of the Six Nations, whose leadership, with the exception of the Mohawk, had pledged neutrality under the Great Peace signed at Montreal in 1701.

Gooch's plan called for four companies of one hundred men each to come from Pennsylvania, raised and led by Captains William Trent, Samuel Perry, John Shannon, and John Diemer.[40] Just before the expeditionary force left Philadelphia, Benjamin Franklin secured an ensign's commission for his teenage son, William. The boy would provide his printer father with information to publicize Pennsylvania's successes, or military shortcomings, in a way that levies could not.

For a time, Pennsylvania's official reports indicated success. As with the Cartagena expedition, the Crown offered inducements to those who enlisted. In his letter to the governor of Pennsylvania dated April 9, 1746, Holles wrote, "As to the Article of Arms and Cloathing for the Men to be raised, His Majesty has commanded me to recommend it to You and the other Governors to take care that the Soldiers may be provided with them; And His Majesty has authorized and empowered Lieutenant General [Sir John] St. Clair to make a reasonable allowance for defraying that Expence."[41] But as with the expedition to Cartagena, the presence of inducements indicates that the underlying motivation for most of the recruits was monetary.

In addition to their uniforms, the Crown authorized accoutrements and bedding, ultimately to be paid out of the royal purse, though the quantity and quality of such articles was never sufficient. The men suffered miserably in the cold New York winter. At some point during the course of the expedition, Governor George Clinton of New York supplied blankets to the four companies, though there were only enough for half the men.[42]

This time, the Pennsylvania Assembly and not the Crown funded stands of arms, consisting of secondhand, obsolete, or contract muskets, belly boxes, waist belts, and bayonet frogs.[43] Belly boxes were small pouches for carrying ammunition. They were cheap and inferior substitutes for the shoulder pouches carried by British regulars. Short swords known as cutlasses or hangers were presumably issued to the men.[44] The men's equipment was really a hodgepodge. The uniforms issued to levies were of poor quality, the muskets were prone to burst when fired, and the general appearance of these would-be warriors was pathetic. Standing alongside the regulars, the provincial levies projected a decidedly inferior appearance. Their cheap weapons and inadequate belly boxes put them at a disadvantage in combat. The winter at Albany probably did little to increase the men's esteem for the ruling establishment in Philadelphia.

The scheduled invasion of Canada never occurred. Moreover, a problem with the men's pay developed. Prime Minister Newcastle had instructed Pennsylvania governor Thomas that "you will assure all those that engage in this Service, as well Officers as Soldiers, that they will immediately enter into His Majesty's pay—the Officers from the time they shall engage in His Majesty's Service, and the Soldiers from the respective Days on which they shall enlist."[45] After a year in service, most of the rank and file and all of the officers had not been paid. It was not until June 24, 1747, that Sir William Shirley intervened. The sergeants and enlisted men received their pay for service to that date. Lieutenants received two months' subsistence, captains nothing at all until after the troops were discharged. The captains may never have been paid.[46] The Pennsylvania Assembly that eagerly furnished arms to the tribes of the upper Susquehanna was unwilling to adequately pay or even properly clothe the members of the Canada expedition. An apathetic assembly, made up mostly of pacifists and elites far removed from the theater of war, callously sent untrained and underequipped men into harm's way. Many of the men decided to go home before their enlistments expired.

Three of the four companies had problems with desertion. Based on notices in the *Pennsylvania Gazette*, Captain Perry seems to have had the smallest problem, or cared the least about them; no deserters from his company were made public. On the other hand, there is so little correspondence from Perry that it is possible he did not march with his company to Albany until much later. Trent lost five men to desertion (three more died in an ambush near Saratoga), while John Shannon lost eight.[47] John Diemer lost thirty-three men in twelve months.[48]

Pennsylvania preserved a muster roll of the four companies that recorded the names, ages, places of birth if outside Pennsylvania, and occupations of the enlistees. A comparison of Trent's company and Diemer's suggests a disparity between the city of Philadelphia and the outlying townships of the countryside. Trent enlisted recruits in and around Philadelphia.[49] Out of a company of 117 rank and file, forty-four professed some kind of trade and fifty-five simply listed "laborer" next to their names.[50] Only four carpenters enlisted in his company.[51] Trent was notorious for harboring fugitive servants.[52] That many of Trent's men were already running away from something or someone most likely explains why so few men from his company deserted. The low rate of desertion might also suggest that Philadelphia recruits possessed different values regarding service, discipline, and defense.

Diemer, on the other hand, suffered tremendously from desertion. His recruits came mainly from the Perkiomen Valley, near the junction of Bucks, Berks, Philadelphia, and Lancaster counties.[53] Many had German surnames.[54] Factors such as ethnic prejudice, religion, occupational interest, and language could have influenced desertion among Diemer's recruits. Assuming that both men were equally capable commanding officers (and assuming as well that Diemer was not possessed of some glaring personality defect not immediately apparent in the official rosters), high desertion rates show that men from the outlying areas, where the economy was mainly farm-driven, were more likely to desert than their urban counterparts. An urban economy like Philadelphia's, with large numbers of undigested immigrants and working poor, was better able to support a military organization.

In autumn 1747, the four companies returned to Pennsylvania mostly intact. The men of the expedition trickled back to their old lives. Some took up an honest trade, others a life of crime.[55] Wherever they went, their experience seems to have followed them. Like the Cartagena levies, veterans of the New York expedition wore their experience as a sort of badge. Notices for thieves and runaways mentioned the culprits' service on the expedition as a mark of identification.[56] Those placing a notice about a deserter looked upon a suspect's wartime service as being as distinctive as his hair color or the clothes he wore. The expedition to Canada quickly became a topic of popular lore. Through the service of a few, the general population gradually became accustomed to war and the experience of war.[57]

An increasing divide was developing between the Quaker elite and the general population. The rank and file of both expeditions seems to have come from that part of the population that possessed relatively little social status, earned low wages, and, like Benjamin Loxley, saw military service as a means to an end. What little is known of their officers suggests that those men at least were economically well-off. William Trent, for example, enjoyed some status as the wealthy son of the founder of Trenton, New Jersey. The year before the expedition, Trent had entered into a partnership with George Croghan, the noted explorer, land speculator, and Indian agent. Philadelphia wholesaler Samuel Perry dealt mostly in imported fabrics and apparel from his establishment on Water Street, at the head of Hamilton's Wharf.[58] William Franklin was, of course, the son of Benjamin Franklin, the prolific pamphleteer and aspiring politician. The younger Franklin became a partner in the Ohio Company and prospered by association with his father and in his own right. None of the officers so far identified appears to have pledged to join the Military Association founded within weeks of the expedition's return to Philadelphia.

In summer 1747, war issues again rose to prominence in Philadelphia politics. Philadelphia merchants enjoyed a brisk business outfitting privateers. The importance of this most prosperous form of commercial warfare throughout the War of Austrian Succession cannot be understated. Carl E. Swanson points out that, "Hundreds of stout colonial vessels worth thousands of pounds sterling were active in the maritime prize war, and thousands of jack tars put their lives on the line."[59]

Indeed, the *casus belli* for the expedition to Cartagena in 1741 and the assault on Louisbourg in 1745 was their use by Great Britain's enemies as home ports for privateers. In Philadelphia, fast becoming the largest port in British North America, the great popularity of privateering and its enormous impact on the maritime trade led to renewed calls for defense.

Despite the successful reduction of Louisbourg in the Gulf of Saint Lawrence the year before, and despite the success of Philadelphia privateers, Spanish and French privateers were active in the Delaware Bay and the river as far up as New Castle, in the Three Lower Counties. [60]

Pennsylvania's political order, meanwhile, showed signs of division.[61] By 1747, many younger Quakers in Philadelphia demanded an equal partnership in the Old Party.[62] Some identified with their non-Quaker neighbors.[63] Even James Logan, a wealthy member of one of the oldest Quaker families in the province, espoused a pragmatic attitude regarding defense.[64] While enemy warships cruised the Delaware Bay and disillusioned levies returned home from New York, factions within the Old Party battled the proprietor for control of the colony's finances.[65] As governor, Thomas Penn advanced proprietary interests in the assembly. He likewise tightened his control over his family's finances.[66] He streamlined the collection of rents and other revenues. He evicted squatters. He mobilized his political beneficiaries, many of whom were managers of proprietary lands.

Benjamin Franklin, a tradesman himself who lived on Second Street in the heart of the city, counted among his neighbors the carpenters, shipwrights, and mariners who were most affected by the depredations of enemy privateers, as well as the merchants and others who had the most to gain from privateering. As clerk of the Pennsylvania Assembly, he observed the political deadlock firsthand.[67] Printing one of the most successful papers in the colonies put Franklin in touch with correspondents up and down the coast, not to mention the British Isles, where volunteers had only the year before entered into military associations to defend the realm against the army of Charles Edward Stuart during the famed Jacobite uprising known as the Forty-Five. In Great Britain, military associations sprang up throughout the countryside, even in the reputedly pro-Jacobite northern cities of Edinburgh, Berwick-Upon-Tweed, and Somerset.[68] If 450 clothiers could volunteer to drill under arms in the city of Plymouth, associated tradesmen could organize harbor defenses in Philadelphia.[69]

Franklin took action. On November 17, 1747, he published *Plain Truth: Or Serious Considerations on the Present State of the City of Philadelphia and Province of Pennsylvania.*[70] *Plain Truth* advocated an alternative to a militia and spurred citizens to action in the absence of effective colonial administration.

In *Plain Truth*, Franklin laid the blame for Pennsylvania's defenseless state squarely at the feet of the Pennsylvania Assembly.[71] Franklin's proposed volunteer defense force would "remind [the assembly], that the Publick Money, raised *from All*, belongs *to all*."[72] Franklin then appealed to all Pennsylvanians to unite, asking, "Is not the whole Province one Body, united by living under the same Laws,. and enjoying the same Privileges?"[73] Franklin also appealed to those whom the proprietor had alienated, as well as those left defenseless by the pacifist assembly, namely the western settlers, some of whom the governor had evicted less than two years before.

Franklin appealed to Philadelphians who drew their living from maritime trades. Protection of that trade, Franklin argued, was reason enough to unite in the colony's defense.[74] Franklin pointed to the importance of Philadelphia as a seaport and warned of the economic ruin that would ensue should enemy warships continue to cruise the Delaware Capes unchallenged.[75] Franklin made no mention of a land-based defense force, but proposed that Pennsylvania commission a warship to patrol the Delaware.[76]

In *Plain Truth*, Franklin claimed to "honestly speak my Mind."[77] But *Plain Truth* was, in fact, full of falsehoods. Franklin tacitly admitted that Pennsylvania had no real need for defense. Indeed, he pointed out that Pennsylvania had "hitherto enjoy'd profound Repose."[78] By Franklin's own admission, the colony had been defended "from the French . . . by the Northern Provinces, and from the Spaniards . . . by the Southern."[79] Franklin founded his entire argument on his suspicion that Pennsylvania's "Enemies may have Spies abroad, and some even in these Colonies." [80] As proof that such spies existed, Franklin cited biblical verse instead of hard evidence.

With his publication of *Plain Truth*, Franklin voiced the dissatisfaction of a substantial number of ordinary Pennsylvanians, to say nothing of veterans of the two expeditions, privateers, and defense proponents. *Plain Truth* appealed to beliefs far more profound than leather apron politics. It claimed that duplicitous French priests threatened the Long Peace by converting members of the Six Nations to Roman Catholicism.[81] Franklin struck a nerve with his appeal to crass anti-Catholicism and racial hatred. Should Pennsylvanians fail to defend themselves, Franklin warned, "Your Persons, Fortunes, Wives and Daughters, shall be subject to the wanton and unbridled Rage, Rapine, and Lust of *Negroes, Molattoes,* and others, the vilest and most abandoned of Mankind."

Franklin concluded his argument with an appeal to his fellow citizens, "the middling People, the Farmers, Shopkeepers, and Tradesmen of this City and Country."[82] Franklin then waxed lyrical, appealing to the British fighting spirit by reminding his readers that "Great numbers of our People are of BRITISH RACE, and tho' the fierce fighting Animals of those happy Islands, are said to abate their native Fire and Intrepidity, when removed to a Foreign Clime, yet with the People 'tis not so."[83] Not one to pass up the support of another constituency, Franklin noted that there were in Pennsylvania "Thousands of *that Warlike Nation* . . . the *brave* and *steady* Germans," blithely ignoring his own anti-German bias and the fact that so many Germans had risked a life-threatening transatlantic voyage to escape the wars in their homeland.[84] Even so, Franklin called on his readers to unite not as Quakers, nor as Britons, Irishmen, or Germans, but as Pennsylvanians against an assembly that, he insinuated, no longer represented them.

In joining the Military Association of Philadelphia, would-be soldiers accepted the Articles of Association.[85] These consisted of a preamble and eight articles. In its opening sentence, the preamble reminded readers that, "Great Britain, to which we are subject, is now engaged in a War with two powerful Nations," France and Spain.[86] The articles were an appeal to those who considered themselves loyal subjects of King George II, and not followers of Pennsylvania's exceptionalist policy. The Associators wanted to perpetuate the myth of "a naked defenceless State, without Fortifications," despite the fact that there was a fort on Society Hill and hundreds of privateers used Philadelphia as a home port to attack enemy warships.[87] The Associators ignored the contributions of the Crown and other colonies to Pennsylvania's defense, declaring instead that "we are at a great Distance from our Mother Country, and cannot, on any Emergency, receive Assistance from thence."[88]

The preamble instead attacked the heart of the matter, stating,

> The Assemblies of this Province, by reason of their religious Principles, have not done, nor are likely to do any Thing for our Defence, notwithstanding repeated Applications to them for that Purpose: That being thus unprotected by the Government under which we live, against our foreign Enemies that may come to invade us, As we think it absolutely necessary, WE DO hereby, for our mutual Defence and Security, and for the Security of our Wives, Children and Estates of others, our Neighbours and Fellow Subjects, form ourselves into an ASSOCIATION.[89]

Philadelphians were willing to take military matters into their own hands.

The duties of chief magistrates, as defined by John Locke in his *Second Treatise of Government*, were "to preserve the members of that society in their lives liberties and possessions."[90] But the author of the preamble to the Articles of Association more likely intended a dual meaning. Not only had the assembly spurned its legal obligation; in the eyes of a growing number of Philadelphians, it had failed in its sacred duty. Associators convened in the very building where the Reverend George Whitefield, the itinerant evangelist of the Great Awakening, had preached only a few years before.[91] They were sure to recall Joshua 1:14 (King James Bible), wherein God commanded the successor of Moses to lead his people in battle: "Your wives, your little ones, and your cattle, shall remain in the land which Moses gave you on this side Jordan; but ye shall pass before your brethren armed, all the mighty men of valour, and help them." Shortly thereafter, another Great Awakening preacher, the Reverend Gilbert Tennent, delivered a sermon in Philadelphia on the lawfulness of the Association, titled "The Lord is a Man of War," published by Franklin's competitor, William Bradford.[92]

The first six Articles of Association remedied most of the shortcomings of the Cartagena and Canada expeditions. Article One required each Associator to provide himself with a musket or fowling piece, a cartridge box, at least twelve cartridges, and a sword "to be kept always in our respective Dwellings, in Readiness and good Order."[93] Article Two organized the Association into companies consisting of fifty to one hundred men each.[94] Article Three provided for the election of officers, to be approved by the governor or the president of the Provincial Council.[95] Article Four required the companies to organize under a regiment.[96] Article Five established a regular training schedule, "not exceeding four Times in one Year."[97] Article Six established a "General Military Council," consisting of four Associators from each county.[98] This council would dictate training schedules and establish regulations, alert mechanisms, and a chain of command answerable to the governor or the highest ranking military officer on the scene.[99] Philadelphia's defense was now well organized, reasonably equipped, and ready, at least on paper, to begin training.

The first six articles contained nothing controversial. They established a voluntary fighting force subject to review by the governor or the president of the Provincial Council, not materially different from those mandated by English law since the days of Queen Elizabeth. But the last two articles revealed a more designing motive. Article Seven limited the Association to voluntary funding only, thus avoiding any interference from the assembly, which controlled public expenditures.[100] Article Eight stated that the Association was to last for the current war against France and Spain, or until the colony was provided with some form of defense, which placed any opponent of the Association in the impossible position of having to argue against militia mandates dating back hundreds of years.[101] According to the Articles of Association, the Associators were neither a militia, nor paid levies, nor professional soldiers; they were a temporary expedient in the absence of a proper defense, and a training institute not unlike the London Military Association, organized during the Forty-Five and subsequently consolidated into the Honourable Artillery Company of London. As events would soon show, the Associators were neither temporary nor a practical defense.

On November 21, 1747, Franklin showed his proposal to "150 Persons, mostly Tradesmen," gathered at a Mr. Walton's school house.[102] Two nights later, he made the same proposal to influential merchants at Roberts' Coffee House. The next night, at a large public hall that eventually housed the Philadelphia Academy, Franklin made his pitch to gathered artisans, shopkeepers, and farmers.[103]

Within a few days, Franklin had more than one thousand signatures. John Swift, a prominent Philadelphian, described the military mania set in motion by Franklin that swept the city during that last week in November:

> A pamphlet [*Plain Truth*] published here a few days ago, set-
> ting forth the miserable calamities that may befall us, if
> something is not done for our security against next spring,
> has raised a military spirit amongst the people. Yesterday
> there was a grand meeting of all ranks and conditions at
> Whitefield building, where they signed an association for
> forming themselves into a militia for the defence of the city.
> And there is to be a lottery set on foot immediately, to raise
> money towards fitting out a vessel, to protect the trade. And
> a petition will be presented to our worthy Assembly (who
> are now sitting), praying them to take it into their consider-
> ation, and do something for the common security. I have
> sent you the pamphlet and a copy of the association, and
> three papers relating to the Quakers' principles of not
> defending themselves, which have been of great service to
> some of them, and convinced them that they have been in a
> mistake about that matter.[104]

Companies organized geographically in order to facilitate training and to encourage the common bond that service in the military wrought. The Association intended to "mix the great and small together in Companies," and sought to dis-courage "peoples sorting themselves into companies according to their ranks in life and their quality or station."[105]

Associators certainly represented a broad cross section of Philadelphia society. Benjamin Loxley was a journeyman carpenter.[106] The regimental commander, Colonel Abraham Taylor, was a prodefense city alderman and presumably enjoyed some degree of social status.[107] As a member of the Common Council of Philadelphia, Captain Septimus Robinson had signed a petition urging King George II to take measures to defend the city in 1741.[108] William Bradford was a lieutenant in one of the companies of foot and, like Franklin, printed a prodefense newspaper, the *Pennsylvania Journal.* Several other members had a vested interest in commerce and defense of the port. Sea captains George Noarth and John Sibbald commanded the first Associator forts at Atwood's Wharf and Wiccacoe.[109] John Sibbald and Thomas Lawrence Jr. were successful privateers.[110] Lawrence had recently purchased *Le Trembleur* at a cost of eight hundred pounds. Pennsylvania commissioned *Le Trembleur* as a guard ship to cruise the Delaware River and Bay from the founding of the Association to the end of the Spanish War.[111] Unlike Loxley and some other Associators, Sibbald also enjoyed a degree of social rank because of his long membership in the Colony in Schuylkill, a prestigious fishing club founded in 1732 that counted among its members some of Philadelphia's wealthiest and most prominent inhabitants.[112] Associators came from all walks of life and were members of a number of religious sects, including the Society of Friends. Benjamin Loxley was an ardent Baptist. Merchant Richard Nixon served as a vestryman at Christ Church, the city's largest Anglican congregation, where on Sunday, December 6, its rector, the Reverend Robert Jenny, "preach'd an excellent Sermon on the Lawfulness of Self Defence, and of Associating for that Purpose, to a very considerable Auditory."[113]

The Association was an ideal vehicle for Franklin. It represented nothing new that might jeopardize his political career. English burghers had organized military associations throughout England during the recent Jacobite uprising. Indeed, Philadelphia's Military Association resembled that of London in name and purpose. In England, military planners coordinated with the associations on defensive works as well as improvements to roads and harbors. Such associations organized in keeping with ancient militia laws without requiring the king or Parliament to embody the militia–a step as politically dangerous in England as it was in Quaker Pennsylvania, as an embodied militia required compulsory military service, assemblies, regular drills, and worse, the presence of a standing army on English soil. During the reign of King Charles I, underpaid English armies had been notorious for plundering the countryside and committing other atrocities so egregious that the very notion of a standing army and the quartering of troops in the homes of the populace had become repugnant to the English.

Franklin and his supporters, "as Englishmen," could easily argue that the Philadelphia Association adhered to ancient principles cherished by the "British race." Franklin's most ardent supporters were the very men whom he counted among his friends and neighbors—affluent tradesmen, or disaffected members of the "upper sort." Because the Association was a voluntary organization, it appealed to wealthy members who might otherwise balk at the idea of mandatory musters. To the established elite and those in the assembly who relied on election returns to remain in office, Associators were a force to be reckoned with: out of a taxable population of about thirty thousand, Associator strength stood somewhere between three thousand and four thousand, or one-tenth of the electorate.[114] This figure is remarkable, given that every Associator was an adult male capable of bearing arms and was therefore able, at least in theory, to vote.[115] By signing the Articles of Association, members had done more than demonstrate their support for the defense of their "wives" and "little ones": they had demonstrated their opposition to Pennsylvania's policy of nonviolent defense in a tangible way.

The result of all this bustle and legal legwork, the Associated Regiment of Foot, the infantry regiment called for under Article Four, first paraded on Monday, December 7, 1747. On that day, six hundred Associators formed under arms in front of the Philadelphia Court House at Second and Market streets.[116] There they divided themselves into eleven groups by ward or township to "mix the great and small together in Companies," and thereby "prevent peoples sorting themselves into companies according to their ranks in life and their quality or station." English law required enlistees and officer candidates to stand before a magistrate for swearing in or commissioning. Alternatively, Provincial Council President Anthony

Palmer told the assembled Associators that "their Proceedings were not disapproved by the Government," and agreed to commission the regiment's officers.[117] Members of the Assembly whose scruples prevented them from supporting such an association abstained in order to let the enabling legislation pass. The Associators had fought and won their first battle.

In accordance with Article Four, members of the regiment elected Abraham Taylor colonel and commanding officer.[118] Taylor was a city alderman and vociferously prodefense.[119] Thomas Lawrence became the regiment's lieutenant colonel, and Samuel McCall its major. The Philadelphia Associators chose eleven captains (see Appendix).

In addition to the city, Philadelphia County raised nine companies, Bucks County nineteen, Lancaster County thirty-three, and Chester County eleven. [120] New Castle County also raised several companies regimented under Colonel William Armstrong, as did Kent County.[121] In a matter of days, the Associators showed what the Quaker elites had failed to act on for decades. In the absence of a militia law, the people of Pennsylvania's eastern counties were willing to form their own defense force. The officers' commissions were handed out on New Year's Day.[122]

In contrast to the impoverished levies that had sweltered in the tropical heat before Cartagena or shivered in the cold of the New York winter, the Associators were relatively affluent. In accordance with Article One, every Associator carried his own privately purchased musket, cartridge box, and hanger.[123] Each regiment from Philadelphia or near Philadelphia designed its own silk color, "painted," according to Franklin, "with different Devices and Mottoes which I supplied."[124] One of the devices bore the motto "Pro Patria" and depicted "a Lion erect, a naked Scymeter in one Paw, the other holding the Pennsylvania Scutcheon," or shield. According to Franklin, Philadelphia women raised funds for the flags, as well as drums for signaling, spontoons for officers, and halberds for sergeants.[125] Pole arms, spontoons, and halberds signified rank and could be used to direct and maneuver soldiers.[126]

The Associators soon tightened some of the requirements laid out in the Articles of Association. Article One merely required that Associators own a firearm and a sword. Shortly after the Association was organized, John Swift wrote to his uncle in London asking for a musket, complaining that "my fowling-piece has no bayonet to it."[127] Article Five stipulated quarterly training, but according to Benjamin Franklin, the Associators "met every Week to be instructed in the manual Exercise, and other Parts of military Discipline."[128] Benjamin Loxley wrote that "at our Fort all through the Spanish War until 1747 I taught the exercise to a great many in this province," and John Swift wrote that "there are upwards of eight hundred men in this city, that bear arms, and are already become pretty expert in the exercise."[129] The Associators showed more than just a casual interest in meeting together and training. Most important, the Associators found muskets, swords, and bayonets to be inadequate. Small arms would vanish into the homes of Associators, never to be seen except on muster days. Something else was needed.

Plain Truth advocated the purchase of a warship able to patrol the Delaware River. Associator Ensign Thomas Lawrence had recently acquired just such a ship. *Le Trembleur* was a handy, fast, and relatively new ship of the type known as a Bermuda Sloop.[130] Pennsylvania commissioned it for the duration of the war.[131] *Le Trembleur* was a practical defense. Mounting fourteen guns, it could challenge an enemy ship long before it endangered Philadelphia. The Association should have disbanded with the commissioning of *Le Trembleur.* According to Article Eight of the Articles of Association, the Associators were to serve only until Pennsylvania made some provision for defense. The Pennsylvania Assembly had done just that, yet instead of disbanding, the Association expanded.

If the Association was to survive, then the Associators needed a permanent home, such as a fort. A fort would give them a place to train and provide the new organization with a visible rallying point. In military terms, the best location for a fort lay near the mouth of the Schuylkill River. James Logan recommended such a site in a letter to Franklin, but the mouth of the Schuylkill sat too far from Philadelphia to serve Franklin's needs.[132] The Associators needed something that could be seen by everyone, especially members of the Pennsylvania Assembly, at a spot easily reached on the muster days stipulated under the articles. For that reason, they chose a spot at the foot of Lombard Street, at Mayor William Atwood's wharf, not far from the site of the old Society Hill fort.

The new fort would need cannon. On December 29, 1747, several Associator officers wrote a letter to New York's governor Clinton requesting guns for the battery.[133] On January 5, 1748, Clinton wrote to decline the request.[134] Franklin, along with Colonels Taylor and Lawrence, and William Allen, a Franklin ally, traveled to New York to dine with Clinton. With the aid of a case of Madeira wine, the delegation soon secured the loan of fourteen guns from the governor.[135] An encouraged Franklin and the officers of the Association continued to seek more artillery, even ranging as far afield as Jamaica to petition that island's governor for cannon.[136] Association members worked directly with the Provincial Council to procure ordnance, sitting in on council sessions and signing their names to the council minutes. Their desire for cannon would ensure their frequent attendance at the State House as issues of funding arose. Once again, the Associators broke their own rules.

Despite the Associators' attendance at council meetings, they sought financial independence. On February 8, 1748, a lottery Franklin organized supported the purchase of cannon from New York and the construction of a timber fort.[137] The Associators intended to become a permanent fixture in the city in a way that an infantry regiment never could. Associator carpenters built the new fort in two days.[138] George Noarth, a prominent sea captain, became its first commander.[139] The fort mounted only fourteen guns. It could challenge a pirate or a privateer but would hardly daunt a more determined foe. Any ship that could get past Ensign Lawrence's *Le Trembleur* could easily destroy such a light battery. Moreover, the fort was poorly located: Windmill Island partially masked its guns (fig. 4, overleaf). Work began on a second and larger battery.

On May 26, 1748, the Provincial Council passed a resolution to fund a stone fort already under construction at Wiccacoe, near Old Swedes Church south of the city.[140] As many hands as possible were to be put to work on this ambitious project. The new fort was meant to augment the existing earthwork at

Fig. 4. Detail from Nicholas Scull and George Heap, "An East Prospect of the City of Philadelphia," 1756. This illustration of the Grand Battery shows the Wiccacoe fort as it appeared to passing ships, bristling with cannon and flying a Union Jack. Note the fort's vertical walls. (*Library of Congress*)

Atwood's Wharf in the city proper.[141] The guns Franklin cajoled from Governor Clinton were mounted at the second stronghold.

Known simply as the "Association" and sometimes as the "Grand" Battery, the fort at Wiccacoe was no great work of military engineering. The Grand Battery lacked such modern engineering features as sloped walls known as *glacis* and outer defenses called *ravelins*. Its walls were too weak to withstand a prolonged attack. The fort mounted twenty-seven twelve- and eighteen-pound cannon, guns large enough to deter an enemy warship, but its location was nearly as bad as the first Associator fort.[142] The Delaware River is over a half a mile wide at Wiccacoe, while the maximum effective range of twelve- and eighteen-pound guns was nine hundred to twelve hundred yards.[143] The Grand Battery's armament would have been largely ineffective in a naval battle should enemy ships hug the Jersey side of the Delaware River.

Franklin remained realistic on matters of defense. As clerk of the Pennsylvania Assembly, he had heard the debates over the Louisbourg expedition firsthand.[144] He had once cautioned his brother James, "Fortified towns are hard nuts to crack; and your teeth have not been accustomed to it. . . . But some seem to think forts are as easy taken as snuff."[145] Moreover,

Associators had built a battery downriver at New Castle, mounted on a temporary wooden platform.[146] In July, Captain David Bush of the New Castle Associators, notified council president Palmer that "we have erected a Battery on the Rocks of Christina," the site of the original Swedish Fort Christina, "with a Magazine that is Bomb proof, &c., for the Defense of this Burrough & parts adjacent." Although the third fort mounted only ten guns, Bush and his officers, John McKinley and Charles Bush, boasted that "it is equall to, if not exceeds, any on the Continent for Strength & Beauty."[147] Any attacker would have to get past it to assault Philadelphia. In April, the Royal Navy dispatched the sloop *Otter*, on convoy duty under a Captain Ballet, to patrol the lower Delaware River.[148] The *Otter*, seven weeks out from Portsmouth, arrived badly in need of careening, a process by which a ship was hauled out of the water, partly dismasted, and stripped of its guns and all contents in order to clean its bottom of the marine growth that inevitably accumulated on a long voyage. Ballet had, moreover, fought a "smart engagement with a very large ship for 4 hours," during which he suffered several casualties to his crew and almost certainly sustained considerable damage to his ship. The little *Otter*, in no condition to take station on the Delaware, also lacked a consort that would have enabled it to effectively mount defensive operations. The gallant Captain Ballet nevertheless put himself, his ship, and his crew at the disposal of the colony, making the existence of the Grand Battery and that of the fort at Atwood's Wharf appear somewhat redundant.

Why, then, did the Associators choose to build the Grand Battery at Wiccacoe? Franklin was well aware of the importance of a fort's location in order that its gun crews might trap ships in a deadly crossfire of round ball and grapeshot.[149] He and James Logan knew that the mouth of the Schuylkill was a more advantageous position, as did Captain Ballet, who, once his ship had been put in order, dutifully patrolled the lower reaches of the Delaware rather than the river directly below the city. The Grand Battery's real strength lay in its ability to project the power of the new Military Association. When finished, the fort would be four hundred feet long.[150] It was easily visible—and its guns easily audible—to Philadelphia inhabitants and to ships approaching the city. Masters of ships sailing up the Delaware, as well as their crews and passengers, would see the fort's masonry walls, bristling with cannon, and the Union Jack flying overhead. Its name evoked the powerful Grand Battery of Fortress Louisbourg, the capture of which Franklin had publicized in the *Pennsylvania Gazette*.[151] Most important, the new fort was built of stone. Its construction on the banks of the Delaware River was material proof that, despite its stated purpose, the Military Association had come to stay.

John Swift wrote excitedly:

> the association for the militia goes on very well here, there are upwards of eight hundred men in this city, that bear arms, and are already become pretty expert in the exercise; and in the province there are near twenty thousand associators, and more daily coming in. The platform for a battery is begun by the swamp below Swedes' church, and we have cannon coming to us from New York, viz: twelve twelve-pounders, and two eighteen-pounders, which are to serve till we can be better provided. With these we shall be able to make some resistance in case of an attack. There is another lottery going to be set on foot, to raise six thousand pounds, which is to be applied for defending the city.[152]

On May 21, Colonel Abraham Taylor reviewed the Associated Regiment of Foot. Five days later, the Association appointed him to be overall commander of both batteries.[153] On the same day, a motion in the Provincial Council recommended the creation of a strong guard at both batteries, for ten men to guard the public powder house in the city, and for pilot boats to patrol the river and bay for intelligence regarding enemy activities.[154]

On June 3, Colonel Edward Jones of the Philadelphia County Regiment inspected five of his companies at Germantown. Three days later, he reviewed four others in Norrington Township.[155] On June 23, the *Pennsylvania Gazette* reported that Colonel William Armstrong reviewed the New Castle County Regiment, which went through its exercise "with the greatest Exactness."[156] Later that month, Taylor and Lawrence recommended forming an artillery company. The Provincial Council commissioned John Sibbald to command the new Association, or Grand Battery.[157] Sibbald, a successful privateer who made two cruises early in the war, understood command and the handling of cannon.[158] Like many who would follow him into the city's artillery, Sibbald had a personal interest in river defense.

The creation of the Associators in general swayed the assembly to acknowledge the Association, to acquiesce in its perpetuation, to fund public works by commissioning a warship and building forts, and to include members of the Associators in the decision-making process of the Provincial Council. The artillery was a specific political statement in the same vein. Artillery was high profile. It was one thing for a company of infantry to exercise in the State House yard or on the common with its own privately purchased muskets, but it was another thing altogether to have to pay for the purchase of artillery pieces and to have forts built. A troop of light horse may have attracted more influential members, but cavalrymen trained in the open spaces outside the city. Companies of foot could exercise in an urban setting, but their equipment required no substantial public outlay. Artillery, on the other hand, shook the window panes. It required the purchase of forts, cannon, and other expensive accessories. Artillery implied permanency. It was also more conspicuous.

In building two forts and commissioning a warship, several hundred Philadelphians had taken matters into their own hands. Proprietor Thomas Penn should have been grateful: the Associators had accomplished what he had failed to do. Moreover, they had done it at minimal cost to him. He should have doffed his hat in gratitude. Instead, Penn raged. Philadelphians had raised a defense force, and without his permission. To Penn, the Association's drills amounted to "little less than treason."[159] Pennsylvania's leaders in the assembly were more comfortable with the Association, perhaps choosing to conduct their affairs "without noise & animosity," as William Penn had once admonished the Provincial Council. Perhaps they had seen Taylor's regiment assembled at the courthouse and thought of what might happen at election time, when voters went there to cast their ballots. At any rate, the Association had accomplished one thing: it had saved them from having to choose between politics and religion.[160]

Religion, or rather the defense of Protestantism, appears to have been one of the more overt motives in the creation of the Military Association, along with the defense of the English realm and one's birthright, and vitriolic hatred of the Spanish and Roman Catholicism. On September 1, 1748, "An ODE, humbly inscribed to the ASSOCIATORS of Pennsylvania," urged its readership, "Inflam'd by noble Patriot Rage/For Lives and Fortunes to engage" to "ASSOCIATE in your own Defence," lest "Pedro's lousy Rout/First seize their Prey, then tack about; And leave the burnt or pillag'd State, To mourn their Cowardice too late: *Too late,* their Wealth and Honour gone, Perhaps their *Daughters, Wives,* undone."[161] Another stanza, echoing *Plain Truth,* appealed to Pennsylvanians' patriotism as Englishmen, "*Heroes* of the *British* Line," and heirs to Cincinnatus, the hero of ancient Rome who had left his plow to defend the republic and then relinquished absolute power to return to his farm.

News of the Peace of Aix-La-Chapelle, ending the War of Austrian Succession, had by that time reached Philadelphia. The war fever of the winter, spring, and early summer died away. Aspiring soldiers went back to their civilian routines. Life in Philadelphia took on its peaceful character again. John Sibbald returned to sea, and John Swift put aside his martial plans.[162] Benjamin Loxley prospered. At his home on South Second Street, his wife, Jane, gave birth to a third son, Abram, on January 16, 1750.[163]

But although the Peace of Aix-La-Chapelle ended the war and much of the drilling in and around Philadelphia, it did not end the Military Association. Throughout the early 1750s, Associators augmented their organization with additional ordnance. The colony in Schuylkill donated its namesake gun, an iron thirty-two pounder (fig. 5). Cast into the top of the breech, the motto "*Kawanio che Keeteru,*" Lenape for "This is my right, I will defend it"–as much as the silk standard bearing the motto "*Pro Patria*" and the doggerel that appeared in the *Pennsylvania Gazette*–attests to the Associators' ongoing commitment to defend land seen as theirs.[164]

A change had been effected along the waterfront. Where there once had been marsh now stood a fort. Its construction represented a change in the outlook of a sizable number of the population. One thousand inhabitants, representing all walks of life and all factions of Philadelphia society, had pledged themselves to local defense. As a promise of permanency, a joint stock company helped manage Associator funds after 1752. The Association lived on, but it would not live on as a mass movement. For despite the egalitarian nature of its first muster, the Association would, for the immediate future, be run by a cadre of expert artillerists.

The Military Association was created out of the shared experience of the War of Austrian Succession. It was natural that a circle of skilled merchants, mariners, and artisans should perpetuate the organization. Artillerists were men who knew the handling of cannon and the principles of construction (useful when building forts and gun carriages), and who shared a personal stake in defending the city from sea attack. Their purpose reflected the social composition and outlook of Philadelphia's busy maritime district. The artillerists were not speculators like William Trent and the Franklins. They made their homes in Philadelphia and their fortunes in the shops within a stone's throw of the river.

Fig. 5. Schuylkill Gun. Cast in England about 1750, this 6.200 pound iron cannon guarded the Delaware River from its mount on the Grand Battery and could fire a thirty-two pound ball over a mile and a half. Typical of British ordnance of the time, a crown is cast on its breech. Below the crown, an escutcheon bears the motto, "Kwanio che Keeteru/ Schuylkill" and the letters "W.P." (*Author*)

The officers of the Cartagena and Canada expeditions came from diverse backgrounds. The officers of the Association tended to come from related occupations. This was due in part to the nature of artillery. Artillery required proficiency in the use of cannon, a highly specialized and esoteric skill, but one that those engaged in the maritime trade would likely have been exposed to. As Marcus Rediker points out, "the maritime trade was often a seasonal, casual occupation."[165] Merchant vessels regularly carried a skilled carpenter and a carpenter's apprentice.[166] Privateers, as well as some merchant vessels, carried a gunner and a gunner's mate.[167] Carpenters and gunners often earned as much as the ship's second in command.[168] Considering that a fort had previously stood on Society Hill, and the number of Philadelphians who put to sea in privateers between 1739 and 1748, there was a sizable pool of knowledgeable artillerists in Philadelphia.[169]

Far more than other branches of the military, the eighteenth-century artillery was a meritocracy. Reflecting the English tradition, commissions at the time were bought or occasionally bestowed based on social standing. Cavalry recruits were frequently young men of relatively high status who could afford a horse, men who had spent a lifetime in the saddle. Infantry recruits tended to come from "the lower sort." They were neither technically proficient nor financially endowed. The infantry lacked the glamour of the light horse and the technicism of the artillery. Where the light horse belonged to clubs that kept rosters, foot soldiers frequented taverns and tap houses, if they could afford the leisure time at all.

Members of the artillery, on the other hand, had a place or many places to meet. They belonged to the Carpenter's Company, the fire companies, and myriad other social and municipal organizations. The memberships of the voluntary associations frequently overlapped. The function of these organizations was of a technical nature. That appealed to tradesmen who possessed those proficiencies and who could hope to excel as artillerists. Through these organizations, doors opened to men who held relatively low social status, as well as more affluent men who had the time and the means to participate in the artillery. Not only could they read and write, they could grasp the complex formulas and mathematical equations found in the artillery treatises of the day. The texts they used contained page after page of complicated tables for the mounting and aiming of cannon.[170] The transportation of coastal guns such as the eighteen-pounders placed at the Grand Battery required the expertise of a rigger. In 1753, an eighteen-pound iron gun was nine feet long and weighed 4,032 pounds.[171] Once such weapons were moved into place, their installation onto wooden carriages required the skills of a carpenter.

Loading the cannon called for skills verging on alchemy. Artillerists belonged to a mysterious coterie that had its own language, traditions, and ritual. It was only natural that tradesmen, who jealously guarded their own trade secrets, kept traditions, and engaged in ritual ceremonies, would join that military arm. For example, the *Prussian Evolutions*, a 1775 tactical manual, contained a table giving the relative weights and measures of gold, quicksilver, lead, silver, brass, iron, tin, stone, and water.[172] It then went on to posit the following problem:

> By the help of this table, having the weight of a ball of any metal with its diameter proposed, it is easy to find the weight of any other ball, either of the same or different metal, whose diameter is given and contra; in order to this, we shall take Dr. Wybard's opinion in his Tactometria, that a bullet of cast iron, whose diameter is four inches, weighs nine pound Averdupois weight; this being granted, suppose the diameter of an iron ball, be six inches, what must it weigh?[173]

Master gunners were valued members of the military. Their rank reflected their expertise and not their wealth or social status. Throughout the eighteenth century, artillerists were often regarded as useful on the battlefield, but hardly worthy of the gentlemen's club that was the British Army. In Philadelphia, the train of artillery attracted tradesmen with technical skill. Affluent tradesmen, such as house carpenters, had the spare time to devote to the frequent and rigorous training demanded by the artillery.

In practical terms, the Military Association organized at the end of 1747 provided adequate facilities in the form of two forts. The forts built in May 1748 served as a training ground for the Associators. At the same time, they acted as tangible reminders of the new movement. The Associators pledged to provide adequate military training to the people of Philadelphia. Skilled tradesmen such as Benjamin Loxley would henceforth help young men prepare for defense, while mariners such as Thomas Lawrence Jr. and Captain Ballet would actually defend the city. The two expeditions created a precedent of military service for Philadelphians. They also served as a shared past. The Articles of Association gave men with a common commitment to harbor defense a forum in which to gather. The forts provided them with a home.

The following spring, on another river hundreds of miles away, another group of men set out to state a political mission of a different kind. French traders had competed with Anglo-American traders in the Ohio River valley for decades. Now, Pierre Joseph Céloron de Blainville led a party of over two hundred French soldiers, allied tribesmen, and Canadian militia from La Chine, on the Saint Lawrence River in New France, down the Allegheny River into Pennsylvania. Under orders from Roland Michel Barrin, le Marquis de La Galissonnière, the governor of New France, the expedition buried lead tablets along the way, inscribed with words that stated his mission: "POUR MONUMENT DU RENOUUELLEMENT DE POSSESSION QUE NOUS AVONS PRIS DE LA DITTE RIVIERE OYO ET DE TOUTES CELLES QUI Y TOMBE ET DE TOUES LES TERRES DES DEUX COTES JUSQUE AUX SOURCES DES DITTES RIVIES"–"To mark our renewed ownership of the said Ohio River and of all those that flow into it, and of all the lands of the two banks as far as the source of those streams"–a shaky claim not based on any purchase or treaty but rather on claims made by French explorer Robert Cavelier de La Salle over a century before.[174] Céloron's act set events into motion that would change Pennsylvania forever.

THREE

WAR IN
PENNSYLVANIA,
1754–1760

In October 1752, William Trent, captain of one of the four independent companies of foot in 1746, and now an agent for the western Indians for Pennsylvania and Virginia, submitted an ominous report to the printer of the *Pennsylvania Gazette*. The previous June, a large party of about 240 French, Ottawas, and Chippewas, attacked the Miami village of Pickawillany on a branch of the Miami River in the Ohio country, home to the Ohio Company's largest trading post. The attackers, commanded by Cadet Charles-Michel Mouet de Langlade, fell on the village with such suddenness that local residents had no time to repair to the fort.[1] After a brief fight, the defenders surrendered the village and their anglophile chieftain, Memeskia, also known as Old Britain, whom the attackers boiled and ate. According to Trent, "Tomahawks and black wampum are continually passing from one Town to another, and nothing but revenge and Blood is to be heard of among the Indians."[2]

The following May, trouble at Pine Creek, near the confluence of the Allegheny, Monongahela, and Ohio rivers, a region known as the Forks of the Ohio, brought James Galbraith of Lancaster County, Trent, and his partner, George Croghan, into council with a delegation representing the concern of Scarroyaday (Monacatootha) and Tanacharison (Half King), two chiefs of the Six Nations. The delegation brought news that a party of about 150 French, Canadians, and Ottawas were building canoes and preparing to receive an additional body bearing eight brass cannon, powder, shot, and provisions.[3] In July, Trent reported the construction of a fort at Presque Isle (Fort de la Presqu'île), on Lake Erie.[4] According to rumors later proven true, two other forts, at Venango and Le Boeuf, were in their early stages. Now, according to Trent, a man known and trusted on the frontier and in the higher circles of Philadelphia society, the French had returned to back the words inscribed on lead tablets with powder and shot.

Despite the direct threat that the French incursion posed to Philadelphia mercantile concerns, not to mention the indirect threat it posed to Pennsylvania's allies among the Delaware and Six Nations, Governor Robert Dinwiddie of Virginia took action first.[5] As a partner in the Ohio Company, Dinwiddie had a personal stake in any development at the Forks of the Ohio. In midwinter, he dispatched twenty-one-year-old George Washington to order the French to withdraw. Inexperienced at statecraft and ignorant of French, Washington returned to Williamsburg with the French commandant's rejection of Dinwiddie's terms.

Diplomatic wheels spun the machinery of war into action. In early 1754, Dinwiddie sent a message to Trent, now building a stone storehouse for the company at Redstone Creek. He granted him a captain's commission in the Virginia militia. Trent and a party of woodsmen proceeded to the Forks of the Ohio to fortify the position.[6] On February 17, Trent arrived there with about sixty men and started work on a fort that he called Prince George.[7]

In April, Trent left the new fort in the hands of his brother-in-law, Ensign Edward Ward, and set off in search of supplies and reinforcements. While he was gone, a superior French force arrived and forced its surrender. French soldiers leveled Fort Prince George and began construction of Fort Duquesne. George Washington, meanwhile, proceeded toward the Forks with reinforcements. When Half King told him of a French party lying in ambush, Washington attacked first, and on the morning of May 28, killed or captured all of them.[8]

Washington quickly put his soldiers to work building a "fort of necessity" at Great Meadows, which he surrendered on July 4.

Two days later and hundreds of miles away, at a council held in Albany, New York, representatives of the Six Nations ceded western Pennsylvania lands to Pennsylvania, including the Conolloway tracts, the valley region occupied by predominantly Scots-Irish settlers for the past ten or fifteen years. By this act, the Six Nations, Pennsylvania's most powerful ally and guarantor of regional stability, walked away from a region that the French and Virginians were turning into a battleground. The Six Nations' cession caused a rift with the Delaware and Shawnees, many of the former still seething over the 1737 Walking Purchase, perhaps Pennsylvania's most famous, but by no means only, land grab. Many Shawnee and Delaware either drifted into the French orbit or pledged neutrality, leaving the defense of the frontier at a critical time, on the shoulders of squatters who had recently been burned out of their settlements by Pennsylvania authorities.

While Washington and members of the Virginia Regiment sweated out a French siege at their makeshift stronghold at Great Meadows, and the Long Peace unraveled at Albany, the officers of the Philadelphia train of artillery mended their forts, chipped rust off shot, enlisted recruits, and exercised their cannon. The imbroglio over the other side of the mountains was between the French, the Ohio Company, and colonial commissioners from Pennsylvania and Virginia. It was not an affair that directly affected the port, therefore the artillerists took no overt action.

The Associators certainly possessed the means to fight in 1754. Besides the original fort at Atwood's Wharf, there was the Grand Battery at Wiccacoe. In October, the *Pennsylvania Gazette* announced that "a sergeant and Corporal of each Company in the Train of Artillery are ordered to go a Recruiting."[9] A third company was in its formative stages. As Benjamin Loxley recalled years later, "a great number of Tradesmen, Carpenters, Masons, Smiths, etc. met at our State House and chose old George North Captain and myself Captain-Lieutenant and John Goodwin 1st Lieut. and James Worrel Second Lieut. We chose all our under officers and formed a company of 107 men, officers included."[10] Sea captain

George Noarth had commanded the first Associator fort at Atwood's Wharf. Lieutenant John Goodwin most likely followed the same occupation as Noarth.[11] James Worrell and Benjamin Loxley were both carpenters.[12]

In late 1754 or early 1755, Loxley borrowed four ship's guns from Philadelphia ship owner Andrew Hodge and modified them for field use.[13] Loxley trained the men in gunnery and the use of small arms, no doubt relying once again on Blakeney's *Exercise*.[14]

For no apparent reason, the Philadelphia Association continued to grow. In telling the assembled Associators back in December 1747 that their efforts would not be opposed, Provincial Council president Anthony Palmer had essentially left them to their own devices.

The British response to the events in the west soon justified their inaction. In September, news of Washington's defeat had reached London, and on February 19, 1755, Major General Edward Braddock arrived at Hampton Roads, Virginia, with the British 44th and 48th Regiments of Foot and a train of artillery. February 23 found him in Williamsburg to execute his plan. Braddock intended to follow Washington's route through the wilderness as far as the Ohio River valley. Once within range of the French, his strategy called for the placement of overwhelming artillery fire on the fort the French had built and named Fort Duquesne. It was a plan that was expected to quickly win the Ohio country for Britain.[15] Having captured Fort Duquesne, Braddock would follow the Allegheny River north to French Creek and thence to Lake Erie, where he would meet Sir William Shirley, who would by then have reduced Fort Niagara with a force built around the 50th and 51st Regiments of Foot.[16] William Johnson would move against the French forts Carillon and Saint Frédéric on Lake Champlain with a mixed force of Mohawks and provincials.[17] Control of the Ohio River would lead to mastery of the continent. To planners in Whitehall, no expense was too large, and Braddock was sure to succeed.

The middle colonies, including Pennsylvania, were naturally quick to lend their support to Braddock's expedition. His plan created a potentially lucrative route to the Forks of the Ohio at relatively low cost to the colonists, who would benefit from army contracts. Benjamin Franklin ensured that Pennsylvania's contribution was substantial. His efforts yielded troops as well as 150 wagons with draft animals and teamsters for each, efforts not lost on the normally antiprovincial Braddock, who noted, "I determin'd before I left Frederick to desire Mr. Franklin of Pensilvania (a province whose people tho' they will contribute very little to the Expedition are exact in their Dealings, and much more industrious than the others) to contract in my name for an hundred and fifty Waggons and a Number of pack Horses to be sent to this place with all expedition."[18] Franklin further ingratiated himself with the British general by means of a bribe, consisting of choice delicacies for the officer's mess that took twenty packhorses to deliver. In return, Braddock advanced the colony several hundred pounds for logistics.[19]

Pennsylvania put a large part of that funding toward the construction of a road that stretched from Shippensburg to the Forks of the Youghiogheny. Once again, monetary gain appears to have been the primary factor motivating the Pennsylvania backcountry, and Pennsylvania's frontier inhabitants seemed as unconcerned with military preparation as the train of artillery at Philadelphia, perhaps even less so. When, on the evening of July 4, 1755, a French war party attacked a convoy carrying provisions in support of the new road, "greatly alarmed" provincial commissaries and road cutters deserted in droves. Despite a British Army escort, nine were killed and several captured in the attack.[20] A few days later, provincial teamsters abandoned a shipment of flour, "the men who conveyed it thither being afraid to proceed any further for fear of the Indians."[21] Eighteen-year-old James Smith, one of the road cutters taken prisoner in another attack about this time, told his captors that the party "had only about thirty guns among the whole of them."[22]

On July 9, 1755, approximately nine hundred French and Indians met Braddock's fourteen-hundred-man force near Fort Duquesne and killed almost two-thirds of it, at the loss of fewer than fifty men. The mortally wounded Braddock died a few days later. According to the *Pennsylvania Gazette*, the Royal Artillery abandoned most of its cannon during the disorderly retreat.[23]

For an army whose stock had been on a steady rise for years, it was an unprecedented military disaster. In Philadelphia, war and the threat of attacks along the Pennsylvania frontier became an immediate reality. If a strong force of regulars could be defeated at the hands of such an enemy, anything was possible.

Never was there a greater need for the Philadelphia Artillery. Due to the losses from Braddock's defeat at the Battle of the Monongahela and the death of so many officers and artillerists, the British desperately needed trained men.[24] Infantry could reach a fort, and light horse could range between settlements, but only artillery could smash down walls, level bastions, and bully defending garrisons into submission. Moreover, trains of artillery were essential to an army on the march, where matrosses filled musket cartridges and artificers maintained traveling forges to repair small arms. Aside from whatever ordnance may have been at Williamsburg or Alexandria, there were few guns or gun crews in the middle colonies, save the train of artillery at Philadelphia.

In late August, managers of the Association stock voted funds to repair the Grand Battery and buy an additional one thousand small arms and ammunition for the Associators' use.[25] Individual Associators, such as Benjamin Loxley, volunteered for service. Captain Harry Gordon of the Royal Engineers "and sundry other of Braddock's defeated men" taught him the elements of gunnery and ammunition making.[26] In addition to the one thousand small arms, the managers of the Association sent to England for two brass twelve-pounders and two brass six-pounders, all completely mounted and fitted.[27] The Association also purchased one eight-inch mortar on a bed, one hundred shells, and accompanying tools and fittings.[28] In addition to the cannon, the Associators ordered 112 fusils with bayonets and accoutrements for the artillery.[29] The Associators spared no expense. Brass field guns were the best of their kind. Properly equipped with the new ordnance and small arms, Loxley taught "great numbers of militia, both officers and men, in the use of the cannon and small arms."[30] Surprisingly, the train of artillery stayed in Philadelphia.

Frontier settlements from New York to Georgia bore the brunt of French offensives. A scouting party eight days out from Fort Duquesne that struck Penn's Creek, near the Susquehanna Forks, early on the morning of October 16, 1755, killing or capturing twenty-five settlers, found the Pennsylvania backcountry unprepared (fig. 6, overleaf). So did the approximately one hundred Delaware and Shawnee warriors under the command of Shingas that attacked settlements in the Conolloway tracts, about twelve miles from Fort Chambers, about midafternoon on October 31, 1755.[31] Attacks on this region lasted several days, killing or capturing forty-seven of ninety-three settlers, as a large force of about fifteen hundred native warriors reinforced by about one hundred French soldiers from Fort Duquesne fanned out over the backcountry.[32] Survivors found refuge at the nearby stockade and Presbyterian meeting house of the Reverend John Steel, erected in the wake of Braddock's recent defeat.[33]

The response from western leaders was swift but ineffectual. From his headquarters, a recently constructed blockhouse in Carlisle, Justice of the Peace John Armstrong ordered Captain Hance Hamilton's company from York to reinforce the northeastern limits of the county.[34] Only the day before, the magistrates of York County petitioned Pennsylvania governor Robert Hunter Morris to authorize Hamilton's company.[35] The signatories, who included Justice of the Peace George Stevenson, Herman Updegraff, Thomas Armor, James Smith, and John Adlum, made it clear that, in an apparent contrast with the Philadelphia Artillery, Pennsylvania's frontier inhabitants were cognizant of their duty but lacked the wherewithal to take the war to the enemy, declaring that "the Company who go, from this Town & the Parts adjacent to Morrow, to the Assistance of the Inhabitants on our Frontiers will take almost all our Arms & Ammunition with them," and offered that "there are Men enough willing to bear Arms & go out against the Enemy, were they supplied with Arms, Ammunition & a reasonable Allowance for their Time."[36]

Three days later, Cumberland County Coroner Adam Hoops reported that Hamilton's company had arrived at John McDowell's mill with two hundred men, plus an additional two hundred Cumberland County volunteers. In his report of November 3, 1755, Sheriff John Potter remarked that, "there is two-thirds of the Inhabitants of this Valley who hath already fled, leaving their Plantations, & without speedy Succor be granted, I am of opinion this Country will be lead dissolute without Inhabitant."[37] Less articulate than their neighbors in York County, but no further from the point, witnesses presented scalps, tomahawks, and the depositions of allied Delawares as evidence of their desperate plight.[38]

Despite the concerted pleas of their neighbors, and the representations of Hoops and Potter, many settlers who remained refused to counterattack. A disgusted Potter, who "would not guard a man that will not fight when called in so eminent a manner," concluded his report with a request that may have also served as a justification for the fortitude apparently lacking in his compatriots. "If our Assembly will give us any additional supply of arms and ammunition, the latter of which is most wanted, I could wish it were put into the hands of such persons as would go out upon scouts after the Indians rather than for the supply of the forts."[39]

Pennsylvania's new governor, Robert Hunter Morris, did not remain idle in the face of such troubling news. Upon receipt of reports from the frontier, Morris dashed off letters to his counterparts in neighboring colonies; to Colonel George Washington in Virginia, who was the ranking provincial officer in the region; and to William Shirley, acting commander of Crown forces in North America, apprising them of the dire situation. Pennsylvania had committed large quantities of grain to Braddock's expedition, to the Virginia provincials, and to the allied Six Nations, where, the previous spring, a late frost had destroyed the grain crop. [40] With food prices already rising, the implication of the French raid was clear to Morris.[41] "Their scheme," he warned, "seems by their motion, to be to take Possession of the Sasquehannah, which We shall not be able to pass without great difficulty, and they will be in that case perfectly at Liberty to destroy all the rich Country beyond that, where there are many thousands of Familys seated."[42]

The local associations raised in York, Cumberland, and Berks County met the immediate defensive needs of their communities. Associators, justices of the peace, or county commissioners could establish local fortifications at regular intervals along the baseline of Blue Mountain to guard population centers, important mountain gaps, or river crossings. But refugees

Fig. 6. "A Map of the Province of Pensilvania Drawn from the Best Authorities by T. Kitchin," 1756. Thomas Kitchin's map shows the location of allied nations relative to the settled parts of Pennsylvania. Note the long line of mountains running from the southwest to the northeast. French and native war parties made good use of the colony's ridge and valley terrain to move rapidly and strike quickly at isolated communities that were poorly served by primitive roads and trails. (*Author's Collection*)

needed escorts, as did convoys carrying grain and arms that had to be provided on a full-time basis. Associators could be expected to do little except establish a local defense and provide rudimentary training while in pursuit of their civilian occupations. What the province, and the region, needed was a full-time force committed to its defense and the destruction of its enemies.

On Monday, November 3, as the Pennsylvania Assembly convened, Morris issued blank commissions to former governor James Hamilton, whom he appointed as a military commissioner, and dispatched Captain Adolph Benzel, a British Army recruiter stationed at Philadelphia, to assist Colonel Conrad Weiser's defense efforts in Berks County.[43] The Supply Act, which the assembly passed a few weeks later, authorized construction of a string of frontier forts and warlike stores that would synchronize Pennsylvania's defenses with those of Maryland.[44]

In the meantime, local authorities associated together to organize training, fortify positions, harbor refugees, and form ranging companies. From his blockhouse at Carlisle, John Armstrong ordered volunteers to reinforce the northeastern limits of the county.[45] Over the next few weeks, Cumberland County officers working in consort with Armstrong improved defenses within a day's march of each other at the Reverend John Steel's meeting house, McDowell's Mill, Chambers Fort, Shippensburg, and Carlisle, in order to secure approaches into Sherman's Valley, the Conolloway tracts, and Conococheague Creek.[46] By the end of November, York County residents followed suit by organizing a military association. Along the Susquehanna River, Associators or local committees fortified Samuel Hunter's grist mill, which they renamed Fort Hunter, and cut loopholes for muskets in the houses at John Harris's Ferry.[47] East of the river, Berks County inhabitants chartered an association that organized a company "to range along the Frontiers of Berks County, from Swetara to Schuylkill."[48] Weiser, who as a frontier diplomat had forcibly evicted squatters a decade before, evacuated backcountry families and organized volunteers to serve as guards at the base of Blue Mountain.[49] Even local religious leaders such as John Steel, Andrew Bay, Thomas Barton, and John Elder raised companies to range between strong points.[50]

Within weeks, frontier leaders, from magistrates to mission-
aries, had completed a rudimentary defensive arc that ran from
within a few miles of the Maryland border to the Lehigh
Valley, with forts, palisades, or strong houses every five to fifteen miles, or about the distance that a patrol could easily
march from sunrise to sundown. Military associations stabilized the frontier, guarded convoys, and harbored refugees. In
contrast to the shiny new guns of the Philadelphia Artillery,
weapons consisted of a few pieces of small arms, light ordnance and powder supplied by the province, and whatever
weapons the Associators brought from home.

On November 14, part of the force from Fort Duquesne
attacked settlements in Berks County within easy striking distance of passes in Blue Mountain. The allied French and native
force roamed at will, operating in parties of about forty fighters
each, more than any one settlement could muster a response
to.[51] Having executed their raid on a settlement, the attackers
could withdraw into the mountains, then reappear several days
later and many miles distant. On November 24, 1755, raiders
struck Gnadenhutten, in the Lehigh Valley about thirty miles
northwest of Bethlehem. Companies under Captain Thomas
McKee ranged the Susquehanna, and companies under
Colonel Weiser and Captains Adam Read and Peter Heydrick
ranged between the Susquehanna and Schuylkill rivers.[52] For
the remainder of the war, frontier leaders would echo Potter's
request that the assembly do what it had failed to do: provide
arms and funding for a force capable of taking the war to the
enemy.

Meanwhile, Benjamin Franklin lobbied for a militia law. The
law, which passed the assembly on November 25, 1755, was a
clear compromise between military proponents such as
Franklin and the Quaker contingent.[53] Like the articles that
created the Military Association, the Militia Act created a voluntary force that was meant for local defense only. To accommodate Pennsylvania pacifists, no inhabitants would have to
serve whose religious scruples prevented them from doing so.
To alleviate financial strains on individuals and communities,
soldiers were not required to spend more than three days away
from home. No unit could be mustered into service for more
than three weeks. In addition to being impractical, the law

proved unconstitutional: King George II vetoed the act on the grounds that it only required local service and that it was not universal. A militia by definition required universal service. The type of campaigning required to win a forest war required long patrols and deep, penetrating raids far removed from settled areas.[54]

Although the Provincial Council accepted the commissions of the nine city companies on December 30, the province had no plan to build a fighting force around the Philadelphia Artillery or any associations organized within the province–if, in fact, the assembly had any plan to defend the province at all.[55] The six- and twelve-pound cannon that Governor Morris ordered for Captain Noarth's company were too large and heavy for use in the forest.[56] The tube of a brass six-pounder weighed 542 pounds.[57] The tube of a twelve-pounder weighed almost half again as much.[58] A six-pounder required seven horses to draw, and a twelve-pounder fifteen.[59] A three- or a four-pound gun on the other hand, required only four horses.[60] For that reason, three- and four-pound guns were more commonly used by the field artillery, especially over the kind of rough terrain found in the Pennsylvania wilderness. Weight was a fundamental consideration in the American forest, where good roads and grassy forage for draft animals were scarce. The Associators' purchase of heavier ordnance indicates that the new artillery company was intended for the defense of the river, not for an expedition to the west.

The arms and ordnance that Pennsylvania authorized for the western counties were likewise inadequate for the sort of warfare, consisting of long patrols and deep penetrating raids, that leaders such as Stevenson, Hoops, and Potter envisioned. Three weeks after Potter's request for arms and ammunition to sustain rangers in the forest, Fort Chambers and the recently fortified McDowell's Mill received four swivel guns and seven quarter casks of powder, defensive weapons, rather than the small arms and funding that would have allowed volunteers to patrol the nearby mountain gaps in force.[61]

In 1755, at a time when the Philadelphia Military Association was augmenting city defenses, frontier leaders threatened violence against the Philadelphia government. In October and November 1755, western threats ranged from taking over Philadelphia to cutting the throats of Pennsylvania assemblymen.[62] Indian attacks on frontier settlements continued, yet Philadelphia did little or nothing to protect the frontier.[63] On November 24, 1755, John Hambright, a Lancaster County tavern keeper, led three hundred to seven hundred men to Philadelphia, demanding protection from the Pennsylvania Assembly.[64] One day, a delegation from the frontier dragged a wagonload of corpses through the streets of Philadelphia to protest the lack of defensive measures.[65] On another occasion, the inhabitants of Paxton Township, near Swatara Gap, petitioned the assembly to keep nearby Fort Hunter in operation.[66]

The fort may have been reinforced at some point with arms allocated by the assembly, but the fifty muskets, four quarter casks of powder, lead, and two swivel guns were hardly adequate to fight a protracted campaign. As things stood, the quantity was likely a trifle, considering that some of it went to Harris's Ferry on the Susquehanna.[67]

Nor did the governor intend for the Associators to serve as full-time soldiers. The Supply Act, passed November 27, 1755, authorized construction of a string of frontier forts that would synchronize Pennsylvania's defenses with those of Maryland.[68] The act authorized funding for forts, warlike stores, and garrisons that provided Pennsylvania with a full-time frontier defense, as did redcoats such as the engineers and artillerists who trained Benjamin Loxley. The assembly had found a way to defend Pennsylvania with the Supply Act, but it still left the colony without a militia law. Benjamin Franklin took his battle to the frontier.

On December 18, 1755, Morris ordered Franklin, Franklin's son William, James Hamilton, and Joseph Fox to inspect the colony's defenses. An earlier arc had been completed under the administration of Governor Hamilton, but Franklin had other ideas.[69]

While on the frontier, he took note of the disaffiliation of the region's Moravian population. The Moravians were members of a religious sect that, like the Quakers, aspires to pacifism. Traditional allies of the Old Party, they had earlier obtained an exemption from bearing arms. On his visit, Franklin found the Moravians arming themselves. He reported

on their preparations, which included the fortification of houses and the organization of several companies. When he commented on the sect's pacifism to its leader, Bishop Augustus
Spangenberg, the latter replied that "it was not one of their
establish'd Principles" and that "on this Occasion, however,
they, to their Surprise, found it adopted by but a few."[70]
Franklin discovered widespread support for defense, even
among professed German pacifists.

In all, the Philadelphia delegation spent six weeks on the
frontier and ultimately recommended construction of a string
of frontier forts, fifteen miles apart, to secure the northern
approaches to Pennsylvania. By the end of January, Franklin
could report on the completion of two forts in northeastern
Pennsylvania and the progress of a third. Thirteen companies
totaling 522 men receiving provincial pay patrolled the northeastern frontier east of the Susquehanna and escorted convoys
of foodstuff.[71]

On January 20, 1756, the governor proposed a force consisting of three hundred soldiers for frontier security, to be stationed at five forts north of Sherman's Valley, "extending from
the Sugar Cabins near Sideling Hill to a Place within about
twenty Miles of the Sasquehannah."[72] By the end of March,
Morris appointed Elisha Salter commissary general of musters.
He was charged with inspecting the companies of the newly
raised provincial regiment and the new forts, and ensuring that
the soldiers, horses, weapons, and equipment shown on rosters
and inventories and paid for under the Supply Act were present and fit for service.[73] The governor cast about for additional
arms and encouraged backcountry inhabitants to find their
own. Two weeks later, in a reversal of a policy in force from
the time of the colony's founding, Pennsylvania declared war
on its erstwhile allies among the western tribes now in confederation with the Shawnee. Philadelphia instituted a bounty of
150 Spanish dollars for every male captive, or 130 pieces of
eight for every scalp, paid for out of the sixty thousand pounds
allocated under the Supply Act. The province offered a lesser
amount for each female scalp, provided the claimant could
prove its owner was dead.[74]

Morris demonstrated a commitment to defending a frontier
in a manner commensurate with the sort of warfare considered

necessary by leaders such as Stevenson, Potter, and Hoops. The governor's measures were implemented none too soon. In late March 1756, a French column marched out of Fort Duquesne to attack the Pennsylvania, Maryland, and Virginia backcountry. The column split into two detachments. One, under the command of an officer reputedly named Donville advanced to within twenty miles of Winchester, Virginia, where volunteers from that colony intercepted the force. Although the "Indians at first endeavoured to surround them," the Virginians, probably reinforced by some Catawbas and Cherokees, maneuvered to higher ground and, in a sharp skirmish, drove the invaders off, killing the French commander, whom they scalped and searched. Inside a leather pouch carried around his neck, the Virginians found orders to destroy supply depots on the Conococheague and harass convoys, which the Virginians shared with their colonial counterparts.[75]

By contrast, the other detachment handed Pennsylvania troops one of the worst defeats of the war a few days later at McCord's Fort, near the West Branch of the Susquehanna. The day after the fall of the fort, thirty-one Pennsylvania provincials under Captain Alexander Culbertson, reinforced by nineteen soldiers under Ensign David Jameson, counterattacked the French and Indian force at their encampment near Sideling Hill. Unlike the Virginians, who had detected the ambush, defeated their attackers, and passed on valuable intelligence, Culbertson's men rushed at the Indian force, which feigned a retreat from its initial position, encircled the advancing provincial troops, killed Culbertson and eighteen others, and wounded Jameson and fourteen others.[76] Lancaster jurist Edward Shippen would lay the blame on a lack of rifles, contending that "the Indians make use of rifled guns for the most part," when it was clear that the native war party had simply outsoldiered the Pennsylvanians.[77]

By May, Pennsylvania had expanded the provincial regiment to three battalions. Conrad Weiser commanded the 1st Battalion, John Armstrong the 2nd, and William Clapham, the 3rd, which was also known as the Augusta Regiment.[78]

Like the Association, the Supply Act promised permanency by authorizing forts as well as soldiers. Unlike the Association, the Pennsylvania Regiment was a publicly funded venture.[79] Its members were provincial soldiers, regularly enlisted and paid for a fixed term of service.[80] The province based its defense on regulars and full-time provincials, not Associators. From Philadelphia, Governor Morris had taken command and coordinated with colonial leaders outside the colony, secured lines of communications, and begun to organize a full-time garrison trained and equipped to patrol the frontier in force, and in a manner suited to destroy rather than merely repel the enemy. While military associations stabilized the frontier, guarded convoys, and harbored refugees using the few pieces of small arms, light ordnance and powder supplied by the province, and whatever weapons they brought from home, the passage of the Supply Act ensured that full-time provincials, rather than the Military Association, would defend the Pennsylvania frontier.

In June 1756, the governor ordered one hundred stands of muskets and two hundred stands of fusils, the latter earmarked for ranging duties, along with ammunition.[81] James Young, who had replaced Elisha Salter as commissary general of musters, inspected Pennsylvania's northern forts.[82] At each one, he checked arms, ammunition, equipment, and the progress of fortification.[83] Where trees grew too close to the fort, Young ordered them cut down.[84] When a noncommissioned officer had failed to do his duty, Young reproved his commanding officer. Provincial companies divided their time between patrolling and manning fort garrisons, and Young noted the number of patrols from each fort and how they performed. Young inspected food supplies and provincial arms, and noted the condition of both. Most important, he ordered the garrisons to the shooting range with their arms so he could inspect the soldiers' proficiency. In August, the arms that Morris had ordered arrived. Young, or some other appointee, issued them to the garrisons on the basis of need, in exchange for unserviceable muskets, which were returned to the provincial stores.[85] Young's hard work ensured that the muskets and fusils would be properly cared for and used.

At the State House in Philadelphia, passage of the Supply Act indicated a continuation of the assembly's struggle with the proprietor, rather than a revolutionary change of heart. The sixty thousand pounds authorized under the Supply Act was funded by taxing Pennsylvania lands rather than taxing Pennsylvanians directly.[86] By funding the act this way, the assembly could appear prodefense while continuing its battle with the proprietor, Pennsylvania's largest landowner. Benjamin Franklin was probably in the majority that favored taxing proprietary lands, since Thomas Penn stood to gain from frontier defense as much as anyone, if not more.[87] On the other side of the debate, proprietary partisans such as the Reverend William Smith, provost of the Philadelphia Academy, and Provincial Secretary Richard Peters opposed taxing Penn's lands.[88] Smith and Peters were no less hawkish than Franklin, but the two men relied on Penn's patronage for advancement, while Franklin did not. The act only passed when the assembly agreed to exempt proprietary estates from the tax.[89] In return, Penn agreed to donate a "free gift" of five thousand pounds, which turned out to be nothing more than the uncollected back rents from his lands.[90]

By 1756, the war had escalated to a general conflict involving the great powers of Europe. That year, Prince William Augustus, Duke of Cumberland, in his capacity as captain general of the British Army, established a plan for the mobilization of provincial forces. The plan called for the wartime establishment of four to six regular regiments, rotating at intervals from the home islands, and three regular regiments to be recruited locally. Two of the three were to be officered by Americans. Cumberland introduced a modified drill for these regiments that facilitated more fluid movement and effective fire. The plan also called for the Crown to pay for the construction, improvement, and garrisons of frontier forts, a corps of engineers, a train of artillery, and the establishment of arsenals.

In conference with assembled colonial governors, John Campbell, the Fourth Earl of Loudoun, lieutenant general and commander in chief of Crown forces in North America, reorganized Cumberland's broad defense requirements during a visit to Philadelphia in late 1756.[91] Loudoun's reforms represented the first major advancement toward continental defense in over eighty years, since the Duke of York's Laws had taken effect in 1676.

Loudoun called for an integrated force of provincials to include four thousand New Englanders to be organized and trained as rangers. New York and New Jersey provincials would garrison forts and were to be used as expeditionary forces should regulars fall below strength. All North American forces were to use a standardized drill authorized by the Duke of Cumberland. His plan worked to the traditional strengths of the respective colonies and did not specifically mention Pennsylvania or any others to the south and west. Pennsylvania nevertheless provided ranger companies and garrisons for the forts on the northern and western frontiers, as well as two barracks, at Philadelphia and Lancaster, that would serve as recruit training depots known as rendezvous for the regiments outlined in his plan. Cumberland's plan implied that regulars, and all of the funding that would make their stay possible, were on the way, and it was with regulars that the Crown intended to win the war in the middle colonies.

The first phase of Cumberland's plan was already in full swing at the time of Loudoun's arrival. The previous summer, several German-speaking officers representing the 4th Battalion of the 62nd Regiment of Foot had arrived in Philadelphia to recruit from the Pennsylvania countryside.[92] Subsequently renumbered the 60th and nicknamed the "Royal Americans," the regiment would constitute one of the British Army's newest concepts. It consisted of four battalions instead of the usual one, and had an authorized strength of four thousand men. Its recruits were mostly, but not all, raised from among German and Swiss settlers in Pennsylvania. The army intended that the 60th should serve in the American colonies, and so the men's training encouraged the use of light infantry tactics then coming into vogue in Europe, tactics that were better suited to forest fighting.[93] As with the levies, the Crown recruited directly from the American population. Young Pennsylvania men who were inclined toward military service or motivated by the promise of steady pay could join the regiment. By December, over five hundred officers and men of the 60th Regiment had assembled in Philadelphia.[94] The formation of the Royal American Regiment was a direct reflection of Britain's resolve to defend Pennsylvania with regulars and not colonial levies, and certainly not Associators.

Lieutenant Colonel Henry Bouquet, commander of the 60th Regiment of Foot, arrived in Philadelphia in 1756 to find the city unprepared to garrison his rapidly expanding battalions, even if the regiment promised to pay.[95] An exasperated Bouquet threatened the most drastic measure then known, that of quartering soldiers in the homes of Pennsylvania civilians.[96] A Pennsylvania delegation headed by Benjamin Franklin intervened with the offer of a nongovernment facility, the newly constructed Pennsylvania Hospital, which Bouquet accepted until permanent quarters could be built.[97] The next step, the Philadelphia barracks, was a commodious structure featuring a three-story officers' quarters, a parade ground, and room for up to three thousand soldiers.[98] Joseph Fox, a politically influential Philadelphia carpenter, became the first barracks master.[99]

The train of artillery now vied with the regular army and the province for manpower. George Noarth remained in command. Benjamin Loxley was its first lieutenant, and John Goodwin the second lieutenant. The artillery company was not to interfere with the garrison at the fort or the company at the Grand Battery at Wiccacoe.[100] Members of the artillery nonetheless contributed to the fort's maintenance.[101] In line with the abortive militia law, the reorganization stipulated that the fort company was for the defense of the city only.[102]

Philadelphia merchant Samuel Mifflin now commanded the Grand Battery.[103] Mifflin's first lieutenant was Oswell Eve, a successful sea captain.[104] The most junior officer at the fort, Ensign William Moore, shared the same name with a William Moore who was a sea captain and merchant in the 1750s and 1760s.[105] The Grand Battery now mounted the thirty-two-pound Schuylkill Gun.[106] This monster could command the water approaches to Philadelphia in a way that its smaller mates could not.

Mifflin's Battery Company had thirty men besides the three officers. Like George Noarth and Benjamin Loxley, Mifflin and Eve recruited from among their peers. Most members of the Battery Company had a direct interest in the Delaware River port: John Anderson, Joseph Brown, Richard Budden, Andrew Carson, Samuel Carson, Samuel Chancellor, James Craig, William Dowell, John Gass, George Houston, John Inglis, Archibald McCall, William Plumsted, George Rankin, Joseph Redman, John Searle, John Sibbald, Archibald Stewart, Charles

Stedman, and George Stephenson were merchants, mariners, ship owners, or all three.[107] Francis Grice built ships.[108]

Some members of the Battery Company were men of means. Three of Mifflin's privates, John Inglis, Joseph Redman, and John Sibbald, had been officers in the Associated Regiment of Foot in 1747 (see Appendix). Privateer captain John Sibbald had commanded the Grand Battery in 1748. John Inglis had been the acting deputy collector for the port of Philadelphia from 1751 to 1753.[109] Joseph Redman served Philadelphia as collector of excise. William Plumsted was the mayor of Philadelphia.[110] In 1741, Plumsted had signed a petition urging King George II to order the Pennsylvania Assembly to fund defense.[111]

The size and composition of the Battery Company indicates the political mission of the Associators. Had it come to a fight with an enemy vessel, Mifflin's garrison was too small to man all of the Grand Battery's fifty-four cannon.[112] Many of its rank and file had either held commissions as officers in the Association, held political office, or occupied high stations in life relative to their military rank.

The Association grew despite its apparently redundant role. By 1756, the Associated Regiment of Foot included a staff, a regimental band, at least one company of grenadiers, a company of pioneers, and a troop of light horse. The train of artillery included two companies, the Association battery, under Captain Mifflin, and another company under Captain George Noarth. Later that year, a third company of artillery may have been raised.[113] Franklin remembered, "We paraded about 1200 well-looking Men, with a Company of Artillery who had been furnish'd with 6 brass Field Pieces."[114]

The officers of the regiment appointed Franklin as their colonel.[115] Upon his return to Philadelphia after touring the frontier, the officers of the Association organized a review.[116] In his *Autobiography*, Franklin wrote, "They came to my door, between 30 and 40, mounted, all in their Uniforms. . . . [A]s soon as we began to move they drew their Swords and rode with them naked all the way. Somebody wrote an Account of this to the Proprietor and it gave him great Offense. No such Honor had been paid him when in the Province, nor to any of his Governors; and it was only proper to Princes of the Royal

Blood."[117] Speaker of the Pennsylvania Assembly Isaac Norris suspected that several of Franklin's allies "are promoted in the Military way and can thence increase their Interest, and are very high in favour of Franklin, the Captains, Officers and Granadiers waiting on him . . . as if he had been a Member of the Royal Family."[118]

Norris had reason to be suspicious. By 1756, the Associators were members of a private corporation that maintained two forts and a vast arsenal of artillery and small arms. Working through the Provincial Council, its members had engineered a legal distinction between the Association and any militia that might be legislated. Franklin had just completed a tour of the frontier. Now the Associators treated him like their king, with a royal procession, resplendent in uniform and drawn swords. They had effectively made themselves independent of the colony's defense structure. The regiment—which included its full complement of eight companies, an honorary colonel, regimental staff, a band of fifes, drums, and oboes, and two companies of grenadiers with attached pioneers—did much to offend the sensibilities of at least some of Pennsylvania's leaders, but little to relieve the beleaguered frontier.[119]

Loxley's gun crews showed marked improvement by this time. As a member of the Library Company, Loxley certainly would have had as much access to published materials as anyone else in the city, and while there is little doubt that he continued to rely on Blakeney's simplified *Exercise*, there is some evidence that he and other Associators began to study other drill manuals and apply them to their training.[120] In early April, the *Pennsylvania Gazette* noted that "the Philadelphia Artillery Company fired one of their Cannon ten times in less than a Minute."[121]

True to its mandate, the Association fielded a trained body of experts who served as an "Expedient for rendering the Use of Arms more universal, and the Province more secure."[122] The day after the *Pennsylvania Gazette* announced the Associators' formal reception of the new governor, William Denny, it announced that they had opened a military academy on the grounds of Philadelphia College, evidently with the full support of its provost, the prodefense Reverend William Smith, and the chairman of the board of trustees, the equally prodefense Provincial Secretary Richard Peters. Located across the street from the city's largest meeting house, the Associator academy offered instruction in three branches: horse, foot, and "the Artillery Exercise belonging to the old Association Battery."[123] Throughout the long summer of 1756, the unmistakable din of military training shattered the peace of William Penn's once "greene Countrie Towne." Artisans and merchants who could ill afford long periods of provincial service that would take them away from their occupations could nevertheless see to basic military instruction, at least in and around Philadelphia.

In 1756, the Philadelphia Associators engaged in several political demonstrations. On March 17, the *Pennsylvania Gazette* reported that more than six hundred members of the Associated Regiment of Foot of the City of Philadelphia treated the city to a military spectacle. Led by "their Colonel," Benjamin Franklin, the Associators formed ranks on Society Hill and marched down Second Street to the New Market, where they demonstrated their martial skills "according to the manner of Street Firing."[124] Street firing was a tactic in which a column of soldiers advanced down a street. As soon as each man in the front rank fired, he executed a right face and marched to the tail of the column, the man behind him taking his place, firing, and then marching to the rear as well, so that an entire company could maintain a continuous fire in a cramped space such as a city street, a narrow wilderness road, or a fort's sally port.

The regiment then marched through the heart of the city, with the band playing and its colors flying, past the governor's house and on to the courthouse. Behind Franklin came two companies of artillery and three bodies of infantry, with special companies of troops known as pioneers, trained to remove obstructions from a regiment's path.

If the purpose of the military procession was lost on any of the gathered crowds, platoons of specially trained soldiers, led by grenadiers, turned out to remind them. Grenadiers had evolved into elite shock troops by the mid-eighteenth century, but their original duty in siege warfare must have been in the minds of some. If not, the pioneers helped get the message across. Pioneers were trained to destroy fortifications such as the French had built at the forks.[125] They were ax-wielding troops whose task was to chop through wooden obstructions in advance of the main body. The French had built forts on Pennsylvania soil. The time had come to remove them.

The artillery had an obvious role in the reduction of enemy fortifications. Little mention was given to the other units. The *Pennsylvania Gazette* failed to describe the marching band, the grenadiers, or the pioneers in any detail. Such sights were great rarities in the American colonial military. But the arrival of the artillery was treated as a sort of grand finale, the culmination of the martial display. The newspaper described the artillery as "consisting of upwards of 100 Men, with four neatly painted Cannon, drawn by some of the largest and most stately Horses in the Province."[126]

In late April, a detachment of Captain Edward Jones's light horse joined officers of Captain William Vanderspiegle's company of foot to provide an escort for Governor Morris as he set out from Philadelphia to review elements of the Pennsylvania Regiment at Harris' Ferry. Jones's troopers and Vanderspiegle's officers, "dressed in their Uniform, made a genteel appearance."[127]

Morris was not the only official so honored. On March 29, Moses, a visiting Mohawk dignitary, suffered a seizure and died at Philadelphia following a conference with the governor and council.[128] "Several Members of the Provincial Council, the Commissioners, most of the Officers of the Militia, and others of the principal Inhabitants of the City" attended his funeral, at which the grenadiers of the Regiment of Foot rendered "all the Honours of War usual on such Occasions," then provided an escort to the gravesite.[129]

On May 14, the Associators demonstrated their tactics in Germantown.[130] The train of artillery was posted on the flanks of the infantry and fired alternately from the left and the right. It was the parent branch of the Philadelphia Association and so deserved favorable mention in print.

The Associators had come a long way since Philadelphia's seven companies boarded transports to join Gooch's regiment in the West Indies, and so had Philadelphia. Then, the *Pennsylvania Gazette* merely mentioned that the soldiers "performed their Exercise to Admiration." Now, it described such intricate maneuvers as street firing and such esoteric military occupations as pioneers and grenadiers. David Hall, the printer of the *Gazette*, obviously expected his subscribers to know whereof he wrote.

The artillery had become a prominent feature wherever the Associators went. In August, "as much of the City Regiment as the Shortness of the Notice would admit of" assembled under arms to honor the new governor, William Denny.[131] An artillery company posted its cannon at the common between Market and Water streets.[132] The guns of the Grand Battery joined the artillery company in a salute.[133] Benjamin Franklin then addressed Denny on behalf of the train of artillery. He expressed the Associators' gratification at serving under a military man such as Denny.[134]

Denny's arrival coincided with military disaster. That very day, word reached Philadelphia of the French capture of Fort Oswego on Lake Ontario.[135] French forces had captured Fort Granville in western Pennsylvania a few days earlier, where they had planted the French colors among its ashes, and Colonel John Armstrong warned of Fort Shirley's defenseless state.[136] There was no money for defense, yet here was a large body of self-trained, self-funded, and largely self-equipped soldiers on parade in Philadelphia.[137]

The artillery was highly trained. In early April, the *Pennsylvania Gazette* noted that "the Philadelphia Artillery Company fired one of their Cannon ten times in less than a Minute."[138] Loxley had learned some advanced tactics. As early as 1560, British artillerists had used linen bags for artillery cartridges. By the early seventeenth century, the technique had become standard practice. Captain-Lieutenant David Hay's crews used flannel-covered cartridges; the Royal Artillery would not introduce metallic cartridges until the nineteenth century.[139] Cloth cartridges facilitated rapid loading, but they had their disadvantages. Because the cloth cartridge casings left smoldering embers in the bore, the use of a corkscrew-like cleaning device, known as a worm, and a wet sponge were necessary to extinguish them.[140] But Philadelphia artillerists chose instead to make cartridges out of metal such as lead, tin, or brass that would melt or fragment on detonation of the main powder charge.[141] Casing the charge in a soft metal such as lead or tin potentially cut two steps out of the loading process, thus allowing a higher rate of fire. The Royal Artillery could have used such expert artillerymen.

By 1756, the guns the Associator Artillery used were stored in wooden sheds at the State House. The sheds were built at both sides of the wing buildings of the seat of government.[142] Loxley was responsible for construction of the sheds and maintenance of the ordnance stored inside.[143] It had been a busy year. The Association had grown. From two forts and three companies it was now a small army complete with uniforms, flank companies of grenadiers, staff officers, and a marching band with oboes. To remind the people of Philadelphia of its existence, the regiment paraded frequently. Loxley saw to it that the great guns were exercised with flash and proficiency. Even when the guns were not in use, the wooden sheds at the State House reminded everyone of the power of the Association in general and the artillery in particular.

On November 4, 1756, Provincial Secretary Richard Peters presented to the Provincial Council a list of Associator companies organized in Pennsylvania. In addition to the train of artillery, Associators in Philadelphia were organized into nine companies of foot. Edward Jones drilled a troop of light horse, and Samuel Mifflin commanded a battery company at the Grand Battery.[144]

Military associations outside of Philadelphia were organized by township. Bucks County raised nine companies of foot in this manner, organized into a regiment.[145] Colonel George Stevenson commanded the York County Associators, which conducted patrols into the nearby mountains.[146] A plan for the defense of Cumberland County, laid before the Provincial Council and dated 1754, but more likely dating to 1756, recommended that two companies conduct regular patrols. The first would be based at McDowell's Mill, twenty miles west of Shippensburg, on the West Branch of Conococheague Creek; the second at an as-then undetermined location.[147] The author of the report, Phillip Davies, pointed out that, "as John M'Dowell's mill is at The most important Pass, most exposed to danger, has a Fort already made about it, and there provisions may be most easily had, for these Reasons let the Chief Quarters be there."[148] Each company would number sixty men and would be organized out of four existing fort garrisons.[149] Davies recommended a five-man guard at three locations, including his own house, which stood eight miles from McDowell's Mill and sixteen and a half miles from Benjamin Chambers's residence.[150] These posts were to be relieved daily "by the patrolling Guards."[151] Ten men would march from McDowell's Mill to the farthest post each morning, and ten would return each evening, stopping at each post. "By this Plan The whole bounds will be patrolled twice every Day, a Watch will be constantly kept at four most important Places, and there will be every Night fourty-five Men at ye Chief Quarters ready for any exigence."[152]

In contrast to the Philadelphia Associators, westerners mustered into provincial service, an indication of the immediacy of the threat and their economic status. The light horse troop and Vanderspiegle's company of foot may have cut a "genteel appearance," but it fell to provincials under "the experienced Colonel Clapham" to build Fort Augusta at Shamokin.[153] Hance Hamilton's company was then in provincial service under the Second Battalion, Pennsylvania Regiment. The York Associators evidently could ill afford the luxury of grenadiers and a regimental band.

No less willing, the Association officers of Saint Vincent's Township, Chester County, on May 8, 1756, notified the Pennsylvania Assembly of their intention to form an independent Associator company designated as the St. Vincent and Puke's Land [Pikesland] Association.[154] Echoing the language of the 1747 Association "and thinking it our bounden Duty as Christians and most Loyal Subjects to our most gracious Sovereign Lord, Georg the Second," these predominantly German Associators pledged "to Save, if possible, Our Lives, Wives, Children, Liberty, and our most holy Religion from the Hands of our most cruel and Merciless Enemy."[155] Once again, Associators evoked sacred duty in defense of the Protestant realm, and natural rights in the name of military service.

On August 21, 1756, Robert Erwin submitted a petition from "Part of the remaining inhabitants of the County of Cumberland" concerning the dire situation on the Pennsylvania frontier. Noting that the French were sure to gather intelligence from prisoners captured in a recent attack on Fort Granville, the petitioners harbored little doubt that "the Enemy will be inform'd of the Weakness of this Frontier, and how incapable we are of defending ourselves against their Incursions."[156] The petition argued that "Great Numbers of the Inhabitants are already fled . . . Finding it is not in the Power of the Troops in Pay of the Government (were we certain of their being continued) to prevent the Ravages of our Restless, Barbarous, & Merciless Enemy."[157] Because the drain on frontier labor affected the economic well-being of the entire colony, not to mention the very survival of the inhabitants of Cumberland County, the petition continued by pointing out that "a part of the immense Quantity of Grain" lay exposed to capture or destruction. It concluded with a request that the assembly ask General Loudoun to order the provincial troops "to make Incursions into the Enemies Country which woul'd contribute greatly to the safety and Satisfaction of your Hon[orable] Pet[itioners]."[158]

Morale sank. On September 17, Colonel Stevenson reported on Colonel John Armstrong's recent raid on the village of Kittanning, expressing his hope that "Care will be taken to pay off these valiant men with Honour, which will be a great means of encouraging others."[159] Stevenson then lamented recent British reverses at Minorca and Oswego, as well as the inaction of the Pennsylvania Assembly. Like other Associators, Stevenson framed the war as a struggle against foreign enemies bent on imposing arbitrary rule and religious persecution in the form of Roman Catholicism when he asked, "must We in very Deed become a Province of France? If so, farewell Property, farewell liberty, sweet Liberty; farewell Religion, instead of the free Exercise of our Holy Religion, must we have Persecution? Images, Crucifixes, &c, &c. Alas! Alas!"[160]

The colony, meanwhile, augmented Philadelphia defenses even further. That summer, Captain Sibbald took the province's ship *Pennsylvania* to sea.[161] The *Pennsylvania* patrolled the mouth of Delaware Bay throughout the summer. It encountered no enemy vessels, underscoring the fact that the colony was under no direct threat from the sea. The threat by this time lay to the west.

Indeed, harbor defense was at any rate a moot point, as neither the French nor the British considered Philadelphia a combat zone. In 1757, the 35th (Otway's) Regiment of Foot, commanded by Major Henry Fletcher, arrived in Philadelphia. The 35th had been part of the garrison that surrendered to the French at Fort William Henry on Lake George.[162] The articles of capitulation stipulated that the regiment remain far from an active theater of war.[163] The safety of British prisoners of war in Canada and elsewhere depended on the integrity of those surrender terms. The sight of the paroled regiment marching through the city should have been an additional argument against the expansion of the Philadelphia Associators, while westerners bore the brunt of French attacks.[164]

On March 29, 1757, the Pennsylvania Assembly passed another militia law.[165] More binding than the 1755 act vetoed by the king, the law addressed many of the concerns raised by the Articles of Association while respecting the sensibilities of Pennsylvania pacifists, but it was in many ways typical of English militia laws dating to the sixteenth century. Taking a page from philosopher John Locke, the new force would "defend their Lives and Fortunes against . . . Hostile Invasion" as well as "quell and suppress any Intestine, Commotions, Rebellions, or Insurrections," the traditional mission of the nation in arms.[166] The militia was to be "well armed and expertly Disciplined in the Military Art" in order to defend the provincial government and the English way of life.[167]

Pennsylvania Associators had the satisfaction of knowing that militia leadership would not be limited to large property owners, or gubernatorial favorites, as it was in nearby colonies. The new law, a modified seigneurial system suited to Pennsylvania's proprietary charter, directed sheriffs to divide each county, ward, and borough into military subdivisions known as districts or divisions, comparable to hundreds in other localities, each capable of mustering a company numbering at least sixty soldiers. Rather than organizing a population into regiments by town or county, the new law enabled commanders to organize a force of eligible volunteers, under elected company officers.

Company officers elected regimental field and staff officers.[168] Lest the elections become a free-for-all, the law introduced property requirements. To be eligible to hold a captain's rank, candidates had to own real estate worth at least 150 pounds or other property worth at least 300 pounds. Lieutenants were required to own land valued at a minimum of 100 pounds, or property worth at least 200 pounds, ensigns 50 pounds real property or 100 pounds of chattel. Owners of eating or drinking establishments were ineligible to hold a commission.

Property requirements and the exclusion of tavern keepers from holding rank were likely insurance against graft and inequity, and reinforced a system of merit-based commissions. During the eighteenth century, professional and managerial credentials were rare. Property ownership at the very least indicated that an officer candidate had some administrative experience. The new law gave sweeping powers to militia officers in time of invasion or civil disturbance, and moreover addressed the concerns of many frontier leaders such as Adam Hoops, John Potter, and George Stevenson.[169] Regimental commanders, for example, could now patrol their jurisdictions with as many soldiers as they deemed appropriate. Sentinels were empowered to fire on anyone who refused to give the proper password, without fear of legal reprisal. Any soldier who knowingly aided or abetted the enemy should suffer death "without benefit of Clergy."[170] Despite such strong language, Pennsylvania's new militia law was relatively mild. Officers and private soldiers who neglected their duty might be fined, but even relatively serious acts such as mutiny or sedition warranted no more than a one-hundred-pound fine. While severe, such a sum, representing several months' worker's wages in a cash-poor economy, was certainly preferable to a firing squad.[171] Striking a superior officer would set a soldier back five pounds.[172] To avoid the public nuisance of heavily armed drunks, the law imposed a summary forty-shilling fine for every case.[173]

The law was equally mild on the point of religious conviction. Addressing the earlier misgivings of Quakers, the law exempted "those Religious Societies or Congregations, whose Tenets and Principles are against bearing arms" from monthly musters.[174] Friends, Moravians, Pietists, and various other pacifist sects who helped fight fires, treated wounded, carried messages, or acted as cooks or guardians to women, children, or the elderly were exempted from service, even in wartime.[175]

The new militia law required that every militiaman muster for no more than six hours every first Monday in June, August, November, and March. The law set the second Monday in October as the regimental muster day, when colonels were expected to drill their regiments.[176] The law also directed militiamen to bring a serviceable firearm; a cutlass, bayonet, or tomahawk; a cartridge box designed to hold at least twelve cartridges; and three good flints. An attached rider required the province to provide arms and accoutrements to those who were without arms, unlike the Association, which mandated self-funding.[177]

The new law did not sweep the Association out of existence. On the contrary, in light of its growing prestige, no regimental limitations governed the organization of an artillery command in the city of Philadelphia.[178] Should "any Number of Men, in or near the City of Philadelphia, not less than Sixty, nor exceeding One Hundred Men, to a Company, including Officers" form a company or companies, "for managing the Artillery belonging to the Province, and the Battery or Fort near the said City," those artillerists needed only to elect their officers in the presence of their colonel, complete a return with his signature, submit the return to the governor, and drill on the same days as the foot regiments.[179] In this fashion, the law authorized the city artillery to organize up to three companies to train with the city ordnance. The law specifically directed that "nothing herein contained shall be construed to affect, alter, change, or take away the right and title of the private owners of the Soil on which the said Battery or Fort is erected."[180] Even within the constraints of the militia law, the train of artillery remained an autonomous and distinct structure, its forts privately owned, its equipment publicly maintained, and its officers and men answerable only to the governor or military commander. Militia companies could alternatively organize as troops of horse, but only with the consent of the regimental colonel.[181]

Pennsylvania had at last passed a militia law that at a minimum addressed the expectations of Pennsylvania's numbered factions. But the act was as temporary as the Association professed to be: it automatically expired, less than eighteen months later, at the end of the term of the Assembly sitting

Fig. 7. Philadelphia map horn. American soldiers at this time often carried powder horns in lieu of cartridge boxes. This horn, a testament to one soldier's service in and around Philadelphia, shows the County Court House at center where the Associators stored arms and drilled. To the right is the steeple of Christ Church. At the far right is the belfry of the Philadelphia Academy. Associators trained at the academy during the summer of 1756. (*Courtesy of Colonel J. Craig Nannos, photograph by John Bansemer*)

March 9, 1758.[182] Significant military operations in Pennsylvania had abated by that time.

In other arenas, Pennsylvania appeared to have moved no closer to a consensus on defense, despite the fact that the October elections had returned only sixteen Quakers to a thirty-six member assembly.[183] Throughout December 1756, Governor Denny wrangled with Pennsylvania representatives over the quartering of the newly arrived 60th Regiment. Proprietor Thomas Penn continued to squabble with the assembly over taxation and monetary policy. The following month, as Denny steadfastly refused to support a tax on proprietary lands, a frustrated assembly proclaimed itself "an English Representative Body," which would allow it to levy taxes on all Pennsylvanians for the common defense, even those who, like the Penns, claimed sovereignty over the colony.[184] In June 1757, Benjamin Franklin sailed to London to ask Penn to relinquish his proprietorship of the colony.[185]

Philadelphia by that time was crammed with soldiers, most of whom had come for no other purpose than the defense of the colony (fig. 7). Captain Sibbald's *Pennsylvania* cruised the Delaware Bay, the Associators marched, and the artillery exercised its cannon. Yet the Crown continued to augment Pennsylvania's defenses. Late in 1757, William Franklin wrote to the editor of the *Pennsylvania Gazette* that "15 Iron Cannon, 18 pounders, were last Year purchased in England, and added to the 50 they had before, either mounted on their Batteries, or ready to be mounted, besides a Train of Artillery, being new Brass Field pieces." In addition to the train of artillery, two thousand small arms were stored in the city for public use.[186] Early in 1758, the Board of War sent another two thousand stands of small arms to Pennsylvania, along with 125 barrels of gunpowder. The board also shipped ten pieces of light ordnance, twelve mortars, and seventy-five barrels of coarse-grained cannon powder for them.[187] Full-time provincial soldiers, paroled regulars in the city, and publicly supplied ordnance should have made the train of artillery superfluous.

On March 15, 1758, the province closed the port of Philadelphia to commercial traffic. On the same day "a letter was wrote to the Commanding Officer of General Otway's Regiment, requesting him without Delay, to reinforce the Guards at the Fort at Wiccacoe, and to use his utmost Endeavors to prevent any outward bound Vessels from Passing the said Fort."[188] Captain Mifflin was directed to cooperate with Major Fletcher's men and to enforce the embargo.[189] Something big was afoot.

On April 14, 1758, Brigadier John Forbes arrived in Philadelphia as commander of a new expedition. All of the martial preparations of the past two years, from the construction of the two barracks buildings, to the arrival of the Royal Americans, to the shipment of ordnance and thousands of small arms now focused on a single goal: the capture of Fort Duquesne.

Forbes found Pennsylvania's logistical situation in shambles. One of his first actions was to secure three hundred fusils to send to the Cherokees then gathered at Winchester, Virginia.[190] Someone must have quickly brought Pennsylvania's considerable arsenal to Forbes's attention. A week after his arrival, he wrote Governor Denny that "there remain in your Store more Arms than will Compleat the Forces proposed to be raised by this Province, besides 2,000 Arms, which I have an

Account of being embarked for the Service of this Expedition."[191] This he followed with a more pointed comment, stating in no uncertain terms:

> As the Situation of these Provinces is such at this Critical Juncture as requires all possible Means to be exerted to clear this Province of the Enemy who have at this Time invaded it, and as there is a great Scarcity of Arms for that purpose, I am under the necessity of requiring your Honour that you will give orders for delivering to me Two Hundred and Eighteen Light Fuzees, which are in your Store, as likewise as many of the 165 Arms as are found to be serviceable after they are Surveyed.[192]

The general was justifiably perturbed. A well-stocked arsenal rusted in Philadelphia while an enemy threatened the frontier less than two weeks' march away. The fusils to which Forbes referred included the 112 carbines belonging to Captain Noarth's artillery company. Despite the fact that the arms in question were housed within feet of the very building in which the province deliberated over public matters, they were no more public property than the fire engines of the Philadelphia Union Fire Company. The arms were the property of the train of artillery, operating under the aegis of a private association, involvement in which the province had absolved itself and over which the assembly had relinquished its authority. Denny justifiably balked at surrendering those arms to Forbes and the regular army. He was powerless to do so and doubtless embarrassed by the fact.

Help for the beleaguered governor came from an unlikely source. According to Loxley, several prominent Associators, including Lieutenant Colonel James Coultas of the Associated Regiment of Foot, informed General Forbes that Loxley knew laboratory work, artillery duty, and military stores.[193] On April 21, Forbes sent Harry Gordon of the Royal Engineers and Army Commissary Henry Ward to fetch Loxley for an interview. Forbes met Loxley in his quarters, where the general asked him "many questions."[194] After the interview, the brigadier placed him in charge of the king's stores at Philadelphia with instructions to issue ordnance to no one except Forbes, Major General James Abercromby (the ranking

British general in North America), or Governor Denny, without the general's permission.[195]

Captain Lieutenant Hay of the Royal Artillery had recently promised to commission Loxley as a second lieutenant in the regular army.[196] Loxley's rank came on the condition that he supply a twelve-man gun crew.[197] A commission in the regular army was highly prestigious, an opportunity at which ambitious colonists often jumped. Any regular army officer above captain automatically outranked a provincial officer, no matter how high the latter's rank.[198]

Despite the allure of such a coveted distinction, Loxley refused Hay's offer and took the storekeeper job.[199] A few days after the interview, Forbes wrote Abercromby that "the Governour has sent me the 218 Fuzees as he has taken the Keys of the Province Magazines into his own hands."[200] In a stroke, the appointment of Loxley as storekeeper of the province headed off a potentially embarrassing situation. The efforts of Coultas and the others had paid off: Loxley and the artillery stayed in Philadelphia.

Loxley took his new job seriously. On May 4, 1758, he produced a complete inventory of the ordnance in Pennsylvania with Hay's help.[201] The list included arms stored at the State House. Four four-pounders, two six-pounders, two twelve-pounders, fifteen eighteen-pounders, and one eight-inch mortar, all belonging to the Association, were now out of the control of the assembly and at the disposal of the British Army, if necessary.

With one of his supply issues solved for the time being, Forbes could turn his attention to the coming campaign. Like General Braddock, Forbes intended to build a road over which he could transport heavy artillery. Like most frontier forts in North America, Fort Duquesne was built of heavy timber reinforced with earth and rubble. It could withstand small-arms fire and even light artillery, but would quickly crumble under the sustained fire of heavy guns. Unlike Braddock, Forbes intended to build a fortified road. Forts were planned at even intervals. Over this road, reinforcements were never more than a night's march from one another. Should an aggressive enemy attack, the army's vanguard need only retreat to the nearest fortification and send for help.

Associators outside of Philadelphia appear to have been less successful when it came to garnering support. The ranger companies organized out of the York County Association had continued to patrol the mountainous frontier of that county during each active campaigning season.[202] Pennsylvania soldiers in provincial service were to uniform themselves with a green shirt, a green jacket, a green blanket, and a green cloth cap.[203] Colonel Stevenson maintained that the Germans would object to purchasing their own uniforms.[204] He proposed linen stockings, red below the knee, petticoat trousers "reaching to the thick of the Leg, made of strong Linnen," and a linen sailor's frock. The proposed uniform made for a cheaper alternative to imported wool and served better for summer campaigning. On May 15, 1758, Stevenson wrote that the companies entering provincial service expected the Crown to pay for "Drums, Colors, & the other Common Instruments of War. Drums they need much."[205]

Captain David Jameson, a physician in civilian life, examined the men according to Colonel Henry Bouquet's direction.[206] Jameson, an experienced soldier who had been wounded in the 1756 battle at Sideling Hill that killed Captain Alexander Culbertson, wrote that the men, who were to escort wagon trains for the Forbes expedition, lacked uniforms, and that only one-third were armed.[207] June found the four York companies waiting on uniforms and essential accoutrements while Benjamin Loxley kept his carbines under lock and key.

Colonel Stevenson meanwhile wrestled with other problems. At least some of his officer candidates were unfit to command, while the viable candidates contended with family and religious bars to service. Stevenson had first recommended Thomas Minshall for command.[208] Minshall's commission was disputed by one Thomas Wright, who supported a Ludwig Myer of the Conococheague Valley. Stevenson described Myer as "a low-lived, worthless fellow, an Inhabitant of the Conedoughela holds under Maryland & never pd one Shill'g Tax, neither to support the War nor for any other publick use whatsoever; he has not Sense enough even to be a Sergeant."[209] Another complication soon arose regarding Stevenson's choice: Minshall's wife opposed his service, as did her friends. Bowing to family pressure, Minshall resigned.[210]

Provincial Secretary Peters recommended that each compa-
ny commission at least one German subaltern "to engage the
German Inhabitants."[211] Accordingly, Stevenson commissioned
Peter Meems.

By September 3, elements of Forbes's army of regulars and
provincials had reached Loyal Hanna, about fifty miles from
Fort Duquesne. By November 12, they had advanced to within
twelve miles of their objective.[212] On November 25, 1758, the
Forks of the Ohio became a British possession. After remaining
a few weeks, most of the army returned over the mountains,
leaving Lieutenant Colonel Hugh Mercer and two hundred
Pennsylvania provincials to build a makeshift fort near the site
of the razed French stronghold. John Forbes died the following
March in Philadelphia, where he was buried with full honors
at Christ Church.

In Philadelphia, things quieted down for the train of
artillery. Loxley continued in his important position as provincial storekeeper, paid twenty pounds per year.[213] As storekeeper, he held the keys to thousands of pounds worth of military
stores, private property that required public funds to be maintained. His office gained him access to the governor and the
Provincial Council. To the supporters of the Association that
owned the cannon, Loxley's position as storekeeper kept the
keys to the provincial stores in the hands of a trusted ally.

FOUR

THE PHILADELPHIA ASSOCIATORS AND THE PAXTON BOYS

On September 26, 1759, Edward Shippen wrote to Colonel Henry Bouquet in response to the British commander's previous request for boat builders, "not being able to procure the Two House Carpenters here which you wrote for, I immediately sent to Mr. Benjamin Loxley at Philadelphia for them and he writes me for answer they are not to be had even at 7/6 p Day without I would promise them Rations and the allowance of Rum."[1]

In early autumn 1759, the outcome of the war in North America was anything but certain. General James Wolfe's victory at the Plains of Abraham on September 13 had allowed his army to occupy Quebec, but only for the time being. On September 18, General Jeffery Amherst replaced Major General James Abercromby as commander in chief of the British Army in North America.[2] Now the powerful force under Amherst's command controlled the northern approaches of Lake Champlain, ready to support the garrison at Quebec in the likely event that an equally powerful army under the able command of François Gaston, Chevalier de Lévis, should attack it from Montreal in the spring, after the Canadian winter had taken its toll on men and animals.

Victory in North America hinged on control of waterways. Armies on both sides of the conflict relied on large numbers of watercraft, including the flat-bottomed boats known as pirogues and bateaux, to move men and supplies to fields of battle, and to build and maintain all manner of fortification when they got there. The bateau, a versatile craft, could be built quickly and cheaply. Bateaux ranged from ten or twelve feet to nearly forty feet long. Hundreds would be needed for the coming campaign, or merely to move supplies to forts the British had already captured. British commanders contracted hundreds of carpenters, joiners, and shipwrights, among other tradesmen, to serve as technicians in the North American wilderness. At Fort Pitt, which commanded the strategically important Forks of the Ohio, there were only fifty-five workers under the command of Harry Gordon of the Royal Engineers.[3] Benjamin Loxley personally knew Gordon. He had previously arranged for the provisioning of the army under Bouquet, and may have arranged for Jehu Eyre to march sixteen ship carpenters and a supply-laden wagon from Philadelphia to Fort Pitt in spring 1760.[4]

Born in Burlington, New Jersey, on January 21, 1738, Eyre, along with his brothers, Manuel and Benjamin, learned the shipbuilding trade at the yard of Richard Wright in Kensington, Pennsylvania, just a few miles upriver from Philadelphia, encompassing the area that William Penn and the Lenni Lenape had known as Shackamaxon, and which still bears that name.[5] By summer 1760, the Eyre brothers were established shipbuilders in their own right.

Eyre's party, which set out from Philadelphia on May 22, 1760, included John Midwinter, Isaac Middleton, Samuel Deninshear, William Flood, Daniel Delaney, Nathaniel Goforth, George Careless, Henry Bragg, Friend Streeton, Thomas Smith, John Barter, Daniel Rambo, David Row, James Tull, William McAllister, and a sawyer, possibly of African ancestry, named George.[6]

In his diary, the young Jehu Eyre kept a record of the party's progress. After stopping at the barracks in Lancaster to draw provisions, the party set out for the Susquehanna by way of Swatara Creek and Harris' Ferry, until recently theaters of operation in the frontier war. At this stage in his journey, the city-bred Eyre, who had grown up on or near the Delaware River, noted that it took an hour to cross the Susquehanna.

After crossing the river, the party followed well-traveled roads to Shippensburg, by way of Carlisle.

Although employed as a carpenter, Eyre carefully noted the distances between each fort, and the number and type of ordnance stored there. On Tuesday, June 3, Eyre and his men reached Fort Bedford and met its commander, Lieutenant Louis Ourry, of the 60th Regiment of Foot.[7] While there, Eyre recorded that there were "six six-pounders in the Fort."[8]

The trip west passed without incident and with some levity. After supervising some construction at Fort Bedford, Eyre took time out to explore the woods, where he went "a-gunning, and . . . caught a turtle" for his party's supper.[9]

On June 18, a rainy day, the shipwrights slogged their way to the top of another geographic landmark, Rhor's Gap, the break in the Allegheny ridge.[10] The next day, the party reached "Colonel John Armstrong's breastworks," built by Daniel Broadhead's provincial rangers a few years before, where it camped for the night.[11] On June 21, the party reached the fort at Loyal Hanna, only recently renamed Fort Ligonier. After drawing twenty-five axes, they set off for Fort Pitt, arriving there on Monday, June 30.[12] Now Eyre's party had reached its destination, and the real work began.

During the Seven Years' War, the Military Association established a distinct role within the city of Philadelphia as a proponent of defense. Pledged, in the words of the St. Vincent and Pikeland Associators, to protect "Our Lives, Wives, Children, Liberty, and our most holy Religion," Associators marched through the heart of Philadelphia, escorted dignitaries, and conducted training at the Philadelphia Academy, while artillerists demonstrated their firepower. However, in 1760, with the war all but won, Pennsylvania still had no militia, the 1757 law having expired in March 1758, a month before General John Forbes arrived in Philadelphia. The colony resorted instead to full-time soldiers to secure its new frontier. Pennsylvanians accommodated large bodies of redcoats, many of them local recruits, along their new western border and in two of their largest cities. Full-time provincials shouldered the day-to-day burden of manning forts and patrolling the frontier. In September 1756, provincials, not Associators, under Colonel John Armstrong wiped out the village of Kittanning, killed the

Delaware war leader Captain Jacobs, and neutralized the village as a base for raids against the backcountry. Throughout 1757 and 1758, the eastern clans of the Delaware Nation under the leadership of Teedyuscung had tried to challenge the validity of the 1737 Walking Purchase in order to reassert their status as land brokers, only to have the authority to do so successfully challenged by their Iroquois overlords at the Easton Conference in October 1758. The Six Nations had renewed their pledge of friendship to the British colonies by brokering a peace between Pennsylvania, New Jersey, and the western Delawares, thereby assuring Forbes's relatively unharassed advance on Fort Duquesne. But for diplomats on both sides of the council fire, the days of the Long Peace were long past.

With the completion of the new barracks and the road built under the direction of General Forbes in 1758, Philadelphia became an important military base for the British Army in North America. Forbes Road permitted wagon transit between the Ohio River valley and Carlisle, Pennsylvania. From Carlisle, improved roads led to the cities of Lancaster and Philadelphia. The port at Philadelphia connected Pennsylvania with other parts of the empire. The fortunes of war had smiled on the city of Philadelphia during the late conflict.

Fortune had not been so kind to James Smith. Born in Cumberland County within a year of Jehu Eyre, Smith had volunteered in May 1755 to help build a road connecting Fort Loudon, part of Pennsylvania's defensive arc, and Braddock's Road near the Youghiogheny River, a tributary of the Monongahela, where he was one of the road cutters captured near Raystown in early July 1755.[13] In his memoir, Smith recalled how a Caughnawaga and two Lenni Lenape took him under guard to Fort Duquesne.[14] There, Smith's captors forced him to run the gantlet, a frightful form of torture in which a prisoner was forced to run between two lines of captors who beat and tormented him along the way. Weeks passed while Smith recuperated from this painful ordeal. During that time, he witnessed the garrison's celebration following Braddock's defeat, saw British artillery wheeled into the fort the day after the battle, and witnessed the torture and killing of Anglo-American prisoners. A few days after the battle, a party of Caughnawagas took Smith to their village and adopted him into their tribe.[15]

In early 1760, almost at the same time that Eyre and his men set out on their western adventure, Smith returned home from six years of captivity to find his betrothed engaged to another man. "My feelings I must leave on this occasion, for those of my readers to judge, who have felt the pangs of disappointed love, as it is impossible for me to describe the emotion of soul I felt at the time."[16]

While Smith attempted to put his life back together, Eyre and his party worked on Fort Pitt's buildings and at building bateaux, work that continued until the middle of September.[17] In October, Eyre and some of his men traveled to Presque Isle on Lake Erie. There they built bateaux or whaleboats for the celebrated Major Robert Rogers, who set off to take possession of Fort Detroit on November 2, with 150 of his equally famous rangers and a company or two of Royal Americans.[18] Only the winter before, Rogers had carried out a raid on Saint Francis, at the northern end of Lake Champlain. The raid, which nearly annihilated his command, exacted a fearful toll on the Saint Francis community, ending the military threat from that quarter.

Rather than fight, Eyre explored the surrounding countryside. On September 1, he and Samuel Deninshear toured the scene of Braddock's defeat, where he recorded his first impression of the war. According to Eyre, "there are men's bones lying about as thick as the leaves do on the ground; for they are so thick that one lies on top of another for about a half a mile in length, and about one hundred yards in breadth."[19] War had been an immediate, brutal reality for westerners like James Smith. For easterners like Eyre, it appears to have been a mere harrowing curiosity.[20]

Nor were the people he met objects of fear or envy. On occasion, he even seemed to try to understand their culture. "Over the river Allegheny where the Indians encamped," and not far from where the teenage James Smith had watched confederated tribes burn and mutilate captured soldiers, Eyre described how "one Indian killed another, and the other Indians were in search for to kill him; for it is their law. It is a Dalloway killed a Mohawk."[21] At another time, the party of shipwrights bought two quarters of venison from them for four shillings.[22] On October 24, "the Indians stole two of our horses, but they gave them to us again."[23] In December, Eyre led his party of artificers back over the mountains.[24]

The experiences of Eyre, the urban shipwright, and James Smith, the frontier settler, illustrate the growing divide between the populous region east of the Schuylkill River and the less-settled western counties through almost a decade of constant wilderness fighting. The two deep-rooted issues of representation and defense lay at the heart of the westerners' grievances.[25] In 1760, the five frontier counties of Lancaster, York, Cumberland, Berks, and Northampton were still represented by only ten members in the Pennsylvania Assembly, while Philadelphia, Chester, and Bucks Counties were represented by twenty-four, and Philadelphia by two.[26] Frontiersmen demanded that Philadelphia should provide better protection and that Indians deemed hostile to the frontier should be expelled from the colony.[27] Most important, westerners wanted to be free of indebtedness to large landowners, especially the proprietor, Thomas Penn, the largest landowner of all.[28] The two worlds would soon collide in Philadelphia.

Unlike the frontier settlements, Philadelphia emerged from the war stronger than ever. The city had not been burned by French and Indian raiding parties. New cannon and small arms were purchased, and military contracts boosted the urban economy, with the result that many Associators profited during the war. Samuel Mifflin had been the captain of the Grand Battery. In 1756, he became a city alderman.[29] John Sibbald commanded the province ship *Pennsylvania*. Others served as commissaries or contracted for lucrative construction jobs, for which the Crown paid a premium in hard currency and rum. For these men, the river represented an identity reflected in their work, their ownership of property, and their service in the artillery. Frequent marches, demonstrations, and escorts, such as that provided by Captain William Vanderspeigle and Captain Edward Jones for Governor Morris in April 1756, reminded those around them of the Association's military might, not to mention its wealth and growing influence.

The war had been especially good to Benjamin Loxley. As a master carpenter, he profited from the construction of new storage sheds and the maintenance of the forts. As an artilleryman, he learned new skills from professional soldiers such as

Harry Gordon of the Royal Engineers and David Hay of the Royal Artillery. In spring 1758, he landed a position as store-keeper of the province that brought him into direct contact with Governor Denny and General Forbes. Military planners turned to him in times of need, especially when it came to his contacts among the Carpenters Company. As a businessman, Loxley owned pasturage on Petty's Island in the Delaware River. He also owned two small ships, one of which he named the *Live Oak*. Loxley's other ship, the *Betsey*, was probably named after his oldest daughter.[30] The ships' names spoke to things that he valued most: his family and his livelihood. Shipbuilders sought live oak for its strength and durability. It is native to the American South and not Philadelphia. To Loxley and men like him, the port and the river that brought it life were more than a source of income or a vested interest: they were a portal to a larger world outside Philadelphia.

In 1760, that world does not appear to have extended much farther west than the Schuylkill River, the western boundary of the land that William Penn laid out for Philadelphia and that was, in 1760, still largely undeveloped commons and wood-land. Across the Schuylkill River, at the Middle Ferry, the Lancaster Road began. It wound its way through Blockley Township on the river's west bank past Darby, where Loxley had spent his first years in America, through villages settled largely by Welsh Quakers, across rolling farmland to Lancaster, another city whose inhabitants the Crown had compensated handsomely during the war. The army of Forbes and Bouquet had marched over this road throughout summer 1758. Ordnance, small arms, and provisions had rolled with them in wagons contracted by local commissaries. Beyond Lancaster, on the western end of Lancaster County hard up against the Susquehanna River, lay the townships of Derry, Donegal, and Paxton. Across the Susquehanna River lay York and Cumberland Counties. From Carlisle, the new Forbes road linked a string of forts as far west as Fort Pitt.

By 1760, an empire in the west had been won, but the British Army was in no hurry to help guard it. The Pennsylvania frontier represented only one link in a vast swath of new lands. Western forts bled off regular troops who were needed all over the world. Regular army garrisons in

Pennsylvania dwindled to a few hundred men, while the Pennsylvania Regiment garrisoned important strongholds. In 1760, the Pennsylvania Assembly and Governor James Hamilton, who had replaced William Denny in 1759, failed to reach a consensus on a new Supply Act that would have allocated one hundred thousand pounds to frontier defense.[31] Over time, the remaining provincial garrisons diminished, sometimes to as few as a dozen men.[32] Their equipment was generally poor and their pay meager.[33] Life at places like Fort Pitt assumed a routine character, as soldiers practiced the timeless art of surviving the boredom of garrison life, and engineers endeavored to keep the walls from crashing down on their heads or washing into the Ohio River.[34] Frontier families who continued to view the Indians and not the French as the immediate threat equated the exodus of the regulars with abandonment. The comparative unguarded state of the frontier stood in sharp contrast to the largess bestowed on Philadelphia.

The frontier settlers were mostly redemptioners or descended from the working poor of Philadelphia who had a generation before been turned out of the overcrowded east to find a home on the frontier. In 1745, the province evicted many families from the backcountry, and it rendered cold comfort during the worst years of the war. Now, having hacked a living out of the Pennsylvania woods, they found themselves once again disowned by a provincial government dominated by land barons and Philadelphia merchants. Many had developed legitimate grievances against the Philadelphia government. Soon their grievances would turn bloody, as once again war threatened the Pennsylvania frontier.

In early May 1763, rumors of trouble in the Ohio country started to reach the Pennsylvania forts. On May 27, Lenni Lenape representatives arrived at Fort Bedford with news of the destruction of Forts Detroit and Sandusky, and the murder of all who were there.[35] Pontiac's War had begun. Ottawa, Chippewa, Huron, and Potawatomi war parties under the leadership of Pontiac moved east to attack white strongholds in the Ohio country.

While the information regarding Fort Detroit proved false, the situation was dismal throughout summer 1763. There were fewer than four hundred regulars in western Pennsylvania.[36]

The garrison at flood-damaged Fort Pitt made frantic preparations. The twelve regulars at Fort Bedford suffered from an extreme shortage of most supplies. Reinforcements were admitted into Fort Bedford only under the condition that they supply their own gunpowder. A shortage of water and an aggressive rodent population tried the fortitude of the fort's young commander, Captain Louis Ourry of the 60th Regiment.[37] As of June 3, no word had arrived from any of the posts to the west. Ninety-three families from the surrounding area had come into the fort, while two companies of local volunteers mounted a nightly guard in the fort and in the outlying town. Ourry faced a logistical crisis.[38]

Approximately two thousand settlers died that spring, and in Pennsylvania, Forts Venango, Le Boeuf, and Presque Isle fell to Pontiac's warriors.[39] Refugees heading east choked roads that had once carried the British Army to victory.

All through June, letters poured into Bouquet's headquarters at the barracks in Lancaster, updating him on the deteriorating situation. On June 5, he notified Captain Simeon Ecuyer, the commander at Fort Pitt, to "Discharge all the Ship Carpenters as soon as they had finished the Twenty Batteaux."[40] On June 8, George Croghan sent word that the hitherto neutral Lenni Lenape had declared for Pontiac. At Fort Augusta on the former site of Shamokin, Colonel James Burd diverted his provincials south to meet the new threat.[41] By July, Bouquet informed the governor that all forts west of Presque Isle had fallen. At Major General Jeffery Amherst's request, Governor Hamilton managed to pass a bill authorizing a home guard of seven hundred men.[42] The Pennsylvania Assembly offered only a token response to the emergency—despite the presence in Philadelphia of the Associator Artillery, the Associated Regiment of Foot, a troop of Associator horse, and a Royal Artillery detachment commanded by Captain David Hay.[43]

Whatever purpose the Associators served mattered little to the frontier families fleeing east. Their situation was desperate. Philadelphia did nothing for them. While Philadelphia carpenters hurried home, Conococheague Valley residents passed the hat in order to fund a company of riflemen, who elected the former captive James Smith their captain. Smith chose other redeemed captives for his officers and dressed his men "uniformly in the Indian manner, with breech-clouts, leggings, mockesons and green shrouds, which we wore in the same manner that the Indians do, and nearly as the Highlanders do their plaids."[44] Smith authorized red handkerchiefs in place of hats and instructed his men to paint their faces red and black. Smith "taught them the Indian discipline, as I knew of no other at the time," and achieved moderate success in defending the valley.[45]

By the end of June, Bouquet was ready to relieve the western forts. He had assembled a mixed force drawn mostly from the 42nd Royal Highland Regiment (the Black Watch), the 71st (Montgomery's) Highland regiments, and his own Royal American Regiment of Foot, along with some provincials and a baggage train. With this force he fought and won the Battle of Bushy Run on August 5 and 6, 1763. Four days later, Bouquet marched his battered column into Fort Pitt. Once again, British regulars and not the considerable might of the Philadelphia Associators had saved western Pennsylvania from ruin.

Instead of sending the city regiment, the provincial government at Philadelphia turned its attention to the plight of the Indians living in the Conestoga Valley and at the towns of Nain and Wechquetank. Philadelphia had long depended on these scattered communities, containing the last remaining pockets of eastern clans who had once treated with William Penn and his agents. Their young men had worked as scouts for eastern traders, or as interpreters for Philadelphia officials. These communities had paid dearly for their loyalty: by the 1760s, the effects of war and disease had reduced their numbers to a few dozen families. In 1763, the fighting to the west made members of the assembly particularly fear for the welfare of the Moravian Indians at the communities of Nain and Wechquetank.[46] Out of concern for their safety, provincial officials moved them to nearby Nazareth. When local courts leveled charges of conspiracy against those Indians, the province disarmed them and moved them to Philadelphia. Two sides in a rapidly developing standoff supported this decision. Members of the assembly favored the removal out of humanitarian concerns, and because it protected old allies. Their opponents supported the decision because it removed potential combatants from the frontier.[47]

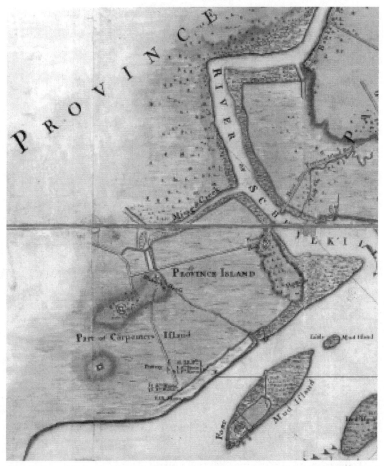

Fig. 8. Detail from P. Nicole's 1777 survey of the city of Philadelphia and its environs showing the remote location of Province Island, on low, marshy ground at the mouth of the Schuylkill River, several miles outside Philadelphia. (*Library of Congress*)

On November 27, 127 Indians arrived in Philadelphia.[48] For their own safety, the refugees were lodged at the Pest House on Province Island, at the mouth of the Schuylkill (fig. 8). The Pest House was normally used to quarantine ship passengers entering the city. It was well removed from most of the population, but relocating the refugees outside the city did not assuage the frontiersmen's animosity.

The frontiersmen turned their anger on the community at Conestoga. In December 1763, Matthew Smith and five men investigated a report that the Conestoga Indians were harboring a hostile fugitive.[49] They found "dozens of strange, armed Indians in the little village."[50] Events moved quickly. A gang formed, and on December 14, fifty armed riders entered Conestoga, killed six Indians, and burned their homes. Fourteen survivors were taken to Lancaster by provincial authorities and placed in the jail.

On December 27, a contingent of twenty-five to thirty men from Paxton, armed with rifles, tomahawks, and scalping knives, rode into Lancaster and murdered the few remaining survivors.[51] Six-year-old William Henry, who was visiting his father's house at the time, arrived at the scene of the crime to find the bodies of Will Sock and his wife near the back door of the prison. In a letter to the Reverend John Heckwelder at Bethlehem written years later, Henry remembered the nightmarish scene. Across the elderly couple lay

> two children of about the age of three years, whose heads were split with the tomahawk and their scalps all taken off. Towards the middle of the yard, along the west side of the wall, lay a stout Indian whom I particularly noticed to have been shot in the breast, his legs were chopped off with the tomahawk, his hands cut off and finally a rifle ball discharged into his mouth, so that his head was blown to atoms and his brains were splashed against and were yet hanging to the wall for three or four feet around. In this manner lay the whole of them, men, women and children, spread about the prison yard, shot, scalped, hacked and cut to pieces.[52]

In response to these brutal murders, Pennsylvania's new governor acted. John Penn had arrived in Philadelphia on October 30, 1763, to replace James Hamilton, who had been appointed for a second term after the departure of William Denny.[53] The thirty-four-year-old Penn was as different from his uncle Thomas as the frontier was from Philadelphia.[54] Unlike the family patriarch, John Penn, a bon vivant, collected art and played the violin.[55] He had spent the last three years in Philadelphia, mostly in the company of an Italian musician.[56] Although a prodigal in the eyes of his family and the Philadelphia elite, Penn proved an able administrator who cared about his constituents and could lead Pennsylvanians in times of crisis. Under Great Britain's Riot Act, any assembly of twelve or more people whom the authorities deemed unruly or even undesirable could be declared rioters and dispersed, by force if necessary. Penn called upon the magistrates of Lancaster, York, and Cumberland Counties to round up the murderers.[57] He persuaded the assembly to authorize funds to move any surviving Conestoga Indians to Philadelphia and to raise one thousand men for their defense.[58] He wrote to Colonel John Armstrong at Carlisle, the Reverend John Elder at Paxton, and Colonel Edward Shippen at Lancaster to suppress the rioting and capture the ringleaders.[59] But Pennsylvania had no real control over the west.[60] Even in Philadelphia, the assembly's decision met with violent opposition. Fearful of a repeat of the Lancaster atrocity, Governor Penn forbade the harassment of Indian refugees on Province Island on December 22.[61]

Penn's edict failed to mollify the surviving Moravian Indians. Armed ruffians had entered a jail and murdered their neighbors under the noses of Pennsylvania officials. How could they be safe on a remote island outside Philadelphia? The Conestoga delegation asked to be sent to England for protection, or at least to Sir William Johnson in New York. He was the British Indian agent for North America, and he was known and trusted by all or most of the eastern tribes. The assembly approved the latter request and tasked a detachment of soldiers from the regular army to escort the Indians through New Jersey.[62] The soldiers were bound to go there anyway and reluctantly agreed to escort the Indians as far as New York City. The mission succeeded, despite friction between redcoats and Indians. But an order from Governor Cadwallader Colden of New York prevented the regular army detachment from taking its charges into that colony, and the refugees stopped at Amboy, New Jersey.[63] William Franklin, now governor of New Jersey, offered to allow the Indians to stay in New Jersey if Pennsylvania would pay their room and board.[64] Franklin was a member of the Ohio Company with vast holdings on the western frontier. As an officer of the Crown, he had to uphold the law, but as a land speculator, he may have wanted to appease the western settlers. Governor Penn decided to bring the Indians back to Pennsylvania. Major General Thomas Gage, the new commander in chief of British forces in North America, offered an escort consisting of a detachment of the 60th Regiment of Foot under Captain John Schlosser.

The refugees arrived back in the city on January 24, 1764, where they were placed under the charge of Montgomery's Highlanders at the barracks, and provided lodging by Joseph Fox, the barracks master.[65] While there, they attempted to retrieve their few belongings, dodge the scrutiny of the curious crowds that gathered, and impart some semblance of normality on their lives through prayer and regular services, which they held at the barracks kitchen.[66] On January 30, missionary Bernard Adam Grube read a passage from 2 Samuel 7:10 that struck a note with his spiritual brothers and sisters: "I will appoint a place for my people Israel, and will plant them, that they may dwell in a place of their own, and move no more: neither shall the children of wickedness afflict them any more, as beforetime." Most of all, the Moravian Indians tried to avoid any involvement with the regulars.[67]

The regulars gave Penn a strong hand, but they were a dangerous card to play. In the western counties, companies of volunteers gathered. Disgruntled frontiersmen stockpiled arms, powder, and shot.[68] Rumors circulated that as many as five thousand frontiersmen had taken up arms.[69] In response, Gage authorized Captain Schlosser to fire on any who opposed him.[70] He also ordered a Captain Murray at Carlisle to move his entire command of regulars to the barracks at Lancaster. Gage next granted Governor Penn direct command over the regulars in his jurisdiction. He authorized Schlosser to prevent unruly acts and to apprehend protestors if necessary.[71]

On Penn's order, Schlosser, on February 1, met with Brother Grube. At the meeting, which was almost certainly held in German, Schlosser admitted that Grube's flock was quite unlike the tribes he had encountered on the frontier. The following evening, Schlosser permitted his first lieutenant and two soldiers to attend prayer services.[72]

On February 4, reports reached Philadelphia of the anticipated arrival of several hundred frontiersmen from the west. Penn asked the assembly for a militia law.[73] The assembly instead passed an Act for Preventing Tumults and Riotous

Assemblies–in other words, an invocation of Great Britain's Riot Act, which empowered magistrates to disperse any group of people for virtually any reason.[74] Captain Schlosser rushed to the barracks and directed Grube to move the refugees into the second story, where they would be safer in the event of an attack.[75]

Governor Penn faced a grave quandary. If the reports were to be believed, most of his constituents supported the armed mob that was even now on the outskirts of Philadelphia. The assembly refused to give any more than nominal support to suppressing what looked like a mounting insurrection. Under the new riot act, Penn could declare martial law. He could then order Schlosser and the garrison at the barracks to open fire on the marchers–then board a fast stagecoach, or better yet, a ship, and write to Gage for help in quelling an armed uprising. If Penn went that far, however, he could never return to Pennsylvania. The 42nd, 60th, and 77th Regiments would not stay in Philadelphia forever. Bouquet was even at that time planning a punitive expedition into the Ohio country that required large numbers of regulars. The governor needed additional military manpower, so he turned to the Association.

On the afternoon of Saturday, February 4, Penn called a meeting at his house on Second Street. He read the riot act and called the Association to arms. Six companies of the Associated Regiment of Foot, with the train of artillery and a troop of horse under Lynford Lardner, the governor's cousin, turned out.[76] The regiment used the nearby home of Benjamin Franklin as its headquarters, where Associators brushed off their uniforms and checked muskets and halberds for rust.[77] At least one of the companies marched under the standard that it had carried on New Year's Day in 1748.[78] The artillery brought out twelve cannon.[79] The Associators formed ranks and marched to the courthouse at the center of town. Arms were stored at the courthouse, and the market, the London Coffee House that William Bradford had opened in 1754, and the big Friends' Meeting House framed the square where Associators had drilled during the French War (fig. 9, overleaf).

The moment had at last come. For the first time in their seventeen-year history, the Associators mustered to defend their city. As Alexander Graydon recalled years later, "Here stood the artillery, under the command of Captain Loxley, a very honest, though little, dingy-looking man, with regimentals, considerably war-worn or tarnished; a very salamander or *fire drake* in the public estimation."[80] Graydon was an aspiring gentleman who studied at the Philadelphia Academy (now the University of Pennsylvania). His description of Benjamin Loxley manages at once to be complimentary and disparaging. Graydon admired Loxley's military skill but also noted his shabby appearance. Shabby or not, Loxley knew his work. He ordered his crews to wrestle eight of the train's cannon into position and load them with grapeshot (fig. 10, overleaf).[81] Troops placed wooden barricades at the courthouse and the barracks.[82] All through that day and night, Governor Penn personally led approximately two hundred Associators alongside regulars and hundreds of volunteers guarding the city, while the refugees spent a sleepless night huddled among the soldiers on the second floor of the barracks.[83]

At midnight, Penn visited the Indians. He played with the children to raise their spirits and engaged in small talk to ease the nerves of the parents.[84] The next day was Sunday, but rather than attend church, the Associators changed and then doubled their guard. Loxley's crews muscled an additional eighteen-pound cannon into place outside the barracks. Upon testing, the report from Loxley's guns shattered some of the barracks windows and frightened many of the refugees inside.[85] Entrance and exit routes to and from the city were blocked.[86] The boats at the Middle (Market Street) and Lower (Gray's) Ferries were ordered to the east side of the Schuylkill to prevent their use by the marchers.[87] Detachments went to secure the ferry at Swedes Ford several miles upriver, but they arrived too late. It was there that the so-called Paxton Boys crossed.[88] By the afternoon, the insurgents, numbering perhaps in the hundreds, had congregated in the market square of Germantown.

As things stood, the westerners were in no hurry to enter the city. Couriers had informed them of the strong reception that awaited them should they attempt to storm the barracks. Despite their bloody rhetoric, there is little indication that the Paxton Boys wanted to start a civil war, especially if it meant a direct confrontation with Montgomery's Highlanders bol-

Fig. 9. "The Paxton Expedition, Inscribed to the Author of the Farce, by HD." Although meant to mock the Associators, Henry Dawkins's cartoon shows the critical moment during the February 4, 1764, standoff when Capt. Benjamin Loxley's artillerists posted in front of the county court house (at center), nearly fired on Lynford Lardner's troop of horse riding down Second Street at right. At least three companies of foot are portrayed, standing in ranks under their colors. Note the market stalls and stocks used to pillory minor criminals. (*The Library Company of Philadelphia*)

stered by Loxley's artillery, Lardner's horse, and the Regiment of Foot. An almost comical standoff developed as the Associators, in uniform and under silk standards, manned their guns in front of the courthouse and the Paxton Boys occupied Germantown's Market Square over six miles away.

On February 6, the crisis began to abate. Along with several unnamed "gentlemen of the city," Benjamin Franklin, Benjamin Chew, Thomas Willing, and Joseph Galloway went out to Germantown.[89] Franklin, like his son, the governor of New Jersey, had to be conciliatory toward the protestors. More than public order was at stake. He, too, owned land in the west and depended upon the goodwill of the rural population for political office. He could not risk offending the countrymen gathered in Germantown. The delegation met the Paxton Boys' leaders in a tavern, and a few hours later, most of the westerners were on their way home. In exchange for Franklin's pledge to present their grievances before the assembly, the protesters dispersed peacefully. A minor stir arose when some of them entered the city, but for now, the province was at peace.

Once again, the defenders of the colony had used words and not gunpowder to wage their war. The Indians stayed at the barracks until March. There they suffered a smallpox outbreak. The survivors were granted land in Wyalusing in far north central Pennsylvania, far from the settled regions of the province.[90] Franklin and his delegation averted a civil war and won a short-term victory. The frontier mob got the removal of the Indians, if not the blood that it wanted. The Philadelphia Artillery most likely got nothing. Franklin did not need Loxley's men in the end, so they paid a final visit to the refugees at the barracks, wished them well, and went home.[91]

The dispute between the settled eastern counties and the western frontier counties soon moved from the streets of Philadelphia to the printing press.[92] In an exchange of pamphlets that lasted several months, the protesters finally aired their grievances formally. Within the context of the frontier, the westerners' demands were not unreasonable: Scalp payments should be renewed (a major source of hard currency on a cash-poor frontier, where wampum and deer skins were considered a medium of exchange). The Indian trade, a major source of arms for the western tribes and a major source of revenue for wealthy easterners, should be abolished. Private individuals and organizations should be prohibited from treating with the Indians.[93] Nothing came of the western demands. The dispute occasionally turned violent. In 1765, James Smith organized a band of westerners calling themselves the Black Boys in the capture of Fort Loudon, and in 1769, they attacked Fort Bedford.[94] The Black Boys' aim on both occasions was the abolition of the Indian trade. Smith stood trial for his life in the alleged murder of John Johnston, a bystander in the Fort Bedford affair.[95]

Fig. 10. Grapeshot. (*Courtesy of Colonel J. Craig Nannos, photograph by John Bansemer*)

These grievances epitomized the schism between east and west. In the eyes of many on the frontier, and to some in Philadelphia, Pennsylvania's leadership had essentially shirked its chartered responsibility by leaving foreign affairs in the hands of individuals. For the westerners, it boiled down to an issue of representation, and in Smith's case, the right to a fair trial.[96] But, as historian James H. Hutson points out, the issue at stake was not the franchise, for "almost anyone who wanted to voted."[97] Many key positions, such as sheriff and justice of the peace, were directly elected. The issue did not stem entirely from matters of faith or principles for or against war, for the Quakers had long ago lost their majority in the State House. Nor did the issue stem from antipathy toward the Indians, and over the almost century-old policy perpetuated in 1764 by the assembly. The Paxton Boys found widespread support for their protest among the people of Philadelphia, but not among the companies of Associators that mustered in its defense, and certainly not in the train of artillery, which nearly fired on Lardner's troop of light horse from Germantown, which had ridden in to help.[98] Simply put, Pennsylvania's leadership did not necessarily reflect the views of the colony's population.

The reason for Loxley's support of Governor Penn, as well as his sympathy for the plight of the Moravian refugees, may have been more complex than one of policy. It may in fact have been beyond words for the "honest" carpenter to express. The Philadelphia artillerists were not wealthy merchants, but they did have money. They were not among Philadelphia's numerous working poor, but they did depend upon work for their living. Unlike the Franklins, Chew, and Galloway, they had few if any commitments to the western frontier. The politics of place—the geopolitical relationship of the backcountry versus the settled eastern counties—created a multifold disparity of which defense was only the tip of the iceberg.[99] Western settlers depended on the eastern-dominated assembly for a voice in government, access to overseas markets, and information from home. Despite the fact that Philadelphia and the Pennsylvania frontier were interdependent, Pennsylvanians perceived a difference.[100] The Paxton Boys did not identify with the port. Philadelphia Associators were not westerners but city men. Their world faced east, toward the river, while the world of the Paxton Boys faced west toward the mountains. In confronting the Paxton Boys, the Philadelphia Associators showed a willingness to defend more than hearth and home.

The February standoff represented a landmark in the life of the Philadelphia Artillery. For the first time, Loxley and his gun crews mustered to defend the city. Loxley, however, makes no mention of the Paxton Boys in his memoir. The year after the Paxton Boys' march, the crisis over the Stamp Act, which imposed a duty on all paper goods imported into the British colonies, would divide the Quaker Party and Pennsylvania. Loxley would become a leader in resistance to the Stamp Act, as would many of his fellow Associators. By 1770, committees set up to promote the boycotting of imported goods would unite the once-antagonistic frontiersmen with the city's artisans.[101] Not long thereafter, Associators in their respective communities would elect Jehu Eyre and James Smith to lead them in resisting the British.

Graydon's description of Loxley as a "*fire drake* in the public estimation" contrasts with descriptions of the Paxton Boys. His words suggest that the train of artillery had become a sort of identity for some of the men it comprised. Graydon remembered Loxley not as a prominent carpenter, nor as an owner of real estate, but for his public service as a soldier.[102] That service came to define Loxley as much as his putting his stamp on the artillery itself.

The Paxton Boys, in turn, defined the frontier culture at the time. On February 5, curious Philadelphians went out to Germantown to see the frontiersmen. They were described as a rough bunch who wore blanket coats and moccasins, painted savages who carried rifles, pistols, and tomahawks.[103] They shocked urban Philadelphians with war whoops and pantomimed scalping. The Paxton Boys had grown up with war and the threat of war as a constant in their lives. The rioters were accomplished showmen, but under the circumstances, they exhibited commendable discipline. Not a weapon was discharged without orders from their leaders. Theirs was a world apart from the commercial hub of Philadelphia. One Philadelphian, George Roberts, later commented that he would rather have his children brought up as Muslims than as *"Pennsylvania Presbyterians,* for I believe no group of mortals under Heaven merit the curse pronounced in Scripture against the 'stiff necked and rebellious' as this people."[104]

In 1764, the Pennsylvania Assembly was unready to address the changes that had transpired in Pennsylvania during the past two decades. That same assembly had grown increasingly out of touch with large and influential sections of the colony's population. On February 4, 1764, two distinct communities within Pennsylvania took up arms in defense of their rights. That the tradesmen and frontier farmers shared a mutual disaffection toward the assembly and yet practically went to war with each other was a harbinger of the crisis to come. Over the next decade, Pennsylvania's traditional leaders would find themselves unable to control the forces of change.

FIVE

THE ASSOCIATORS
AND THE MAKING
OF REVOLUTION

On June 4, 1766, the Philadelphia Artillery fired a salute in celebration of King George III's birthday.[1] In the decade since Great Britain's victory in the Seven Years' War, sentiment toward the king had oscillated, at times favoring violent revolt, at other times loyalism. The Royal Proclamation of 1763, which barred settlements west of a line along the Alleghenies, had renewed the long-simmering resentment many western Pennsylvanians felt toward Philadelphia, resentment that flared into violence in 1764 with the riots of the Paxton Boys, their march on Philadelphia, and the seizure of trade goods by James Smith's Black Boys the following summer. Henry Bouquet's valiant relief of Fort Pitt during Pontiac's War assuaged some worries in the interim. But in 1765, American colonists boycotted goods imported from Great Britain in protest of the Stamp Act. The act, which imposed a duty on imported paper goods, created a drain on currency in a historically cash-poor economy. The boycott of imported goods, known as nonimportation, united Philadelphia's artisan population from the middle of April 1765 until the act was revoked in May 1766. Word of its repeal renewed Philadelphians' faith in their king.

For the time being, Britain's prestige rode high in the minds of many Americans. Yet within a year of the artillery's salute, many of those same Philadelphians organized resistance to the Townshend Act duties. Although the duties were tied to the cost of maintaining the empire in North America, concerned Americans known as Whigs regarded them as arbitrary policies enacted without their consent. Whigs resisted what they saw as a trend on the part of the ministry toward an increasingly autocratic rule. Instead, they sought at least a return to the salutary neglect with which the Crown had traditionally treated the American colonies, or, preferably, a change to a form of representative rule that would include Americans as full members of the British nation, rather than colonists.[2] Committees formed in every colony. This time, the pendulum would swing farther toward open revolt than it ever had.

Several Associators were early supporters of resistance to Crown policy, including Benjamin Loxley and Samuel Mifflin. In November 1765, Mifflin sat on a committee that enforced compliance with boycotts.[3] Loxley belonged to a similar committee in 1770.[4] Loxley also belonged to the Tea Committee in 1773.[5]

What Mifflin and Loxley articulated in committee, the artillery underscored with gunpowder. When Parliament repealed the Stamp Act in May 1766, the Philadelphia Artillery fired a salute to celebrate.[6] A month later, the artillery saluted the king. When the Townshend Act imposed new taxes on imports, longtime artillery officers joined new nonimportation committees. In March 1768, the guns of the artillery boomed to mark the revocation of the Glass Act, one of the Townshend duties on finished goods.[7]

Loxley's early career offers clues to his politics. His papers reveal a deeply religious man, devoted to church and family. He was a prominent member of the First Baptist Church in Philadelphia.[8] Upon his release from indenture on May 7, 1742, his former master, Joseph Watkins, gave him a Bible and a psalm book in addition to the tools of his trade.[9] Loxley was an ardent supporter of the Reverend George Whitefield, the famous traveling evangelist.[10] On March 28, 1743, Loxley married his first wife, Jane Watkins, the sister of his master, who bore three sons.[11] The first son died shortly after birth. The second, Benjamin, was born June 16, 1745, and, like his father, took an active role in the First Baptist Church. A third son,

Abram, was born January 16, 1750. He served in his father's artillery company during the Revolutionary War. In all, Loxley fathered fifteen children by two wives.

Loxley put down deep roots in Philadelphia. He owned several properties in and around the city.[12] He was a member of the Carpenter's Company, which encouraged improved construction and support for his fellow artisans; the Library Company of Philadelphia, a cooperative that promoted the importation of publications; the American Philosophical Society, dedicated to the dissemination of knowledge; and the Society of the Sons of St. George, a philanthropic organization pledged to support English immigrants and their descendents.[13] He donated money to the Philadelphia Almshouse.[14] He owned a wood frame house on Second Street, at the southeast corner of Little Dock Street, "above the drawbridge."[15] Ironically for a man whose life flew in the face of the Philadelphia establishment, the house was a relic of Penn's original vision of a "greene Countrie Towne," wherein homeowners were encouraged to build at the center of their lots in order to prevent fires and encourage tree growth. Set back from the street and painted blue, the house had a second floor balcony, typical of the older homes in the neighborhood.[16] Tradition holds that Reverend Whitefield preached from this balcony before moving to the hall, or academy building, built by Loxley and others under Benjamin Franklin's patronage.[17] Though a dissenter in faith and in politics, Loxley dedicated his life and work to Philadelphia's future. He wrote his name on the map of the city.

The motto cast onto the Schuylkill Gun, "*Kawanio che Keeteru*," or "This is my right, I will defend it," must have served as a constant reminder to Loxley of his pledge to defend Pennsylvania dating to the day he put his name to the Articles of Association in 1747. In 1755, Loxley had dutifully modified ships' guns for the artillery, and espoused a broader view than most in his support for the British Army in North America. In 1764, Loxley had put on his "war-worn" regimentals and led the Philadelphia Artillery to defend his city against the Paxton Boys. Yet within a few years, he switched to battling new British taxes. Loxley had little to gain from nonimportation. Most of his income came from lumber sales, real estate, and shipping. But he supported his fellow artisans, as well as the "Wives, Children and Estates of others." Philadelphia was his home. He had sworn a sacred oath to defend it.

From the end of the Seven Years' War to the start of the War for Independence, Loxley remained active in the artillery and as province storekeeper working with another man he had known for decades, Captain David Hay of the Royal Artillery.[18] In 1758, Loxley briefly accepted a commission in Hay's artillery company. After Loxley turned the commission down in favor of the storekeeper position, Hay and Loxley often worked together maintaining Pennsylvania's arsenal.

By 1763, the year the British Army ceded control of its military hardware back to Pennsylvania, that relationship was in transition. The British consolidated their ordnance at this time, and the province stopped paying Loxley his annual stipend of twenty pounds per year.[19] According to Loxley, Hay and his men schemed to secret away Philadelphia's prized ordnance, the four "neatly painted Cannon" that Loxley and his gun crews fired with such precision. The British officers likely considered them to be British property. Governor John Penn anticipated the guns' removal. He ordered Loxley to keep the Philadelphia arms away from the regulars. Loxley was able to save all but the mortar, which the British spirited away.[20] Loxley thereafter labored to keep Pennsylvania's arsenal out of the hands of the British.

Instead of brawls and street fighting, Loxley fought a battle of books. When counting Pennsylvania's military hardware, he made a clear distinction between what belonged to the province and what belonged to the Crown. Throughout 1772, Loxley transferred Pennsylvania's remaining stores over to his direct control. On May 16, 1772, an entry of "£36.14.0"–thirty-six pounds fourteen shillings–in his ledger marked the settlement of his account with the Royal Artillery for items he had sold to Hay.[21] On December 26 that year, he noted that Hay delivered two old swords from the regular army's stores.[22] That same day, Loxley refurbished several cannon "by Order of the Commissioners," working at the direction of Governor Penn.[23] A month later, Loxley received Pennsylvania's four brass cannon at the State House storage sheds.[24] Within months, the Philadelphia Artillery had broken its ties with the British Army.

Contact between Loxley and the British officers further illustrates the abstract nature of the Philadelphia Artillery's resistance. The artillerists' demonstrations in support of non-importation were no mere reactions to overt policy. They were highly refined acts of protest carried out in committee, in the orderly exercise of the artillery, or official salutes fired to celebrate the repeal of an unpopular act. Their actions paralleled the character of resistance in Philadelphia.

To men like Loxley and Mifflin, resistance was nothing new. Members of the artillery had long used the organization as a means of obtaining a political voice. During the War of Austrian Succession, Associators lobbied for military preparedness. Throughout the Seven Years' War, opposition to the ruling oligarchy translated into defense of Crown policy in North America. During the standoff with the Paxton Boys, Associators aligned themselves with Benjamin Franklin and Governor John Penn, but in 1765, Franklin was voted out of the assembly by a slim margin.[25] He sailed for London on November 7, 1765, leaving his longtime compatriot, Joseph Galloway, in control of the Quaker Party.[26] John and Thomas Penn thereafter mended fences with the assembly.[27] By the early 1770s, when Galloway was known as a reactionary politician, most of the Philadelphia Artillery's leadership identified with the politics of Charles Thomson, a nonimportation pamphleteer and community organizer, and other leading Whigs.[28] Following the Boston Massacre, on March 5, 1770, American revolutionaries increasingly viewed the British soldiers in North America not as defenders but as agents of oppression. A gulf thus existed between the Philadelphia Artillery and the British Army by the early 1770s. Loxley, for one, concluded that the British plotted to disarm the colonists: "They gave us plain hints that it would not be long before the British Army would visit America in a different manner than they had done to fight the French," he would later write.[29]

Loxley's rancor may have reflected his mindset in 1789, the year he recorded these words, rather than the early 1770s, when they were supposed to have been uttered. Indeed, such anti-British sentiments were by no means universal prior to the war. Philadelphians in particular tolerated and even accommodated the redcoats. The Philadelphia Artillery certainly did not seek confrontation with the king's troops, but it maintained a distance from them. On June 4, 1772, Hay's gun crews fired a royal salute at their barracks in honor of King George III's birthday.[30] The *Pennsylvania Gazette* mentioned no similar demonstration by the Philadelphia Artillery.

The redcoats provided ample opportunity for friction in Philadelphia. In addition to Hay's artillery company, elements of the 18th (Royal Irish) Regiment of Foot garrisoned Philadelphia between 1767 and 1774.[31] In early 1771, Major General Thomas Gage ordered Captain John Montrésor of the Royal Engineers to Philadelphia. Montrésor began work on a stone fort on Mud Island at the mouth of the Schuylkill River, a far more defensible site than any previously chosen. In contrast to the 1748 Grand Battery, the new fort was designed according to the latest military principles, consisting of a star-shaped redoubt that could house thirty-two cannon, four mortars, four howitzers, and a garrison of four hundred soldiers.[32] The fort's construction signaled a protracted British presence in the city. Its construction should have been inflammatory in the wake of the Townshend duties and the Boston Massacre. The British Army nevertheless enjoyed cordial relations with many Philadelphians prior to its departure in 1774.[33]

Relations between Great Britain and the thirteen colonies became polarized that year, following the passage in Parliament of a series of punitive measures known collectively as the Coercive Acts or Intolerable Acts. These included the Boston Port Act, which closed that port following the seizure and destruction of tea belonging to the British East India Company in Boston Harbor; the Quartering Act, which authorized the quartering of British soldiers in the homes of Boston civilians; the Administration of Justice Act, which allowed the governor to remove royal officials accused of crimes to stand trial in Great Britain rather than face the judgment of an American jury; and worst of all, the Massachusetts Government Act, which revoked the charter of the Massachusetts Bay Colony and placed it under the direct rule of the king or his ministers. The elections of 1774 swept Philadelphia's revolutionaries into power soon after the last British regular army regiments left the city to concentrate at Boston.[34] More than a hundred Philadelphians served on Whig committees.[35] Nine out of ten had never held public office.[36] That autumn, delegates from thirteen colonies convened a Continental Congress in Philadelphia to renounce the Coercive Acts and the Townshend duties, organize support for the people of Boston, coordinate an organized resistance as a single body, and declare the constitutional rights of the American people.

The Military Association stepped up training following the adjournment of that first Continental Congress. In late autumn and winter 1774, Pennsylvania Associators organized new companies to serve as training cadres and as a temporary defense expedient. In addition to Loxley's train of artillery, Abraham Markoe's light horse associated on November 17. Additionally, John Cadwalader's Philadelphia Greens, Joseph Cowperthwaite's Quaker Blues, and Thomas Hartley's York Blues, associated by April 1775, their names determined by the color of the coats they wore. Former Black Boy James Smith may have commanded a company as early as 1774. Having elected their officers, the new companies typically voted on a uniform and arms. The companies established a training site, known as a rendezvous, where they conducted training twice daily under veteran instructors, who were either hired or appointed from among the ranks.

Several of the twenty-eight Philadelphians who associated under Captain Abraham Markoe were active members of the Committee of Correspondence, including James Mease and Samuel Caldwell.[37] Lieutenant Andrew Allen had served on the Provincial Council for several years. Lieutenant Samuel Morris, a noted equestrian, had served as a commissioner to audit, liquidate, and settle the accounts of wagons, teams, and horses contracted for Braddock's expedition in 1756.[38] Two of Morris's cocommissioners at the time, Edward Shippen and Alexander Stedman, likely served in Lardner's light horse troop during 1756. Another, Samuel McCall, served as major of the first Associated Regiment of Foot.

Having elected its officers, the newly formed light horse troop voted on a uniform and weapons. The troop hired a trumpeter as well as a "Mr. Moffit, who had belonged to a Corps of Horse in Ireland," as a horse handler and fencing instructor. The troop drilled several days a week.[39]

The composition of Cadwalader's company indicates that it, too, provided a cadre for future officers and prominent leaders in the Revolution, including Alexander Graydon, John Lardner, Thomas Peters, Samuel Howell Jr., John Maxwell Nesbitt, and David Conyngham.[40] John Lardner was the well-connected son of Lynford Lardner, who came to Pennsylvania in the 1740s as receiver general to the proprietors and who commanded the light horse from 1756 to 1764.[41] The occupations of the others indicates that Cadwalader, one of the wealthiest men in the colony, associated with "gentlemen of fortune," investors who speculated in maritime trade and other risky ventures with the prospect of financial growth. [42]

Graydon provides a description of the Greens' training program: "There were about seventy of us. We met morning and evening . . . in the course of a summer's training, became a truly respectable militia corps. This was in the afternoon, and the place of rendezvous the house of the captain," not far from Loxley's house, on South Second Street, at the foot of Society Hill.[43]

Captain Joseph Cowperthwaite drilled the Quaker Blues.[44] As with the light horse and Greens, aspiring "gentlemen of fortune" such as Clement Biddle made up Cowperthwaite's company. According to Graydon, the Quaker Blues maintained a friendly rivalry with the Philadelphia Greens. As the designation suggests, Quakers made up most of Cowperthwaite's company.[45]

The York Blues, a similar company associated in that town in 1774, may have even looked beyond Pennsylvania's borders for expertise. Baltimore merchant Bernard Eichelberger, son of the York County magistrate, helped drill the company at first. Eichelberger may have been enlisted in the Baltimore Independent Cadets, a volunteer unit organized December 3, 1774, that served as the nucleus for the troops of the Maryland Continental Line, Maryland's component of the Continental Army.[46] York resident John Adlum later recalled how the York Blues then "chose an old soldier named Dytch, who had served in one of the battalions of the Royal American Regiment," to serve as a fugleman, a model soldier who demonstrated maneuvers in front of a body of troops. [47] Dytch may also have been one of the original Baltimore Independent Cadets.[48]

Adlum also remembered that "we chose another old soldier for our first lieutenant."[49]

On January 16, 1775, Bucks County Whigs organized a committee of safety.[50] Such committees initially set standards in all military matters at the local level and later ensured that soldiers' equipment, training, and discipline conformed to standards established by the Continental Congress. Additionally, committees of safety ensured that measures adopted by Congress were carried out at the local level. As one of its first official acts, the committee approved funds to relieve the "poor inhabitants of the Town of Boston," who many feared were in danger of starvation, the Boston Port Act having shut down much of that city's commerce.[51] Following news of the battles of Lexington and Concord, Massachusetts, on April 19, the committee recommended that the people of Bucks County organize military associations in their respective townships to begin military training.[52]

In Lancaster County, the city of Lancaster and the townships of Hanover, Middletown, and Lebanon resolved to join the Philadelphia committees of correspondence in resisting Crown policies in Massachusetts. Like their compatriots in Bucks County, the chairmen of the respective committees, Timothy Green of Hanover, James Burd of Middletown, John Phillip De Haas of Lebanon, and George Ross of Lancaster, had already organized or would subsequently organize Associator battalions.[53]

Following news of the battles of Lexington and Concord, each of these companies in their respective counties (the light horse excepted) expanded to two companies numbering from 100 to 170 soldiers. In conformance with British Army practice, the two companies served to supply the battalions, once formed, with trained recruits.[54] According to John Adlum, "the boys of the town also formed a company."[55] Once battalions organized in Pennsylvania, they usually consisted of a veteran, or "gentleman" company, and the others "boys" or student companies.[56]

Associator training intensified in the first weeks following the battles of Lexington and Concord. Out of the train of artillery, Pennsylvania established the Philadelphia Artillery Battalion on May 1, 1775.[57] Major Samuel Mifflin, who had commanded the Grand Battery in 1756, now commanded four companies under Benjamin Loxley, Joseph Moulder, James Biddle, and Thomas Procter.[58] Mifflin's battalion crewed thirteen cannon.[59] Loxley commanded the 1st Company, which numbered 174 men.[60] The sizes of the other companies is not known.

Many of the officers and noncommissioned officers of the Philadelphia Artillery Battalion had interests in common with Loxley. Joseph Moulder commanded the 2nd Company, Philadelphia Artillery Battalion, in 1775. Like many artillerists, Moulder worked in a trade related to carpentry or shipbuilding: he was a sailmaker.[61] Like Loxley, he was a Baptist and might have seen Loxley on Sunday mornings.[62] He shared Loxley's interest in city welfare. In 1771, Moulder was elected city street commissioner.[63] He served in that office until at least 1773.[64] In 1774, Dock Ward elected him to a revolutionary committee.[65] He also ran for office on the mechanics' ticket with Samuel Mifflin in 1775.[66]

James Biddle commanded the 3rd Company, Philadelphia Artillery Battalion. He was long active in city affairs and the interests of the port. In 1770, he helped update Nicholas Scull's 1766 map of Pennsylvania.[67] The Scull and Heap map includes one of the only known contemporary engravings of the Grand Battery. In October 1774, Biddle was elected to the city council on the Whig ticket.[68] On July 4, 1776, as a vestryman at Christ Church, he would sit on a committee that voted to omit prayers for King George III from the liturgy.[69]

Loxley's ledger records several other close associates in the Philadelphia Artillery Battalion. They included neighbors Benjamin Armitage and Lawrence Shiney.[70] Armitage and Shiney rented property from Loxley.[71] Armitage was Loxley's second-in-command.[72] Shiney was a 1st Company wagon master.[73]

Thomas Nevell was Loxley's supply clerk.[74] The two men also shared club memberships. Nevell was a member of the Carpenters' Company. In 1768, the company appointed Loxley and Nevell to buy the land on which Carpenters' Hall was built. They both belonged to the Society of the Sons of St. George, the philanthropic organization that worked on behalf of recent English arrivals.[75] On October 2, 1772, the members elected Loxley vice president. Nevell was an officer in the society.[76]

Mariner Joseph Stiles may have been an officer in the Philadelphia Artillery as early as 1774.[77] During the 1750s, 1760s, and 1770s, he taught writing, arithmetic, accounting, and navigation at his school in Philadelphia.[78] As president of the Sons of St. George, he knew Loxley and Nevell.[79] He had also known Major Mifflin for several years: during the early 1770s, Stiles and Mifflin were managers of the Society for the Relief of the Poor and Distressed Masters of Ships, their Widows, and Children.[80]

Francis Grice became an officer in the Philadelphia Artillery Battalion on June 5, 1775.[81] Grice had first served under Samuel Mifflin at the Association Battery in 1756. His shipyard, Francis Grice and Company, would be one of four Philadelphia firms contracted to build frigates for the Continental Navy in 1776, along with the Eyre brothers' shipyard in Kensington.[82] The other two shipyards were Wharton and Humphreys, and Warwick Coates.

William Thorne served in the Philadelphia Artillery from 1775 to 1777.[83] He was an elected officer of the Sons of St. George in 1772.[84] Thorne, Joseph Stiles, and Thomas Nevell also belonged to the Committee of Privates, a radical group of Associator officers, in 1775.[85]

More than membership in various organizations linked these men to one another. Many of the artillery officers were also neighbors. A survey of all males sixteen to fifty years old living in Dock Ward includes Joseph Moulder, Thomas Nevell, Lawrence Shiney, Benjamin Loxley, and Abram Loxley.[86] The list includes the names of other men known to have served in the Philadelphia Artillery during the Revolutionary War.

Thomas Procter, on the other hand, was a relative newcomer to Philadelphia. A carpenter by trade, Procter arrived in the city sometime before the end of 1766. He most likely served, along with his brother Francis, as an artillerist in that component of the British Army known as the Irish Establishment, which was authorized, raised, and equipped from a centralized headquarters at Dublin Castle rather than the Tower of London, like the English Establishment.[87] Soldiers serving in the Irish Establishment were regulars just as much as those

Fig. 11. Button from a uniform coat, 3d Battalion, Philadelphia Associators. (*Courtesy of Independence National Historical Park, Philadelphia, Pennsylvania, Archaeological Collection. Photograph by Jed Levin*)

serving in the English Establishment. The Association likely commissioned the Procters on the basis of their prior service, as no evidence, apart from Thomas's trade, has been found to link him to other known prewar artillerists or to membership in any of the Whig committees.

Captain Jehu Eyre, who carefully recorded the size and type of ordnance during his march to Fort Pitt in summer 1760, commanded an additional company from Kensington, known as the Associator Artillery of the Northern Liberties. Eyre's artillery guarded the remaining artillery stored in many of Philadelphia's public buildings.[88] In 1775, more than one hundred cannon were stored in and around Philadelphia, including the State House, the courthouse and jail, the Grand Battery, Fort Mud, and a storage site near Gray's Ferry.[89] Loxley's sawmill supplied cedar planks, pine boards, and other ship fittings to the Eyre brothers' shipyard.[90] Loxley built Eyre's home.[91] Through the early 1770s, barely a week passed in which the two men were not in contact.[92] In 1775, Eyre and his men repaired cannon under Loxley's supervision.[93]

In addition to the artillery, Philadelphia raised three smartly uniformed foot battalions, following the latest trend in military deportment.[94] Colonel John Dickinson's 1st Battalion sported brown coats faced with buff, Daniel Roberdeau's 2nd Battalion wore brown coats faced red, and Colonel John Cadwalader's 3rd Battalion brown, faced white (fig. 11). Each apparently wore round hats festooned with feathers and ribbons that matched their facing colors, rather than the more conventional—and less practical—cocked hats. White linen smallclothes, or vests and knee breeches, and short leggings known as spatter-dashes or half gaiters completed the uniform. Associators carried their ammunition in large black cartridge boxes marked "Liberty," with the number of the soldier's battalion on the flap (fig. 12).[95]

Like the artillery, the foot battalions each initially consisted of four companies, with two majors and a battalion adjutant authorized for each. A provost guard secured training areas and maintained camp discipline. The public spaces in Philadelphia soon filled with drilling Associators. They trained twice daily on the commons west of the city, at 5:00 a.m. and 5:00 p.m.[96]

A rifle battalion rounded out the structure. Rifle battalions elicited considerable comment wherever they trained, dazzling onlookers with their feats of marksmanship that only a decade before had been considered riotous activities. The rifle battalions represented an innovation based on lessons learned in the Seven Years' War. Rangers and light infantrymen had favored rifles and carbines since at least the early 1750s, and by the early 1770s, they favored the well-known linen hunting frock, an innovation that appears to have been introduced from the Virginia backcountry. [97]

The officers of Philadelphia's foot battalions were a virtual who's who of Philadelphia society and politics. Noted jurist and statesman John Dickinson commanded the 1st Battalion, chaired the Committee of Safety, and represented Pennsylvania in the Continental Congress.[98] Dickinson's staff included Majors Jacob Morgan and William Coats. William Will, James Irvine, and a Captain Smythers commanded three of the four companies.

The 2nd Battalion, under the command of Colonel Daniel Roberdeau, included companies under the command of Captains Francis Wade, a Captain Peters, and William Bradford. Adjutant Thomas Hanson administered the battalion.[99]

Colonel John Cadwalader expanded the Philadelphia Greens to four companies, designated as the 3rd Battalion.[100] Joseph Cowperthwaite is listed as a captain in one of the companies of the 3rd Battalion. As he had previously commanded the Quaker Blues, it follows that he should have commanded the light company after Cadwalader attained field grade rank.

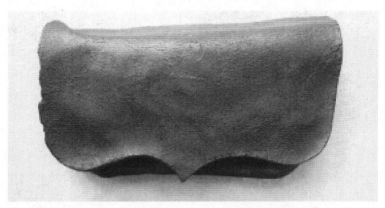

Fig. 12. Cartridge pouch, similar to the type adopted by the Pennsylvania Committee of Safety. (*Courtesy of Colonel J. Craig Nannos. Photograph by John Bansemer*)

He was elected to the active roll of the Light Horse of Philadelphia on March 16, 1776.[101] Cadwalader's second in command, Lieutenant Colonel John Nixon, had been a lieutenant in the regiment of foot that had made such a stir throughout summer 1756, with its grenadiers and its impressive show of street firing.[102] Nixon's father had commanded one of the original companies of foot organized in 1747. Major Thomas Mifflin, no relation to Samuel Mifflin of the artillery, graduated from Philadelphia College in 1760. He represented Pennsylvania as a delegate to the First and Second Continental Congresses in 1774 and 1775.

Other officers of Cadwalader's battalion included Thomas Wharton, Richard Peters (the son of the former provincial secretary), John Shee, and a Captain Fitzsimmons, who was most likely Thomas Fitzsimmons.[103] The colonel's brother, Lambert Cadwalader, commanded the battalion's light company.[104] Light companies trained to skirmish, patrol, reconnoiter, and man outposts ahead of the main army. Artist Charles Willson Peale, newly arrived from Maryland, enlisted as a private in Captain Richard Peters' company.[105] Peale rose to the rank of captain when the Associators organized a fourth battalion sometime between late 1775 and early 1776.[106] Philadelphia County additionally organized four battalions.[107]

Other counties organized in a similar fashion. Colonel John Patton commanded the Berks County Battalion of Foot.[108]

This battalion consisted of four companies under Captains John Lesher, Michael Furrer, George Miller, and Michael Wolf.

In pursuance of a resolution reached in Lebanon on June 25, 1774, Major John Phillip De Haas organized a four-company battalion in western Lancaster County townships in summer 1775.[109] Timothy Green organized a battalion of riflemen in nearby Hanover Township.[110]

The York Associators expanded in May 1775 as the 1st Battalion, York County Associators, under Colonel James Smith and Major Michael Swope.[111] Apparently no relation to James Smith of the Black Boys, Colonel Smith was likely one of the magistrates who petitioned the province for frontier defense in 1755.

As Pennsylvania had done under the 1757 Militia Law, and as Maryland had done since the 1600s, Cumberland County organized four military districts, each responsible for raising a battalion of foot.[112] Robert Callender commanded the lower district and the 1st Battalion, William Thompson commanded the upper district and the 2nd Battalion, John Montgomery commanded the middle district. James Wilson, who would also represent Pennsylvania in Congress, commanded a district comprising all of Cumberland County beyond Kittatinny Mountain, excluding the Path Valley.[113] The Path Valley parallels the Cumberland Valley to the west and north of Kittatinny and the Blue Mountains. The region had been the scene of brutal fighting since 1755 and produced several ranger companies over the past twenty years. The York County Committee of Safety created five districts, and there is some indication that Philadelphia also organized military districts at about this time.

On May 16, 1775, the Westmoreland County Association organized two battalions, the 1st under Colonel John Proctor, and the 2d under Colonel John Carnahan. The Associators commissioned ranger James Smith as major of Carnahan's battalion.[114]

From these organizations, the Pennsylvania Associators had, by August 1, created battalions consisting of eight line companies and one light infantry company. [115] Line companies maneuvered in standard, close-order tactics as part of the battalion. Light infantry companies consisted of select soldiers who demonstrated superior marksmanship, greater strength, and higher intellect to serve as skirmishers, marksmen, and scouts for the line battalions. On August 26, the three foot battalions expanded to accept three existing training companies until new battalions organized.[116] Properly organized, thousands of Pennsylvanians received a minimum of three months' training, in contrast with previous mobilizations for service outside the colony in 1740 and 1746, when Pennsylvania recruits went off to war with as little as a few weeks' training.

Associators were quick to affirm their new loyalty. On September 6, 1775, former joiner Robert Jewell ran for Philadelphia County Coroner. He ran the following notice in the *Pennsylvania Gazette*:

> To the FREEHOLDERS, and others, ELECTORS of this city and county, THE subscriber being disabled from following his trade, by an accident generally known, finds himself under the necessity of throwing himself on the generosity of the public, to enable him to procure a decent subsistence for himself and family: He therefore takes the freedom to solicit the votes and interests of the freeholders of this city and county, in returning him for the Office of Coroner, for this city and county, at the ensuing election. As his misfortune befel him on a public occasion, he humbly hopes for a proper share of public favour and compassion. ROBERT JEWELL[117]

The broadside illustrates the political shift in Philadelphia's civil-military relations. A year earlier, on September 16, 1774, a premature discharge blew off Jewell's hand while he was loading one of the brass six-pounders in the State House Yard.[118] The accident effectively ended Jewell's careers as an artillerist and a joiner. The Philadelphia Artillery had by this time replaced the Royal Artillery as an instrument of government policy. By 1775, Jewell considered artillery drill as public service. He expected Philadelphia voters to share his view and compensate him for his disability.

William Bradford published the *Journals of Congress* in 1775. Its title page showed an engraving of three soldiers dressed in uniforms and swearing on the Bible (fig. 13, overleaf).

That summer, John Dickinson, commanding the 1st city battalion, co-wrote "A Declaration by the Representatives of the United Colonies of North-America, Now Met in Congress at Philadelphia, Setting Forth the Causes and Necessity of Their Taking Up Arms" with fellow delegate Thomas Jefferson, which read in part:

> In our own native land, in defence of the freedom that is our birth-right, and which we ever enjoyed till the late violation of it—for the protection of our property, acquired solely by the honest industry of our fore-fathers and ourselves, against violence actually offered, we have taken up arms. We shall lay them down when hostilities shall cease on the part of the aggressors, and all danger of their being renewed shall be removed, and not before.[119]

Benjamin Loxley, who had quietly but steadfastly distanced himself from his former relationship with the Royal Artillery, was no less emphatic when it came to affirming his new loyalty. In 1775, Dock Ward elected him to the Committee of Safety.[120] After the Revolutionary War, he justified his decision in a carefully worded passage:

> I thought it was dangerous for me on account of the oaths of allegiance I had taken to King George at the three times when I had taken [a] commission under him and that I should be perjured. But some of my old comrade officers through the French War, who were also chosen committee-men, and I met and considered the matter well and we judged that King George had broken his coronation oath with us, wherein we engaged to protect all his subjects in free liberty of conscience and lawful rights, and now he had broken his promise and we were free from ours.[121]

His words reveal a great deal about his values, and the values of his fellow officers. King George III had broken the covenant between government and governed. Loxley had taken his commission "in free liberty of conscience and lawful rights." He considered it his duty to rebel against his former sovereign.

Loxley associated with like-minded Philadelphians. Many of the men he met on a regular basis through work or in civic organizations and political committees later took commissions in the Philadelphia Artillery Battalion. They in turn demonstrated remarkably similar political views, occupational pursuits, and outlooks.

Printer John Dunlap drilled as a trooper in the Philadelphia Light Horse. Early in the war, Dunlap's *Pennsylvania Packet, or General Advertiser,* printed the "Pennsylvania March," a stirring ditty set to the tune of "Coming Thro' the Rye," whose second stanza called on Philadelphians to take up arms:

Fig. 13. "Journals of the Proceedings of the Congress, held in Philadelphia May 10 [1775]." Its title page showed an engraving of soldiers. (*The Library Company of Philadelphia*)

> We'll not give up our
> birthright,
> Our foes shall find us men;
> As good as they, in any
> shape,
> The British troops shall ken.
> Huzza! brave boys, we'll beat them
> On any hostile plain;
> For freedom, wives, and children dear,
> The battle we'll maintain.[122]

If the lines were indeed written by Dunlap or another member of the light horse, they speak to values of courage, country, and liberty not unlike those expressed so many times since 1747.

Associators outside Philadelphia echoed these sentiments. In Lancaster County, where the Hanover Township Committee had so famously left its cause "to heaven and our rifles," the Articles of Association adopted on May 3, 1775, noted that

> the enemies of Great Britain and America, have resolved by force of arms to carry into execution the most unjust, tyrannical, and cruel edicts of the British Parliament . . . and have flattered themselves from our unacquaintance with military discipline that we should become easy prey to them. . . . We do most solemnly agree and associate under the deepest

sense of our duty to God, our country, and ourselves, and posterity, to defend and protect the religious and civil rights of this and our sister Colonies.[123]

The Westmoreland County Association likewise resolved that

the Parliament of Great Britain, by several late Acts, have declared the inhabitants of the Massachusetts-Bay to be in rebellion, and the Ministry, by endeavoring to enforce those Acts, have attempted to reduce the said inhabitants to a more wretched state of slavery than ever before existed in any state or country. Not content with violating their constitutional and chartered privileges, they would strip them of the rights of humanity, exposing lives to the wanton and unpunishable sport of a licentious soldiery, and depriving them of the very means of subsistence. There is no reason to doubt but the same system of tyranny and oppression will (Should it meet with success in the Massachusetts-Bay) be extended to every other part of America; it is therefore become the indispensible duty of every American, of every man who has any publick virtue or love for his Country, or any compassion for posterity, by every means which God has put in his power, to resist and oppose the execution of it; that for us we will be ready to oppose it with our lives and fortunes. And the better to enable us to accomplish it, we will immediately form ourselves into a military body.[124]

To Philadelphia grocer and patriot Robert Lettis Hooper Jr., the Associators' martial skill would surely prevent "those servile engines of Ministerial power" from viewing "those high topt Mountains which seperates the lower plains from *our Canaan.*" To this obvious reference to Joshua, Hooper added a reference to Locke, predicting that "should their folly or madness prompt them to attempt it," the Americans would march "Thousands and tens of thousands with Guygantick strides to wash the plains with the blood of those degenerate invaders of the libertys of Mandkind." James Armstrong, the son of Colonel John Armstrong of Kittanning fame, characterized the Associators of the Kittatinny district as "a noble Battalion indeed as marks-men, many of them able to vie with the Tribe of Benjamin," a tribe of ancient Israel reputed to be great archers.[125]

Strong as their words may seem, Associator rhetoric appears to have softened in at least one respect. Despite an ongoing commitment to defend a land considered their birthright, and despite a continued religious zeal, Associators by 1775 appear to have dropped their anti-Catholic cant in favor of an appeal to a broader constituency. At least one Associator officer, Thomas Fitzsimmons of Cadwalader's battalion, was a practicing Roman Catholic, as were other prominent supporters, most notably mariner John Barry, late of Wexford, Ireland, who would soon gain fame as one of the new nation's first naval heroes, and merchant Stephen Moylan, soon to serve as the quartermaster general of the Continental Army and later as colonel of the 4th Continental Light Dragoons.

Though fiery rhetoric put Pennsylvanians on the march, words alone would not drive the redcoats out of Boston. Benjamin Loxley's memoirs illustrate Philadelphia's military transformation. Throughout 1775 and 1776, Loxley supervised large numbers of artillerists and laborers readying the artillery.[126] He spent long hours making carriages, mounting gun tubes, and making them fit for service.[127] In addition to readying the ordnance, Loxley also built mobile blacksmith shops to maintain the battalion in the field.[128] He outfitted fortifications, batteries, and ships for the Pennsylvania Navy.[129] Twice daily he trained his artillery company at the State House. He also trained members of the Associator foot battalions in artillery and small-arms exercises. He taught gunpowder manufacture and the use of fireworks. He surveyed pine logs and recommended their purchase by the Committee of Safety to be used in building antiship obstacles known as chevaux-de-frise in the Delaware River.[130] In 1776, Loxley offered to cast cannon and was directed to do so.[131] He was tireless in support of the Revolution.

Such duties reflected skills accumulated over decades of service to the train of artillery, but they also overextended the hardworking carpenter. At their July 1775 meeting, the members of the Sons of St. George voted to postpone their next quarterly meeting.[132] Both Joseph Stiles, the president, and Benjamin Loxley, the vice president, were busy with committees and mobilizing the artillery command. Loxley was so busy with mobilization that in August 1775, he relinquished his job of provincial storekeeper to Robert Towers.[133]

Loxley was not the only member of the artillery with new and varied responsibilities. Captain Eyre's shipyard built gunboats.[134] Major Mifflin was heavily involved with the Pennsylvania Navy, and Captain Biddle was active in preparing river defenses. Captain Moulder purchased sail cloth, sails, cables, and rigging for the Pennsylvania Navy.[135] He made canvas carriage covers for the artillery battalion's cannon and purchased coarse linen to make tents and haversacks for the city battalions.[136] The modifications Moulder made to his gun carriages were adopted by all Associator commands in the city, as well as the Pennsylvania Navy.[137] Major Mifflin supervised the changes.[138] Thomas Nevell built gun carriages for the cannon at Fort Mud.[139] The duties assumed by each of those men reflected their civilian occupations, or skills learned in the train of artillery. The Committee of Safety conversely sought the skills of artillery officers such as Mifflin, Loxley, Moulder, and Biddle. Over the past decade most had been active supporters of nonimportation, Whig candidates, or members of the Committee of Safety. All had an entrenched interest in their city. Their accumulated expertise was invaluable to the city's defense.

These men in turn relinquished their duties to younger men who showed promise. Loxley, along with other Associator officers, helped advance military knowledge in Philadelphia by subsidizing the publication of a uniform tactical manual and regulation. Thomas Hanson, battalion adjutant to Colonel Roberdeau, published the *Prussian Evolutions* in 1775.[140] The frontispiece lists the names of the subscribers, which included several Associator officers.[141]

The *Prussian Evolutions* marked a departure from earlier tactical manuals used in Pennsylvania. Indeed, the new manual marked a departure from manuals used in other colonies as well, combining a manual of arms and maneuver compatible with the British system, derived from the 1756 Prussian Army manual, with an advanced tactical treatise and regulations. The manual consisted of two books. The first contained the manual of arms, infantry tactics, and military law; the second covered artillery tactics. The *Prussian Evolutions* soon became the

Fig. 14. Pennsylvania Committee of Safety Musket. (*The State Museum of Pennsylvania, Pennsylvania Historical and Museum Commission*)

standard tactical manual throughout the Pennsylvania Military Association.[142]

The new Articles of Association, adopted statewide August 17, 1775, lacked the heady rhetoric, and particularly the anti-Catholicism, of their predecessors.[143] A total of thirty-two articles served as articles of war, or military law, and reflected the vast military service of many Associator officers schooled by soldiers such as John Forbes and Henry Bouquet and who read a number of tactical manuals. Articles Sixteen and Seventeen, for example, stipulated that enlisted soldiers sit on courts-martial, a practice then current in the Prussian Army and one that would not be adopted in the British Army for many decades.

William Bradford, who had expressed prodefense politics through his *Pennsylvania Journal* and had served as an officer in the 1747 and 1756 Association, also served in Roberdeau's 2nd Battalion. Bradford printed two thousand copies of the new Articles of Association in July 1775. Shortly thereafter, the Committee of Safety instructed Roberdeau to print five hundred copies in German.[144]

No detail was too small for the Associators who mobilized Pennsylvania. In addition to Moulder's modified gun carriages, subcommittees of the Committee of Safety introduced several innovations. On July 3, the committee resolved that John Cadwalader of the 3rd Battalion and Samuel Morris of the light horse provide patterns for cartridge boxes, muskets, bayonets, and knapsacks to the different counties.[145] The new musket departed from that of the British land pattern in having a forty-four inch barrel bored for seventeen balls to the pound.[146] The Committee of Safety contracted with local gunsmiths to build the new weapons, a number of which survive (fig. 14).[147] John

Nicholson also made pattern muskets for each of the Pennsylvania counties to use as templates.[148] In August, Robert Lettis Hooper boasted that the city battalions were "generally well furnished with Arms."[149] Contractors delivered nearly two thousand small arms by year's end to augment surplus stocks from the last war. On March 6, 1776, the Committee of Safety authorized a gunlock factory at Philadelphia to correct a major shortage of that key component.[150]

Despite the adoption of a standard-pattern arm, Associators who reported to rendezvous carried muskets bored to several different diameters. To correct a potential logistical nightmare, the Pennsylvania Committee of Safety on May 29, 1776, ordered each Associator battalion to maintain a size book.[151] The size book recorded the number of muskets in a battalion by bore size. The Committee of Safety also standardized the charge of each cartridge at this time, at two-fifths the weight of each ball to a charge of powder. Muskets were stamped with a number designating their bore, and cartridges were to be rolled and tied in bundles, with the bore number marked on the outside.[152] On July 2, 1776, the Committee of Safety ordered that the cartridges in the future have an addition of three buckshot in each cartridge.[153] On February 10, 1776, the Committee of Safety authorized six powder mills at French Creek, Lancaster, Swedes Ford, and Northern Liberties.[154]

On July 18, the committee resolved that the standard cartridge box would contain twenty-three cartridges. Two bundles of cartridges to a box containing twenty-three holes enabled a soldier to ram the remaining cartridge into his musket, ensuring that his weapon was properly loaded. On the same day, the committee ordered patterns for muskets, cartridge boxes, and knapsacks sent out to the twelve counties.

To supplement Pennsylvania's rapidly expanding military, the committee took the unprecedented step of requiring all who did not actively serve to surrender arms issued during the last war to those who did serve.[155] Pursuant to this order, the Bucks County Committee of Safety on July 10, 1776, ordered Matthew Bennett and Jared Irwin to seize the arms of non-Associators and mark the breech pin or lower end of the barrel with its bore size.[156] Several other counties followed suit.

Fig. 15. Wooden canteen of the type authorized by the Pennsylvania Committee of Safety, carried by a 1st Battalion soldier. (www.*historicalimagebank.com*)

Economic disparities between Associations first became apparent in the 1750s. As Steven Rosswurm has observed, these inequalities persisted into the 1770s.[157] In 1776, the Pennsylvania Committee of Safety censured cooper Jacob Brandt. He had contracted to make canteens but sold them to Associators at inflated prices, which the Associators could evidently afford (fig. 15).[158] Western Associators lacked the resources that Philadelphia Associators had. Few Associator battalions outside Philadelphia and larger towns appear to have purchased uniforms. When Cumberland County Associators scrounged surplus arms and accoutrements, "leaving a Parcel of Rubbish" that was sent to Lancaster, "some of the poorer Associators" cleaned and refurbished them.[159] But where complaints of shoddy or half-hearted defensive measures had previously fallen on deaf ears, Associators now had their local committees of safety to mediate their grievances. When the committees failed to satisfy the more zealous Whigs in the ranks, disgruntled Associators could form their own committees, such as the Committee of Privates, which organized in September 1775.[160]

On June 14, 1775, Congress authorized six rifle companies from Pennsylvania, two from Maryland, and two from Virginia for the new Continental Army besieging British-occupied Boston. Provincial veteran William Thompson of Carlisle commanded companies recruited under Captains Michael Doudel of York, James Chambers, Robert Cluggage, Abraham Miller, George Nagel, and John Lowdon. They marched to Boston to join the Continental Army. Rifleman Aaron Wright of Northumberland County, a private in Lowdon's company, likewise styled the Continentals as "Sons of Liberty" and the redcoats as "Philistines" and "parliamentary tools," and defined the struggle very much as Loxley did, citing Voltaire and Martin Luther in his reflection on the war with Great Britain.[161] The Pennsylvania battalion was among the first units from outside New England to arrive at Cambridge, Massachusetts.

Pennsylvania's Executive Council, the Provincial Council's successor, authorized Colonel John Bull to command the 1st Battalion on October 12, 1775, and ordered William Allen, Jonathan Jones, William Williams, Josiah Harmer, Marien Lamar, Thomas Dorsey, William Jenkins, and Austin Willet, newly sworn in as company commanders, to report to the Philadelphia barracks. There, Joseph Fox and Samuel Caldwell issued whatever items were in storage and entered the captains' names, as well as the names of any soldiers present, onto the rolls. Congress would soon make Caldwell's appointment as paymaster general official; for the time being, he acted on behalf of his partner and fellow trooper, Cornet James Mease.

Congress had authorized a felt hat, pair of yarn stockings, pair of shoes, hunting shirt, and blanket to state battalions in Continental service, but not weapons or any other items, known as necessaries, vital for a soldier's comfort and survival.[162] The firm of Mease and Caldwell, acting on behalf of the Committee of Safety, reimbursed company commanders' purchases of weapons.[163] At the barracks, the 1st Battalion learned how to drill together as squads, platoons, and companies, while providing security along the Philadelphia waterfront. Its commanders recruited troops and acquired weapons, and the Committee of Safety issued equipment necessary for active campaigning. By December 15, 1775, Pennsylvania had authorized the 2nd, 3rd, 4th, and 5th Battalions for Continental service. Pennsylvania had by that time organized six foot battalions for Continental service, in addition to Thompson's.[164]

On January 10, 1776, Congress ordered the Committee of Safety to issue enough mittens, musket slings, stockings, warm waistcoats, leggings, shoes, breeches, and blankets to sustain Bull's battalion in the field, as well as nine wagons to carry additional baggage.[165] Congress had two days earlier resolved to order Benedict Arnold to reinforce his army in Canada.[166] Each of Pennsylvania's three battalions of foot supplied two companies. An attached rifle company rounded out each battalion.[167] In January 1776, one of De Haas's officers, William Allen, a Loyalist, resigned. Pennsylvania commissioned Benjamin Davis to replace him. John Bull, cashiered for selling furloughs and other conduct unbecoming an officer, had been replaced in command by John Philip De Haas. On January 19, 1776, the 1st Battalion received orders to march, and on the twenty-second, two companies left Philadelphia, elegantly dressed in brown jackets and round hats reminiscent of the city foot battalions. Colonel De Haas and his battalion staff set out not long after.[168] On February 12, the Pennsylvania Committee of Safety applied to the Continental Congress to replace the arms carried by the battalion of foot and the rifle company in Continental service.[169]

On October 27, 1775, Captain Procter had reported to the Philadelphia barracks, where his men drew bedding left there by the Royal Artillery detachment.[170] On December 27, 1775, Procter's garrison moved to Fort Mud.[171] By this time it numbered ninety men.[172] The company manned six eighteen-pound cannon.[173] On August 14, 1776, the Committee of Safety created the Pennsylvania State Artillery Battalion and promoted Procter to major.[174] The new command had an authorized strength of two hundred men in two companies.[175] Two Pennsylvania marine officers, Captain John Martin Strobaugh and Captain Thomas Forrest, transferred into the artillery to command the 1st and 2nd Companies.[176] The Philadelphia Artillery now fielded three battalions under Colonel Mifflin, Major Procter, and Captain Loxley.

The departures of Thompson, De Haas, and Procter left three foot battalions, a rifle battalion, the light horse, and four artillery companies in Philadelphia, commanded by the most politically active Associator officers, who continued to train Associators and mobilize resources, both human and material. Numerous overlapping networks tied the other Associator officers to one another. Those networks motivated the Philadelphia Associators to support the Revolution.

By 1775, Associator companies had expanded, first to two, then four, and finally eight company battalions for Philadelphia's defense. The enthusiastic support for the Revolution shown by so many Associator officers demonstrates that the organization continued to be what it had been for decades: a politically motivated military organization serving the needs of its members and their community. Thus Associators put Pennsylvania on a wartime footing commensurate with the twelve other colonies. Due to their efforts, few Pennsylvania battalions mustered into service with less than three months' training. Pennsylvania's mobilization included six companies of the first battalion outside of New England to march to Boston. Pennsylvania additionally mobilized commercial resources that produced munitions of every kind. Pennsylvania battalions were well equipped, at least at first.[177]

The Associators considered military service a natural right. Time and again, the Articles of Association, letters, broadsides, and personal declarations spoke to a remarkably consistent tradition of volunteerism, patriotism, and a commitment to civil and religious liberty. Common service as Associators and provincial soldiers, not to mention administrative experience as contractors, prepared Pennsylvanians who were willing to pass before their "brethren armed" to take leadership roles in the Revolutionary committees and the battalions, regiments, and other units organized after May 1, 1775. The 1776 campaign would stretch that determination to the limit.

SIX

TO TRENTON
AND PRINCETON

In late afternoon of November 16, 1776, Colonel Robert Magaw, commander of Pennsylvania's 5th Battalion, surrendered the garrison of Fort Washington on the upper end of Manhattan Island. Numerous Associators or former Associators, now enlisted in Continental service, surrendered with Magaw, including Corporal John Adlum, Major John Beatty, and camp follower Margaret Corbin. If Corbin marched out of the fort, she did so with great difficulty: enemy grapeshot had torn away part of her face, an arm, and one of her breasts. The defense of Fort Washington had been a costly failure that would go down as one of the worst defeats the Continental Army suffered in the war. In addition to the human cost, the British captured or destroyed large stocks of warlike stores. With the loss of Fort Lee, Fort Washington's sister fort on the west bank of the Hudson River a few days later, even more supplies fell into the hands of the British. Moreover, the relative ease of the forts' fall, the last American defenses on Manhattan, gave newly arrived British and Hessian soldiers a false sense of invincibility and contempt for American arms.

John Adlum, John Beatty, and Margaret Corbin represented a cross section of Pennsylvania society. Adlum had enlisted in the boys company of the York Associators in 1775. Prior to associating, the teenager lived an average townsman's life in York, the son and grandson of York County public servants.

Adlum's father had been among the first managers of the York Association in 1755. In 1776, the younger Adlum marched to New Jersey with Major Michael Swope's York County Associator Battalion.

Twenty-seven-year-old Bucks County native John Beatty first served with the Pennsylvania Regiment in 1756. After graduating from the College of New Jersey, in Princeton, Beatty practiced medicine in Warwick Township, Bucks County. In 1775, he took command of the 2nd Battalion, Bucks County Associators, organized at Buckingham, Wrightstown, Warrington, Hilltown, Plumstead, Solebury, Upper Makefield, Warminster, New Britain, and Warwick.[1] He helped train young recruits using the *Prussian Evolutions* before he, too, marched off to New Jersey.[2]

Twenty-five-year-old Margaret Cochran Corbin grew up on the Pennsylvania frontier among ever-present war and hardship. She followed her husband, John, to war with the Philadelphia Artillery in 1776, where she performed camp duties and doubtless gained familiarity with the intricacies involved in servicing a field piece. That summer, the Corbins, with other Philadelphia Artillerists, reinforced the defenses of New York City. What motivated Adlum, Beatty, and Corbin, given such diverse backgrounds, to cast their lot with the Revolution?

In previous conflicts, Associators were often reluctant to enter service. In 1775, they went to war with alacrity. Pennsylvania mobilized resources of all types. Foot battalions, riflemen, and gun crews marched to Quebec. Thomas Procter's company garrisoned Fort Mud. In 1776, Pennsylvania promoted him to major and expanded his command to a battalion. Had the HMS *Syren* not captured Francis Procter and his company of Continental artillerists at sea in summer 1776, the Philadelphia Artillery might have played some role in bolstering Charleston's defenses.[3]

Effective July 1, 1776, Pennsylvania reorganized its battalions as regiments, in conformance with Continental Army standards. Associator battalions, interestingly enough, mustered six companies into service, leaving two to three companies at home, presumably to receive and train the new recruits needed to make up for losses in the field due to combat, illness, or desertion. County battalions that failed to recruit the required companies were augmented by companies from other counties and even other states.[4] These companies stayed in service until no longer needed, at which time they rotated home or served as replacements in state battalions in Continental service.

Elements of the Pennsylvania Associators and state troops were soon scattered across the map. The five foot companies assigned to Colonel De Haas's battalion reported to General Philip Schuyler, commander of the Northern Department of the Continental Army at Albany on February 14, 1776.[5] From Albany, the battalion proceeded up the Hudson River and Lake Champlain to Canada, augmented by Captain John Nelson's rifle company. On March 30, the 1st Battalion reported to Arnold's army before Quebec.[6] A part of the battalion fought at the Battle of Trois Rivières on June 9, where a number of soldiers were captured.[7]

The Philadelphia Light Horse, under Captain Samuel Morris, escorted payroll and other important dispatches between Congress and the Continental Army. The light horse additionally reconnoitered the Delaware River, delivering intelligence reports to Pennsylvania president Thomas Wharton and to William Bradford at his London Coffee House.[8]

In July, Michael Doudel and many of his company of riflemen, fresh from Continental service, returned home, where they transferred into one of York's Associator battalions.[9] Other Associators guarded British prisoners interned at Reading. British soldiers–at least some of whom were from the Saint Johns garrison captured by Arnold's army in Canada, and had been accorded the honors of war and were allowed to keep their weapons. In autumn 1776, a number of these prisoners attempted to escape. The revolt failed, and Captain Conrad Geist's company, 7th Battalion, Berks County Associators, subsequently mustered into state service in 1776 to guard and escort them from Reading to Lancaster.[10]

The war's evolving operational tempo quickly changed the configuration of the Philadelphia Artillery. On May 6, Pennsylvania dispatched Captain Thomas Read with the Pennsylvania Navy to counter a British force sailing upriver toward Philadelphia. Captain Loxley's 1st Company, Philadelphia Artillery Battalion, sailed in shallops, small, light-draft cargo craft, to Read's flagship *Montgomery*, anchored off Fort Mud.[11] Read ordered Loxley to join the 3rd Battalion, under the command of Lieutenant Colonel John Nixon, at the fort, Thomas Procter's 119 artillerists having left Fort Island to man the Pennsylvania galley *Hornet*.[12] During the inconclusive defense of Fort Mifflin on May 8-9, 1776, Loxley's 1st Company served under Nixon, and Procter's company fought as sailors and naval gun crews under Read. Any number of factors could account for this switch: Loxley's age relative to Procter's (Loxley was nearly twenty years senior to Procter); Procter's previous service; or Loxley's experience at building Fort Mud's still incomplete fortifications.

The defense of Fort Mifflin would not be the last duty for the Philadelphia Artillery. Shortly after the Delaware River battle, wartime exigencies again called the Philadelphia Artillery Battalion away from the city. On June 25, 1776, a massive British amphibious force, commanded by Major General William Howe and his brother, Admiral Richard, Lord Howe, launched a long-awaited offensive against New York City. New York's deep harbor would provide the Royal Navy with a base from which it could control much of the Eastern Seaboard. From New York City, the British could mount offensives up the Hudson River in order to meet a force under Sir Guy Carlton that was advancing down Lake Champlain. Control of the Hudson and Champlain valleys would in turn isolate New England, with its large fighting population and stocks of cattle and horses, from the rest of the rebelling colonies. All available assets from neighboring states rushed to the theater of operations.

In response to the emergency, Congress on June 3 authorized the Flying Camp, which consisted of ten thousand troops drawn from Pennsylvania, Maryland, and New Jersey. It was organized into battalions deployed to defend the water approaches to New York City until state and Continental regiments could be recruited, trained, and organized to take its place. Congress set Pennsylvania's quota at six thousand soldiers under the command of two brigadier generals.

Translated from the French *camp volant*, a flying camp was a strong body of horses and sometimes infantry that was kept in constant motion to cover a garrison or a geographic strong point and in turn keep the enemy on constant alert.[13] According to Lancelot Théodore Turpin de Crissé's two-volume tactical treatise, *Essaie Sur L'Art de Guerre* (*Essay on the Art of War*), with an enemy nearby, a general should place mounted troops and infantry close enough to protect and support troops engaged in fortifying a position.[14] In other instances, Crissé recommended harassing the enemy with small detachments of mounted defenders. Nearby states, especially Connecticut, known for its horse breeding, had mounted troops available. George Washington, now general and commander in chief of the Continental Army, was familiar with Crissé's writings. But as Washington pointed out to Connecticut governor Jonathon Trumbull, the army lacked forage sufficient to keep the needed cavalry in service. This forced Washington to rely on dismounted horse, riflemen serving as light infantry, and small detachments of artillery posted at strategic points.

Pennsylvania, by contrast, along with Virginia and Maryland, had trained hundreds of light troops using Crissé's doctrine, under commanders who had served with or under Washington. In partial compliance with the six thousand-man quota request, Pennsylvania ordered Colonel Samuel Miles to march the State Rifle Regiment, consisting of two battalions of six companies, and Samuel John Atlee's Battalion of Musketry, to New Jersey. The two men had known one another since at least spring 1756, when they held commissions in the same battalion of the Pennsylvania Regiment. Miles had trained the 9th Battalion, Philadelphia County Associators during the previous summer, but that July, Atlee and Miles's commands had drilled together less than four months.[15]

Responsibility for mustering the remainder of Pennsylvania's quota of four thousand five hundred troops fell to the city of Philadelphia and the counties of Philadelphia, Bucks, Berks, Chester, Lancaster, Northampton, York, and Cumberland. Congress instructed Pennsylvania to send the Flying Camp levies to Philadelphia by increments as soon as they were raised. Those of Bucks, Berks, and Northampton were to proceed directly to Brunswick, New Jersey.[16]

On July 2, 1776, at the State House in Philadelphia, Congress voted to declare independence from Great Britain. Among the Pennsylvania delegates was George Ross of Lancaster and three former Associators: James Smith of York, James Wilson of Carlisle, and George Clymer of Philadelphia. A fifth delegate, John Dickinson, abstained from the vote. Having concluded his civil affairs in Philadelphia as a delegate to Congress, Ross set out for Lancaster to preside over a body that, despite its military purpose, was no less democratic.

Just as Congress had declared that "governments are instituted among men, deriving their just powers from the governed," the Lancaster convention of Associators, consisting of two officers and two enlisted soldiers from each of the Associated battalions in Pennsylvania, convened to select the two brigadier generals who would lead them in battle. When a quorum was reached, the convention voted on a succession of motions. "A question was put whether the Officers & Privates would ballot singly. Resolved unanimously in the affirmative." Should the brigadier generals be voted for at the same time, with the two highest vote-getters being named commanding generals? The president's gavel dropped. Resolved. Daniel Roberdeau, James Ewing, Samuel Miles, James Potter, Curtis Grubb, George Ross, Thomas McKean, and Mark Bird stood for election. All motions on the floor having passed, the convention took a brief recess. Upon its return, the floor appointed Colonel Mark Burd of the 2nd Battalion, Berks County Associators, and Captain Sharp Delaney of the 3rd Battalion, Philadelphia Associators, as judges of the election.[17] Ballot boxes passed through the hall. When the votes were tallied, Daniel Roberdeau and James Ewing were proclaimed winners and appointed brigadier generals for Pennsylvania.

The convention then resolved to "march under the Direction & Command of our Brigadier Generals to the Assistance of all or any of the free, independent States of America," and granted Roberdeau and Ewing the full power to draft Associators out of the several counties.[18]

The Military Association had executed an about face. Where it had once petitioned an inattentive assembly for funding to defend the province, Associators now served as delegates in the Continental Congress and exercised the power to mobilize Pennsylvania soldiers for service outside the state. As a young man, Benjamin Franklin had coveted the office of printer to the colony, a position he held from 1730 to 1766. Franklin now deliberated over the prosecution of the war. Two other Associators, John Dunlap and William Bradford, served Pennsylvania and Congress as official printers. The next day, July 5, while Dunlap's Philadelphia printing office readied copies of the Declaration of Independence for distribution to the states, Congress ordered all Associators into service until they were relieved by the Flying Camp battalions that were then organizing. On Monday, July 8, 1776, Colonel Nixon read the Declaration of Independence to a crowd of about two thousand gathered in the State House yard. Associators now held positions of leadership and public trust at all levels.

On July 20, the Continental Congress called on Pennsylvania for four additional battalions for the Flying Camp. Three weeks later, Pennsylvania ordered the commanding officers of the several counties, excluding battalions belonging to the frontier counties of Bedford, Northumberland, Northampton, and Westmoreland, to New Jersey "with their whole battalions" and attached companies of guards and carpenters.[19] Associator battalions that provided their quota to the Flying Camp were permitted to return home after six weeks of service. The Pennsylvania Convention, which had replaced the assembly upon statehood, appointed three commissioners to go to New Jersey to organize the Flying Camp and to nominate the officers. On August 12, the convention raised the additional four battalions for the Flying Camp from the city of Philadelphia and the counties of Philadelphia, Berks, Chester, Lancaster, York, Cumberland, and Northampton. The next day, the convention authorized the Flying Camp commissioners to commission the Flying Camp officers, using blank commissions supplied by the convention.[20]

From the time of the Seven Years' War, western leaders had pleaded, petitioned, and even threatened by force of arms for a full-time defense force. When Pennsylvania raised that force, as it did for over a decade in the form of the Pennsylvania Regiment, westerners made willing and effective soldiers. Commensurate with these needs, Aeneas Mackey's battalion organized in July and August 1776, in Westmoreland and

Bedford, specifically to garrison Presque Isle, Fort Le Boeuf, and Kittanning. Unlike other Pennsylvania battalions, Mackey's battalion organized on the Continental establishment of eight companies, enlisted for one year of service. At roughly the same time, six Continental companies were raised in Northampton and Northumberland for the defense of those counties. An additional two companies were raised in the Connecticut settlement at Wyoming.

By July 10, 1776, the Bucks County Association had organized its quota.[21] Also known as the Bucks County Battalion, it had an authorized strength of four hundred Associators organized into five companies and was commanded by Colonel Joseph Hart and Lieutenant Colonel William Baxter.[22] Colonel John Beatty served on the battalion staff. Captain James McClure's company of the Chester County Flying Camp Battalion probably completed Baxter's battalion, bringing his total up to six companies.[23]

In July, Pennsylvania ordered all of the York County Associators into the Flying Camp. Once there, they organized into a battalion under the flag of Major Michael Swope. Swope's battalion was a composite recruited from all York County Associators in the Flying Camp assembled at Amboy. Westmoreland County organized a battalion and commissioned former Black Boy James Smith as its major.[24] In similar fashion, Chester, Berks, and Lancaster Counties organized battalions for Continental service in the Flying Camp.

General Washington, commanding the Continental Army in New York, had few cannons with which to defend the city.[25] Congress promoted Samuel Mifflin to colonel and ordered the Philadelphia Artillery Battalion into Continental service at the end of June. On July 2, 1776, the Philadelphia Committee of Safety directed storekeeper Robert Towers to "deliver to Capt. Loxley such of the Ordnance & Military Stores required for his Artillery Company as he can supply, & Capt. Loxley is authorized to procure the remainder on the most reasonable terms, and bring his account to the Committee."[26] Within a few weeks, the Philadelphia Artillery Battalion was outfitted and accoutered.[27] Loxley and his crews were tasked with defending the port town of Amboy and monitoring Staten Island Sound. The sound was an important water approach to Manhattan, so

Loxley chose two twelve-pounders from Philadelphia's train of artillery. Twelve-pounders, while harder on horses and men to transport and maneuver into battle, threw a ball heavy enough to smash a ship's timbers and wreak serious damage.

On July 21, 1776, "by order of the Honourable the Continental Congress & Col. Mifflin," Captain Benjamin Loxley marched his artillery company from Philadelphia, reaching the Rising Sun Tavern in northern Philadelphia County that evening.[28] The tavern evidently could not support Loxley's company, which instead billeted in a church, where Loxley's men heard prayer services. The company continued its march, ferried across the Delaware River at Bristol, and marched across New Jersey to Amboy.

The rest of the battalion soon joined Loxley and his men.[29] Captain Moulder commanded the 2nd Company. Lieutenant Joseph Stiles was promoted to captain.[30] He replaced James Biddle as commander of the 3rd Company. Procter's 4th Company was already a separate command, and Captain Eyre was busy with important naval contracts at his shipyard in Kensington.[31] Accordingly, two companies from New Jersey, the 1st Company of Artillery of West Jersey under Captain Samuel Hugg and the Eastern Company, New Jersey State Artillery, under Captain Daniel Neal, were added to the Philadelphia Artillery Battalion. They brought it up to full strength with six additional guns and 120 men.[32]

The battalion made camp in and around Amboy "within Gun Shot of the Enemy."[33] Loxley's company defended the waterfront while the other companies secured the town from land attack. The Philadelphia Artillery Battalion was stationed in northern New Jersey until September 5, 1776. By the end of July, Colonel Mifflin commanded thirteen gun crews scattered over several miles.[34]

On July 22, 1776, Pennsylvania again reorganized the Philadelphia Artillery Battalion.[35] Joseph Moulder's 2nd Company, consisting of about fifty men crewing two cannon, transferred to the Flying Camp.[36] Moulder's guns were soon followed by Colonel Mifflin and the two New Jersey companies.[37] By the end of August 1776, Philadelphia gun crews serving in two administrative commands fortified New Jersey shore points at Amboy, Passaic, Elizabeth, and Newark, as well as Woodbridge, an inland crossroads.[38]

Despite the Philadelphia Artillery's dispersed deployment, it still functioned as a unitary command in matters such as administration, personnel, and logistics. On July 22, 1776, Loxley met Mifflin at the battalion headquarters.[39] A few days later, Loxley delivered forty-eight cannon primers, known as portfires, and three hundred metal cartridge tubes to Captain Moulder (fig. 16).[40] Moulder distributed the ammunition to the other artillery companies. Mifflin, Loxley, and Procter swapped gun crews and may have even supplied gunners to the Pennsylvania Navy. Loxley's rolls, for example, list twenty-six privates "at sea or at publick work" during the Amboy campaign.[41] Reinforcements from Philadelphia increased the divided Philadelphia Artillery Battalion to sixteen crews in July.[42] When Loxley's battalion was ordered home on September 4, 1776, it left a gun and crew with the quartermaster at Amboy.[43]

The Flying Camp performed a vital and occasionally hazardous service. In August, Lord Howe's powerful fleet passed in the distance. A few days later, a Hessian artillery detachment placed guns at the Billopp House on Staten Island, just within the effective range of Loxley's twelve-pounders. Over the next several days, the Hessian and American gun crews engaged in a deadly game of cat-and-mouse. One day, in an effort to find the range, Loxley's men fired across the sound, putting one of their shot down the chimney of the house, "greatly distressing the inhabitants within." On Saturday, August 25, "the enemy gave us three shot from abreast Billop's house, and then took the gun up into an orchard on the next farm," where it was evidently safely out of range. In August, Loxley received news of the death of a fellow Associator, Trooper George Fuller of the light horse. Fuller had been riding in column alongside Samuel Caldwell when one of Caldwell's pistols accidentally discharged into his thigh. After several hours of agony, Fuller bled to death.

On September 5, the balance of the Philadelphia Artillery Battalion commenced its march home. Loxley ended his service with the battalion following his arrival in Philadelphia on September 7. His return from Amboy marked his effective

Fig. 16. Portfire. Consisting of a waxy combination of combustible materials, portfires functioned like a flare to touch off cannon. (*Courtesy of Colonel J. Craig Nannos. Photograph by John Bansemer*)

retirement as a citizen soldier. The Amboy campaign had been a physical hardship for the fifty-six-year-old veteran, punctuated by the occasional terror of combat.[44] Loxley nevertheless continued to dedicate his time and talent to the Revolution. He built a boring mill and furnace for the production of brass cannon. All through fall and winter 1776, he cast cannon and made gunpowder.[45] While he continued to serve the cause of independence, Loxley's retirement was a detriment to the train of artillery. The Philadelphia Artillery Battalion had lost its most experienced company commander.

On October 5, 1776, Procter ordered Captain Strobaugh and fifty men to reinforce the Flying Camp in New York.[46] John Corbin was probably one of the reinforcements who marched with him.[47] Corbin had been a mattross, or private, in Procter's Fort Mud Garrison on July 31, 1776.[48] Margaret Corbin accompanied her husband. Strobaugh's detachment was originally ordered to defend Fort Montgomery on the Hudson River north of New York City. At least some part of it, including the Corbins, was soon diverted to reinforce Fort Washington on Manhattan Island.

The Philadelphia Artillery played an active and sometimes crucial role in the battles that followed the Amboy deployment. Unfortunately, few Flying Camp rosters survived the defeats and arduous marches that characterized the main Continental Army's retreat across New Jersey.[49]

Pennsylvania's mobilization had been anything but seamless. Following a training period characterized by spectacular feats of marksmanship, and a march to Boston remarked upon by many for its speed, Thompson's battalion of riflemen soon proved something of a headache for General Washington. Ordered into Continental service during Pennsylvania's summer rendezvous of 1775, Thompson's men may have lacked cohesion and a clear understanding of what their duty required—both of which unit training might have provided.[50] Some of the soldiers took the law into their own hands during the march to Boston. Rifleman Aaron Wright of Northumberland County recorded how he and his comrades stopped and searched a suspected Tory named Charles Smith.[51] A few days after that, "the men took a girl out of jail," and then, near Hartford, Connecticut, tarred and feathered Joseph Brooks on the grounds that he forwarded military intelligence to General Gage at Boston.[52]

After Thompson's battalion arrived at Boston, its lawless behavior continued. The battalion took up positions along the American lines that surrounded the city, at Prospect Hill and Ploughed Hill. On September 10, 1775, Wright noted "great commotion," at the former location, arising from the arrest and detention of a sergeant in the battalion.[53] On September 14, rifleman John Kelly shot another soldier in the head. A month later, the provost guard confined two sergeants of the battalion for drunken behavior.

Back in Pennsylvania, Associators in Bucks and Chester Counties were responsible for arming and equipping themselves, and some resorted to confiscating arms from non-Associators to do so. On February 27, 1776, the Bucks County Committee of Safety petitioned the Pennsylvania Assembly to levy an additional property tax on non-Associators. Non-Associators were previously assessed a personal tax, but Associators viewed this as a mere exemption fee for those who hoped to avoid military service. Because Associators were not compensated for furnishing their own weapons and accouterments, nor for the personal danger military service subjected them to, Associators deemed the property tax to be just, since they were providing for the common defense. The county committee further petitioned the Pennsylvania Assembly to direct the battalion commanders to mobilize only a part of their battalions, consisting of volunteers, or those whose circumstances enabled them to go.[54] Should entire battalions march, the county would be left bare of any soldiers to defend it. Indeed, the committee noted that "large tracts of country will be left destitute of men, except those who either hold all resistance unlawful, or such as are disaffected to the present measures."[55] In May, the committee directed all townships that had not already done so to elect representatives to confiscate the arms of non-Associators.

When Colonel De Haas's battalion reported to General Philip Schuyler, commander of the Northern Department of the Continental Army, at Albany on February 14, 1776, the battalion was "much thinned by sickness and desertion," over half its arms required repairs, and the entire battalion had to requisition shoes, socks, and mittens. The items authorized by Congress only a few weeks before had worn out, if the Pennsylvania Committee of Safety had ever issued them at all.

The nature of the Flying Camp rotations, coupled with the democratic culture that prevailed among the Associators, produced a rash of unexcused absences, prompting Washington to issue a proclamation appealing to their patriotism and urging them to complete their pledge to serve until sufficient Continental battalions could be raised. At other times, the revolutionary zeal the Associators displayed at the expense of military bearing tested the patience of their commanders. By August 1776, the lack of discipline the Associators exhibited in the Flying Camp drove Governor William Livingston, serving as commanding general of the New Jersey troops at Amboy, near distraction: "the worst men (was there a degree above the superlative) would be still perjorated by having been fellow-soldiers with that discipline-hating good-living-loving too eternal-fam'd damn'd coxcomatical crew we lately had here from Philadelphia. My antient corporeal fabric is almost tottering under the fatigue I have lately undergone."[56]

In 1775, ideologically charged Associators had mobilized thousands of Pennsylvanians into training battalions. Associators had mobilized resources of all types to field Continental and state battalions for service in temperatures that ranged from near tropical in the summer to below freezing in the winter. Campaigning in North America required men and animals to march over roads that ranged from poor in the settled areas to nonexistent in the wilderness. Taverns, barracks, and other support facilities that were common in Europe were rare in North America, or incapable of supporting the armies that marched across Pennsylvania and New Jersey that summer. Poorly disciplined soldiers, rushed into service in compliance with congressional resolves, soon proved intractable. Shoes wore out from constant wear; leather cracked from repeated exposure to heat and water. Weapons broke in training or in action against the enemy, or were lost as deserters carried them off. All proved difficult to replace.

It was under these conditions that Washington, in summer 1776, prepared to defend North America's most strategically important harbor against an enemy assault. He soon attached all the regular troops belonging to Pennsylvania and Maryland, plus two Flying Camp regiments and a battalion of Associators to the main army. Many fought at the disastrous Battle of Long Island on August 27. Following British victories there and at Kip's Bay on September 15, the Americans abandoned New York City at the lower end of Manhattan. Fort Washington was the Continental Army's last bastion on Manhattan Island.

Fort Washington was a vital segment in a line of defenses extending across upper Manhattan and the Hudson River to Fort Lee in New Jersey.[57] Like most harbor forts, Fort Washington's strength lay in its well-positioned artillery. The fort sat on a commanding hill at a narrow spot on the Hudson where gun crews could also observe enemy movements on the Harlem River. Steep cliffs dropped almost two hundred feet to the two rivers. Defenders sunk chevaux-de-frise in the Hudson, between Forts Lee and Washington, to prevent British ships from passing the forts. By early November, thirty-seven cannon, including two brass howitzers and at least one eighteen-pound cannon, bristled from Fort Washington and its outlying defenses known as redoubts.[58] A redoubt was a small, enclosed fortification built to guard the approaches to a fort or large encampment. Experts on both sides, including the garrison commander, Colonel Robert Magaw, considered Fort Washington a strong post.[59]

General Washington was less optimistic about the fort's prospects.[60] It was constructed almost entirely of earth. It lacked bombproof shelters for the fort's garrison, and its situation exposed defenders to fire from British positions on land and on the Hudson River.[61] Those defenders had no secure water supply inside the fort. The sheer cliffs that appeared to give the fort's artillerists such an advantage in fact created a dead space, or shelter to any attacker able to get in under the cannons' arc of fire.[62] The chevaux-de-frise proved an ineffective barrier when, on November 7, the HMS *Pearl* and two other warships sailed upriver past the forts.[63] In light of these deficiencies, Washington recommended that Major General Nathanael Greene, the overall commander of the two forts, order Magaw to evacuate Fort Washington.[64]

Greene, however, shared Magaw's enthusiasm regarding the fort's defensibility. The 3rd and 5th Pennsylvania State Battalions garrisoned the fort.[65] Greene reinforced them with Colonel Moses Rawlings's Maryland Rifle Regiment, Major Michael Swope's York County Associators, the Bucks and Chester County Associator Battalions commanded by Lieutenant Colonel William Baxter, and elements of the Philadelphia Artillery.[66] Though many of the fort's thirty-seven guns were idle at the time of the battle, other artillery companies must have been present to man them.[67] Their numbers have been calculated into the overall totals. By November 14, Magaw commanded nearly two thousand seven hundred men.[68] Greene decided to stand and fight.

Magaw positioned his troops. Rawlings took his regiment and Swope's York County battalion to defend two redoubts containing three cannon about one-half mile north of the fort.[69] Approximately a quarter of a mile to the east of Rawlings's position, Baxter's Associators occupied two positions overlooking the Harlem River.[70] The Philadelphia Artillery detachment supported Baxter's exposed position with one four-pound cannon.[71] Colonel Lambert Cadwalader commanded most of the 3rd and 5th Regiments and one six-pound cannon in an outlying position south of the fort.[72] Magaw commanded a small force inside the fort. Many of the troops, especially Rawlings's men, but at least a company within each Pennsylvania battalion, were armed with rifles. Although rifles had greater range and were more accurate than muskets, they lacked bayonets–a grave weakness in case of a determined assault, even if stiffened by battalion companies armed with land service muskets. Artillery fire would be critical in repelling the British and Hessian attackers, provided the Maryland and Pennsylvania riflemen kept them at bay long enough.

On November 14, General Howe marched approximately eight thousand men into position around the American fort. He planned a three-pronged attack. Following an artillery barrage, Lieutenant General Wilhelm Freiherr von Knyphausen would lead almost five thousand highly trained, professional German troops in a frontal assault launched from the north against Rawlings's 250 riflemen and three cannon.[73] Major General Hugh, Lord Percy would simultaneously attack Cadwalader's eight-hundred-man position from the south with one brigade of Hessians and several British battalions. Brigadier Edward Mathew would strike Colonel Baxter from the northeast with two battalions of light infantry, two guards battalions, and two battalions of grenadiers. The guards battalions came from the Brigade of Foot Guards, organized from three elite regiments, the 1st Guards, the 3rd Guards, and the Coldstream Guards.[74] Although they had only trained together for a few weeks, the soldiers of these battalions sported some of the latest uniform innovations in the British Army.[75] Shortly before the brigade's departure for North America, Mathew consulted with Lord Loudoun, a man with considerable North American campaign experience as well as an innovator who had introduced Cumberland's reforms to the American colonies in 1756. At Loudoun's recommendation, Mathew modified the uniform and the equipment of the detachments under his command, introducing short coats, round hats, and short gaiters, not unlike the uniforms sported by the Philadelphia Associator foot battalions in 1775.[76] Major General Charles, Second Earl Cornwallis, would support Mathew with the 33rd Regiment of Foot. Nearly three thousand British troops, most of them elite light infantry, grenadiers, and guards freshly arrived from the British Isles, would face Baxter's Pennsylvanians. Colonel Thomas Sterling would lead the 42nd (Royal Highland) Regiment in a diversion from the east. Not only did Howe's force vastly outnumber Magaw's, his troops were better equipped and better trained—especially for the sort of shock tactics needed to overwhelm the American fort.

Early on November 16, the guns of the *Pearl* and land-based British artillery began to bombard Fort Washington.[77] Following the barrage, the main attack, Knyphausen's five thousand Hessians consisting of the regiments von Lossberg, von Rall, von Bünau, von Huyn, and his own von Knyphausen, in one column, and the Grenadier-Battalion Köhler, and the Regiments von Wutginau, von Stein, von Wissenbach, and the 3rd English-Waldeck Regiment in the second column, advanced on Rawlings's riflemen.[78] A short time later, Lord Percy struck Cadwalader's position.[79] Sterling's Highlanders began their attack in late morning.[80]

By midday, three British assaults were pressing Fort Washington's defenders. Many of the American artillerists were exposed to British cannon fire, the enemy having erected temporary batteries to support the assault columns.[81] The Fort Washington defenders also found it difficult to depress their cannon sufficiently to bear on the advancing enemy. Mathew's light infantry overwhelmed Baxter's Associators. Philadelphia artillerymen from the Flying Camp nevertheless put up stiff resistance. John Corbin was killed while serving on a gun crew.[82] Margaret took his place but fared little better. In the course of that action, she suffered the loss of a breast, the near loss of one arm, and severe facial injuries. Her wounds reflect the desperate fighting that took place at this point in the battle, as well as the artillery's exposed position. American gun crews at the fort, seeing that the British had taken the redoubt, soon fired on it.

Knyphausen pressed his attack against Rawlings's riflemen.[83] Despite vigorous resistance, Knyphausen's Hessians forced the Marylanders to retreat into the fort.[84] Percy was equally successful. American soldiers who were not captured retreated to the main fort as Magaw's outer lines collapsed. Magaw soon surrendered to Knyphausen.

The loss of Fort Washington was one of the worst American defeats of the Revolutionary War. Its surrender cost the Continental Army nearly three thousand soldiers.[85] British losses were only about three hundred killed and wounded.[86] In addition to the human cost, the British captured all the fort's cannon, ammunition, and rations. Its loss and the evacuation of Fort Lee a few days later marked the abandonment of the lower Hudson to the British, leaving only the thinly garrisoned Forts Montgomery and Clinton to defend the river.

The nation was truly in a state of crisis, as Thomas Paine noted in his pamphlet of the same name. The Continental Army in nearby states was divided among Washington's Pennsylvania command, Major General John Sullivan's contingent in northern New Jersey, and Major General Horatio Gates's regiments headquartered at Albany, New York.[87] Sullivan and Gates marched their commands to reinforce the main army, but their combined forces would only augment Washington's dwindling force by two thousand five hundred men, raising it to about five thousand.[88] Numbers told only half the story: most of Washington's army was worn out from months of fighting, long marches, and exposure to the weather. It lacked shoes, clothing, and every other type of equipment necessary for survival in the outdoors, including tents.[89] The British Army facing Washington numbered almost twelve thousand well-fed, well-equipped troops.[90]

The British had beaten the Americans in nearly every encounter of the 1776 campaign in the middle states. They had captured New York City in September and now controlled nearly all of northern New Jersey. British agents traveled through the occupied territory, distributing handbills that urged the Americans to swear an oath of allegiance to King George III. Many New Jerseyans complied.

As Washington's army retreated to the west and south, and the "summer soldiers" of the New York campaign decamped by the hundreds, twenty-two Philadelphia light horsemen elected instead to join Washington's force. Sporting the brown coats of the Philadelphia city regiments and commanded by Captain Samuel Morris, they urged their horses north through roads clogged with deserters and refugees heading in the other direction. They arrived at Trenton on December 2, 1776, and immediately went to work reconnoitering the British at New Brunswick, New Jersey.

Washington decided to put the Delaware River between his army and the British. On December 7, with part of Major General Charles Lee's command still in northern New Jersey, the Philadelphia Light Horse provided a rear guard as Washington ferried the last of his men across the Delaware River to Pennsylvania as the British entered Trenton.[91] Congress abdicated its war-fighting power to Washington five days later and fled Philadelphia for Baltimore. Thomas Rodney, the brother of Delaware congressional delegate Caesar Rodney, marched into Philadelphia at the head of a company of Delaware light infantry. To him, the city "made a horrid appearance, more than half the houses appeared deserted, and the families that remained were shut up in their houses, and nobody appeared on the streets."[92]

Washington nonetheless had reason to plan a counterstrike. Continental forces in the northern and southern departments had thwarted British offensives on Lake Champlain and at Charleston, South Carolina. The British under General Howe could not easily attack him from New Jersey. Under orders from Washington, boat handlers ensured that every watercraft on the Delaware River was safely in American hands on the Pennsylvania side.[93] New boats for a British assault would take days to build or to carry over from the fleet anchored in New York Harbor. Moreover, Howe had declared the 1776 campaign at an end.[94] He ordered his army to stand down and go into winter quarters, and granted leave to senior officers such as General Cornwallis to return home to Britain.[95] Crossing into Pennsylvania bought Washington time to plan an attack, but that time was limited. Many of his soldiers, their enlistments about to expire, were due to go home within weeks or even days.[96]

Reinforcements from Philadelphia, Delaware, and other states provided Washington with further incentive to attack. On November 23, the Pennsylvania Committee of Safety asked the Associators to volunteer for service. Following a precedent established in the Flying Camp the previous summer, the Associators ordered all available strength to a central rendezvous and then asked for volunteers, rather than draft indi-

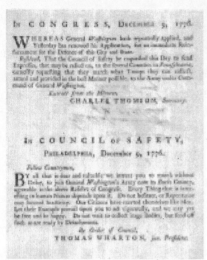

Fig. 17. Broadside. President Wharton issued this proclamation the day after the Continental Army evacuated New Jersey. Lacking the authority to order the Associators into service, Wharton called on them to voluntarily march to the army's headquarters at Newtown in Bucks County. (*Library of Congress*)

vidual soldiers or units.[97] The Association then organized the volunteers into deployable battalions or brigades, under officers of their choosing.[98] The artillery followed suit, its nature likely necessitating that entire gun crews volunteer for service. In all, Colonel John Cadwalader mustered at least one thousand Philadelphia Associators from the foot battalions to reinforce Washington's shattered army. Major Thomas Procter dispatched Captain Forrest's 2nd Company from the Pennsylvania State Artillery, Captain Eyre's company, and a company commanded by Wingate Newman. Marines and sailors from the Pennsylvania Navy under Captains Isaac Craig, William Shippen, William Brown, Andrew Porter, and Thomas Read brought additional guns (fig. 17).[99]

Cadwalader's brigade formed ranks and sailed or marched north to join the main army. Captain Charles Willson Peale marched at the head of one of the Philadelphia companies. He described the preparations taking place at the Associator camps. Having drawn additional arms and accoutrements from state commissary Robert Towers on December 4, Peale's company sailed up the Delaware by shallop, arrived at Trenton in the middle of the day December 7, and crossed into Pennsylvania that night.[100] There, Washington established the army's headquarters at Newtown in lower Bucks County, at the head of navigation on the Delaware River, with access to the New York, or York Road (the main highway into Philadelphia), and close to ferry points into New Jersey. Cadwalader's brigade camped at nearby Bristol, Pennsylvania.[101] On December 15, Cadwalader sent the brigade's heavy baggage and extra ammunition back to Philadelphia, issuing each man an additional thirty-six cartridges.[102] Following Prussian and British doctrine, Associators drilled daily in line tactics.[103] Additionally, soldiers of the brigade drilled in open tactics as light infantry.[104] Peale noted shortages in food, clothing, and other essential supplies, but the army continued to train in preparation for a counterattack across the river.[105]

By December 18, reinforcements from Delaware, including Captain Thomas Rodney's company, had arrived at Philadelphia on their way to join the main army. In all, approximately one thousand six hundred Philadelphians joined Washington's defeated army, bolstering its ranks with a brigade of trained and determined fighters.[106] Two days after his dismal description of an abandoned city, a reassured Rodney could report the Philadelphia "streets full of militia and hundreds pouring in every hour."[107]

On December 23, Washington formulated a daring, three-pronged, surprise attack on the Hessian garrison under Colonel Johann Gottlieb Rall at Trenton (fig. 18, overleaf).[108] He ordered the main Continental Army to cross the Delaware at three locations. He would cross at McConkey's Ferry, about nine miles north of Trenton, with the main body of roughly two thousand four hundred men. Brigadier General James Ewing, commanding roughly one thousand Pennsylvania and New Jersey levies, would cross directly opposite Trenton to block Rall's escape and prevent his receiving reinforcements. Colonel John Cadwalader and his Associators were to execute a feint near Trenton to draw off reinforcements from the British garrison at Bordentown.[109] His artillery by this time included Captain Eyre's Northern Liberties Artillery and Captain Newman's company.[110] The Pennsylvania Navy, commanded by Commodore Thomas Seymour, sailed up the Delaware to support the crossing.

Washington's plan put competent boat handlers at a premium. Fortunately for the general, many Philadelphia artillerists worked in maritime trades. On December 23, Captain Eyre ordered seven men from his company to Trenton Ferry. There they readied boats for the attack.[111] Second Lieutenant Anthony Cuthbert of Captain Moulder's 2nd Company helped Colonel John Glover's Marblehead Regiment ferry Washington's main body across the Delaware.[112]

The crossing commenced just after sunset on December 25, 1776.[113] All three columns had great difficulty. Tides, ice, driving sleet, and strong winds made the crossing extremely hazardous at the lower ferry sites.[114] General Ewing's command never risked a river crossing. Eyre helped supervise the landing of about six hundred of Cadwalader's men from two of his battalions but would not risk the loss of his two cannon.[115] With "the ice gathering so thick at a considerable distance from the shore, there was no possibility of landing, and they were ordered back, with all the troops that had landed."[116] Cadwalader canceled his feint. Conditions were more favorable at the main crossing site. By 3:00 a.m., approximately two thousand four hundred men were across the river.

Once the main column had formed on the New Jersey side of the river, Washington ordered it to march to the town of Birmingham. There he regrouped his forces. The winter storm conditions had continued unabated, with the result that more than half of the American army had failed to cross the Delaware. His column was still several hours from its objective and risked discovery by Hessian patrols at any time. Washington split his main body into two columns and ordered the army to converge on Trenton from the north.

Major General John Sullivan commanded the right, or southern column, which consisted of three brigades. The

Fig. 18, opposite. "Sketch of the engagement at Trenton, given on the 26th of December 1776 betwixt the American troops under command of General Washington, and three Hessian regiments under command of Colonell Rall, in which the latter a part surrendert themselves prisoner of war. [By] Wiederhold Lieut: from the Hessian Rgmt of Knÿphauss." This map, drawn from Hessian sources, shows the position of American artillery at the head of King and Queen streets, as well as the final position of the regiments von Rall, Lossberg, and Knyphausen at the eastern edge of town. (*Library of Congress*)

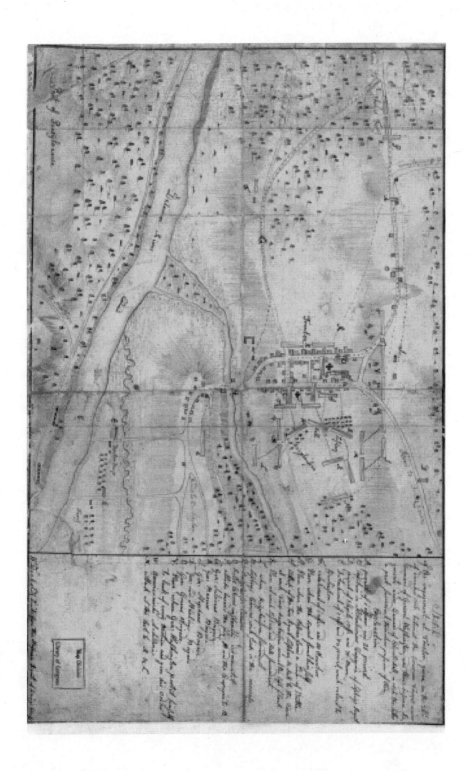

Philadelphia Artillery Battalion consisting of Moulder's 2nd Company, Neal's Eastern Company, and Hugg's 1st West Jersey Artillery provided Sullivan with direct fire support.[117] Elements of this battalion had been in the Flying Camp since August. The Philadelphia Artillery Battalion was augmented by Captain Lieutenant Winthrop Sargent's company of Massachusetts artillery.[118] Sullivan followed the Lower, or River Road, to his objective. He would attack Trenton from the south.[119]

Three companies of artillery and Captain Samuel Morris's Philadelphia Light Horse troop supported Major General Nathanael Greene's left, or northern column.[120] Greene's artillery consisted of Captain Thomas Forrest's 1st Company, Pennsylvania State Artillery Battalion, with two reserve companies from New York under Captains Sebastian Bauman and Alexander Hamilton.[121] Some artillerists attached to Greene's division were designated as teams to capture or sabotage Hessian cannons.[122] Sullivan's right column was to swing around to the south and advance along the River Road through Trenton's southern outskirts.[123] It would then attack through the town. The Hessian garrison would be caught between two fires. Effective artillery would be critical to the success of Washington's hastily activated attack.

Trenton had two main north-south thoroughfares. From east to west, they were King Street and Queen Street. Four east-west roads intersected them. Front Street ran parallel to Assunpink Creek. North of Front Street ran Second and Fourth streets. The River Road ran from east to west and terminated at Front Street, near Assunpink Creek.

At about 8:00 a.m. on December 26, advance elements of Greene's column made contact with a Hessian outpost north of Trenton.[124] The Hessians fired a volley and withdrew to their main encampment at the northern edge of town.[125] With the wind increasing, and hail mixing in with driving rain, Greene ordered his column into position.[126]

The Philadelphia Artillery had trained in advanced tactics for many years. Using metallic cartridges of lead or tin, Philadelphia gun crews had been able to fire as many as ten rounds per minute. Their cartridges, moreover, were less susceptible to the severe weather conditions experienced during the crossing of the Delaware and subsequent march on Trenton, with the result that the American artillery would prove devastatingly effective. Forrest's company led Greene's column. Colonel Henry Knox ordered Forrest's two brass six-pounders to the heads of King and Queen streets.[127] Forrest's artillery opened fire on the Hessian regiments as they tried to form in the streets.[128] As Forrest's gunnery took effect, Knox ordered Hamilton's reserve company into action.

At almost the same time, General Sullivan's advance guard overwhelmed a fifty-man outpost on the River Road south of Trenton.[129] Many of Sullivan's men could not fire their muskets because their gunpowder had become wet in the stormy weather overnight.[130] Sullivan ordered his men to fix bayonets and take the town with cold steel.[131] The winter weather, however, had little or no effect on the effectiveness of the artillery, due to its use of waterproof cartridges. Captains Moulder, Neal, and Sargent's companies provided fire support for Sullivan's advancing infantry.[132] The artillery made Sullivan's attack a success.

American forces quickly took control of Trenton. On the eastern edge of town, between Second and Fourth streets, Colonel Rall attempted to rally two of his regiments.[133] Moulder positioned his company at Second and Queen streets.[134]

His fire made any kind of Hessian counterattack impossible. Rall ordered a retreat to an orchard outside town, where he was mortally wounded.[135] Sullivan's men surrounded the surviving Hessians, who quickly surrendered.[136]

The Battle of Trenton ended before midmorning. The Continental Army captured nearly one thousand prisoners, six brass field pieces, and about one thousand small arms.[137] Following the victory, Washington ordered his army back to Pennsylvania.

Washington's gamble at Trenton proved a brilliant success. In addition to the captured arms, Washington showed the American people and his own army that the Hessians could be beaten. Artillery had played an important role in the victory. Half of that artillery had come from Philadelphia.

Washington kicked off a second successful offensive within days of his victory at Trenton.[138] Meetings with his top officers convinced him to capitalize on the recent victory with another foray into New Jersey. Beginning on December 29, 1776, the Continental Army recrossed the Delaware. Reinforcements, including much-needed artillery, arrived daily. Thomas Procter joined the army from Philadelphia with two guns and extra troops. By the end of December, Washington's army numbered almost five thousand men. His available artillery had increased from eighteen to forty guns.[139]

On December 30, 1776, Colonel Joseph Reed led a twelve-man detachment of the Philadelphia Light Horse in the vicinity of Princeton. [140] Trooper Thomas Peters recalled that "we advanced as near them to gain information as was consistent with our weak forces."[141] At great risk to life, limb, and liberty, the patrol determined that some of the Crown forces had marched from Brunswick and occupied Princeton, with the objective of attacking the Continental force at Trenton. While conducting this dangerous mission, the patrol came within a few hundred yards of a foraging party from the 16th (Queen's) Light Dragoons, consisting of wagons escorted by mounted and dismounted troops. Reed's heavily outnumbered detachment waited until the enemy dragoons had passed, and upon resuming its patrol, observed some of the enemy plundering a stone farmhouse. Seizing the moment, Peters wrote, "we immediately rushed on them who to the number of Eleven Soldiers came out of the House formed in the Yard with Muskets in hand a new post and rail fence between us we compeld them to surrender." [142] The troopers mounted their prisoners behind them, and, with their captured arms, set off, with a party of enemy dragoons in hot pursuit. Despite the extra riders and the additional burden of the captured weapons, the patrol reached the safety of the American pickets, the only apparent mishap occurring when Trooper James Caldwell's mount threw him. The reconnaissance performed by the Philadelphia Light Horse provided the commander in chief with vital information leading to the victories that followed. The British prisoners informed Reed that General Cornwallis had reinforced Princeton and was on the march toward Trenton with the main body of the British Army.[143] Washington implemented his plan.

Washington ordered a brigade commanded by Brigadier General Matthias Alexis de Roche de Fermoy to delay Cornwallis's advance. De Fermoy's brigade included experienced skirmishers of the 1st Pennsylvania Regiment, now commanded by Colonel Edward Hand. Many of Hand's soldiers, being riflemen, lacked bayonets. Thomas Forrest's 2nd Company, Pennsylvania State Artillery provided support for these men. Washington ordered de Fermoy to prevent Cornwallis from gathering knowledge of the main Continental Army's strength and exact whereabouts, and delay battle by twenty-four hours.

Meanwhile, Cornwallis departed Princeton and marched toward Trenton with two battalions of light infantry, the 42nd Royal Highland Regiment, and a battalion of Hessian grenadiers.[144] He left Lieutenant Colonel Charles Mawhood in command at Princeton with the 4th Brigade, consisting of the 17th, 40th, and 55th Regiments of Foot.[145] Mawhood also had three troops of the 16th Light Dragoons. Mawhood's reinforced brigade numbered about one thousand two hundred soldiers.

At about midmorning on January 2, 1777, General de Fermoy made contact with Cornwallis just south of Maidenhead.[146] The Americans began an orderly retreat into Trenton, contesting the British at every opportunity.[147] De Fermoy had accomplished his mission. The British wasted an entire day in a series of sharp skirmishes and artillery duels with Pennsylvania riflemen and Forrest's Philadelphia artillerists.

By sunset, de Fermoy's brigade was safely behind pre-prepared positions across Assunpink Creek from the British. Captains Moulder and Thomas Read of the Pennsylvania Navy reinforced Forrest. Washington had lured the British into a trap in which Philadelphia gun crews pinned down the British in Trenton.[148] The artillery bought additional time for the Continental Army.

Cornwallis believed it was he who had Washington trapped. The Continental Army lay with its back to the Delaware River. Cornwallis had a marginally superior force of about five thousand two hundred men. Strong British outposts stood between Washington and the ferry crossings that could take him into

Pennsylvania. Cornwallis dispatched a message to Mawhood, ordering him to bring reinforcements from Princeton. The earl then ordered the British troops opposite Trenton to eat and rest. Cornwallis planned to destroy Washington's army the next day.

That night, Washington convened a council of war with his senior officers. He ordered a flanking movement around Cornwallis's main force. The Americans would march east toward Princeton, and attack the British rear guard there. Washington hoped in this way to achieve his initial objective and at the same time thwart Cornwallis's advance.

Sometime after midnight on January 3, Brigadier General Hugh Mercer started the advance guard toward Princeton.[149] His brigade was supported by Captain Neal's Eastern Company, New Jersey State Artillery. Washington followed with two brigades under Colonel Cadwalader and Colonel Daniel Hitchcock. Captain Moulder's artillery and Samuel Morris's light horse supported Cadwalader's three infantry battalions of Associators. General Sullivan followed with the main body of the army and the rest of the artillery, including Eyre, the Pennsylvania sailors and marines, and Procter's company. A five-hundred-man rear guard with two iron cannon stayed behind to deceive the British with built-up campfires and the sounds of digging while Washington's main body slipped away to the east.[150]

Early on the morning of January 3, 1777, Mawhood left Princeton with part of the 17th and 55th Regiments of Foot, numbering about seven hundred men, to reinforce Cornwallis as ordered.[151] The 40th Regiment of Foot stayed in Princeton to guard supplies and wounded soldiers.

Washington's column, meanwhile, prepared to attack Princeton. At Stony Brook, a creek a few miles west of Princeton, Washington ordered the light infantry to file off the main road. Sullivan's main body advanced on Princeton from the right. Hitchcock's and Cadwalader's brigades were ordered to surround the town on the left. Washington directed Mercer to march straight into Princeton without leaving the road.[152]

Before this was done, Mawhood discovered Mercer's column, or rather, the two opposing forces blundered into each other. Both sides raced for a nearby orchard sitting on high ground. Mawhood got there first, and at about forty yards distance, point-blank range, the two sides opened fire.[153] Then the British fixed bayonets and charged. Captain Neal had unlimbered his two guns and fired. Though he caused heavy casualties, Neal's effort did nothing to check the British advance. The redcoats killed him and disabled his cannon.[154] The fighting degenerated into a hand-to-hand melée as Mercer's brigade and Mawhood's troops crashed into each other. A British soldier clubbed Mercer with his musket. Other redcoats bayoneted him several times.

With its commander mortally wounded and lacking artillery cover, Mercer's brigade fell back in confusion. Washington, meanwhile, advanced with Cadwalader's brigade, but not before Mercer's line collapsed and began to retreat into Cadwalader's advancing column. It was only the quick action of Moulder's artillery that saved the American line from complete rout. Light infantry Captain Rodney of the Delaware militia fought a few yards away from the 2nd Company's guns. He related in his journal that Moulder's "two pieces of artillery stood their ground and were served with great skill and bravery."[155] Washington, who arrived with Hitchcock and Cadwalader's brigades, took personal charge of the battle. Part of Morris's light horse troop dismounted and formed a cordon around the artillerists, while the rest of Morris's men stayed with Washington. Moulder's barrage momentarily stemmed the tide of battle, and Mawhood retreated to a fence and extended his line so that every British soldier could fire without obstruction.[156]

The two brigades under Cadwalader and Hitchcock counterattacked. Mawhood regrouped and ordered a charge that singled out Moulder's guns. Undaunted by the line of glittering bayonets, Moulder's Philadelphia artillerists stood their ground, firing grapeshot into the enemy ranks. Mawhood's counterattack failed, his redcoats recoiling with heavy loss of life.

Mawhood's line broke. The shattered British force retreated east with the 17th and part of the 55th Regiment, heading toward Maidenhead to join the roughly one thousand two hundred men of Brigadier General Alexander Leslie's 2nd Brigade.[157] American soldiers collected equipment discarded by the British in their disorganized retreat.[158]

The remaining British, including the 40th and part of the 55th Regiments of Foot, with some assorted British and Hessian wounded, made a stand at Nassau Hall but were soon dislodged and retreated to the north.[159] The Continental Army entered the town of Princeton and took 194 prisoners after a short fight around the main college building. The remainder of the British force escaped to the north. The Americans helped themselves to many of the supplies they found. Other soldiers plundered baggage, or picked up muskets thrown away by the retreating British.

Cornwallis had by this time learned of the clash at Princeton. He reacted to the news by ordering an advance party to go there. Captain Samuel Morris's troop of Philadelphia Light Horse and Moulder's two artillery pieces covered the American rear as the main Continental Army advanced in the direction of Brunswick. The Queen's Light Dragoons came upon Moulder's men. Moulder opened fire, but refused to abandon his guns. His men pulled them by hand, with forty men to a gun. As they had during the British counterattack, Morris and his troopers dismounted and formed a line across the road and drove back the attacking British cavalry.[160]

Washington's losses were seven officers and forty enlisted men killed.[161] The British suffered more than four hundred killed, wounded, or captured. The Americans captured two brass six-pound field pieces, large quantities of ammunition, and other military stores. [162] The two American victories forced General Howe to concentrate his army closer to New York City, between Brunswick and Amboy.[163] The threat to Pennsylvania had ended, and Washington could spend the winter at Morristown monitoring an enemy that had been contained in New York City. Most important, the two American victories inspired the army, keeping it intact long enough for new recruits to fill its ranks.[164]

The 1776 New Jersey campaign had come to a close. Procter marched his battalion to Morristown. Moulder's company joined him for a time before returning to Philadelphia to reorganize. In Continental service almost seven months, Moulder's Philadelphia artillerists had contributed to at least two major victories.

The Battles of Trenton and Princeton marked the high point of the Associator artillery's active military service.[165] Lieutenant Patrick Duffy of the Pennsylvania State Artillery Battalion assured Colonel Procter that "the Artillery got applause."[166] An eyewitness to Moulder's defense outside Princeton wrote, "Our cannon played very briskly."[167] The Continental Army's precarious situation in 1776 called for cannon and skilled artillerists to bolster the army's bayonet-deprived infantry battalions.

John Donnaldson concluded his account of the battle this way:

> At a time when gloom pervaded the land, & hope had yielded to despair, it should never be forgotten that Captain Samuel Morris with twenty one gentlemen of Phila., most of them with families & all of them in independent circumstances did, in an inclement season take leave of their domestic happiness & personal comforts, to rally around the standard of their country, & furnished an example as rare as it was disinterested & patriotic.[168]

To George Washington, the Philadelphia Light Horse demonstrated "a noble Example of discipline and Subordination, and in several Actions have shewn a Spirit of Bravery which will ever do Honor to them and will ever be gratefully remembered by me."[169] Safely, if not comfortably ensconced at Morristown, Continental Army elements continued to harass the enemy in the vicinity of Woodbridge, as the Americans settled down to the less glamorous business of an army in winter quarters: reorganizing, refitting, recruiting, training, and observing the enemy and harassing his supply lines.[170]

Washington dismissed most of the Pennsylvania and Delaware troops on or about January 23. Many began their march home in stormy weather, with words of praise from their commanders ringing in their ears. The next day, under orders from General Washington, Colonel Reed prepared a dispatch for general circulation in Philadelphia newspapers. After disposing of some personal business involving two of his blankets that the elder Bradford had in his possession, Reed reported on continuing fighting in northern New Jersey and concluded with the following comments on the conduct of the Associators:

> General Cadwalader has conducted his command with great honour to himself and the Province, all the field officers supported their characters, their example was followed, by the inferior officers and men, so that they have returned with the thanks and praises of every general officer in the army. . . . The Light Horse, tho' few in number, have rendered as essential service, as in my opinion, the same number of men ever performed to their country in the same time. They thought no duty beneath them, and went through it with a generous disregard of fatigue and danger, which entitles them to the kindest notice and attention of their fellow citizens. We hope that some of the artillery officers who have engaged in this temporary service may be induced to enter into the Continental army as the specimen they have given shows that they may be exceedingly useful to their country in a line of service which every day shows to be more and more important.[171]

With these words, the discipline and technical proficiency displayed by the Associators at the Battles of Trenton and Princeton, became a matter of public record.

Conclusion

A generation after the Revolution, city growth in Philadelphia had obliterated much physical evidence of the Association. In the 1790s, Congress Hall and a new city hall went up on the site of the old artillery storage sheds built during the French War. The US Navy built the Philadelphia Navy Yard on the site of the Grand Battery. By 1830, the Pennsylvania State House, known to a younger generation as Independence Hall, had become a shrine, hallowed as the meeting place of the Continental Congress and the Constitutional Convention of 1787. Most Americans were too young to remember the heady days of the Revolution and were less likely to know of the events that preceded them. In 1830, the State House, which had been built by Philadelphia carpenters and masons between 1732 and 1753, showed signs of age. The city contracted workers to renovate the structure, replacing the graceful wing buildings, connected to the main hall by arcaded passages, with modern office buildings. While digging on the site, workers uncovered several objects near the western wall of the main building. The master mason sent for John Fanning Watson, just then compiling data for what would become the three-volume *Annals of Philadelphia*. Watson examined the find, which he listed as a "keg of excellent flints," a sword, musket, cartridge box, buckles, and over a dozen powder-filled bomb shells. The objects posed a mystery to the chronicler Watson, who knew little or nothing of the storage sheds, the decades of struggle for recognition on the part of the Associators, nor of the site's past as the training ground of the Philadelphia Artillery.[1]

Americans born after the Revolution were less interested in the dynamics of past political conflict than they were in stories of great men and great deeds. Watson wanted to remember Philadelphia's glorious Revolutionary War past, but Philadelphia's military history following the close of the 1776 campaign was less than glorious.[2] Following Washington's brilliant victories at Trenton and Princeton, the British Army under Sir William Howe returned to the Delaware Valley in late summer 1777, bypassing Philadelphia's formidable river defense at Forts Mud and Mercer by marching overland from Head-of-Elk, Maryland. After beating General Washington at the Battle of Brandywine on September 11, redcoats occupied the city, where the likes of Joseph Galloway and William, John, and Andrew Allen–former Associators or supporters of the Associators–provided his army with aid and comfort. In October and November, Americans defended Forts Mifflin and Mercer with valor. The Army metamorphosed into an engine of victory at Valley Forge that winter, but these noteworthy events occurred outside the city. Watson had little material with which to work, but he nonetheless took great pains to emphasize the city's role in the war, gathering information on Philadelphians who served in the Revolution, including Benjamin Loxley.

Unfortunately for Watson, Loxley died in 1801, but he did leave a legacy of fine buildings, children who carried on in his footsteps, and a memoir of over thirty years of service to his adopted homeland. Loxley's oldest daughter, Elizabeth, married the Reverend Morgan John Rhees, a prominent Baptist minister from Wales.[3] During the Civil War, Loxley's great-great grandson, Benjamin Ogden Loxley, would volunteer with the 58th Pennsylvania Infantry. While he remembered Loxley as "a military chieftain of an earlier day," Watson placed as much or greater emphasis on his house as the residence of Lydia Barrington Darragh during the Revolutionary War (fig. 19).[4] Tradition holds that Darragh, Loxley's caretaker tenant, secreted information to the Continental Army at Whitemarsh that alerted Washington of Howe's plans to attack there on December 7-8, 1777. Loxley's service to the city had been exemplary, but Darragh's heroism provided Watson with a stirring wartime anecdote. Harbor defense and cannon casting,

LOXLEY HOUSE, SECOND STREET.

Fig. 19. The master carpenter Benjamin Loxley House stood on Second Street just to the south of Society Hill on what was then Philadelphia's main thoroughfare. Nearly every event that defined the Philadelphia carpenter's life occurred within an easy walk of this house. (*Author's Collection*)

after all, could hardly compete with tales of whispered plans overheard in the dead of the night, messages sewn up in cloth-covered buttons, and daring journeys through enemy lines.

Benjamin Franklin founded the Military Association in 1747. He thereafter used it to propel himself into public office. In 1756, the Associator officers gave him a royal escort. Two years later, he used the Associators to curry favor with General John Forbes. In 1764, he again used the Associators, this time against the Paxton Boys. Franklin was elected to the Philadelphia Committee of Safety shortly after his return to the city from London in 1775. Over the next year, he busied himself with committee matters, including warship design and weapons development. Now that war had begun, the one-time printer was less interested in the Associators as a fighting force than he had been when the Associators could fight for him.

The Philadelphia Artillery, which of all the various Associator organizations should have left the most tangible evidence of its service in the form of ordnance, fortifications, and storehouses, rendered reliable and at times distinguished service to Pennsylvania and to the Continental Army, but its service was often overlooked by higher-ranking revolutionaries. Benjamin Franklin, John Adams, Silas Deane, and George Washington were all in Philadelphia at the beginning of the war. All were deeply involved in military affairs. Each, for different reasons, failed to mention the Associator Artillery in his correspondence.

Their omission is understandable. The Associator foot soldiers, distinctive in their short coats and round hats, were something new. The Associator uniform reflected innovations dating to the French and Indian War, when Anglo-American soldiers had first cropped their uniform coats and hats to allow greater freedom of movement for forest warfare. Deane described another American innovation, the riflemen, as they held tomahawk-throwing contests outside the city.[5]

Adams and Deane knew all three commanders of the infantry battalions. Roberdeau, Cadwalader, and Dickinson were, like Adams and Deane, members of the wealthy elite, or comers at the very least. Deane socialized and consulted on military and political matters with them.[6] In his letter to his wife Elizabeth, written from Philadelphia on June 3, 1775, Deane discussed the battalions and their commanders by name.[7] He then added that "I know not of the others."[8] The officers of the Philadelphia Artillery Battalion moved within their own social and business circles. They did not dine with Revolutionary leaders. Deane, therefore, did not know them. Deane's omission points to a demographic disparity dating to the time of the Paxton Boys or even earlier.

The city's foot battalions, light horse, and light infantry, on the other hand, provided a remarkable spectacle for the delegates. On June 7, 1775, Adams observed, "There are in this City, Three large Regiments, raised, formed, armed, trained, and uniformed under Officers consisting of Gentlemen of the very first Fortune and best Character in the Place."[9] Adams neglected to mention the train of artillery until three days later, when he described a grand review of the Philadelphia Associators, which he called "A Field Day, on which three Battalions of Soldiers were reviewed, making full two thousand Men."[10] Adams grouped the train of artillery with "Battalion Men, Light Infantry, Grenadiers, Rifle Men, Light Horse, Artillery Men, with a fine train, all in Uniforms, going thro the manual Exercise and the Maneuvres with remarkable Dexterity."[11] As far as Adams was concerned, artillery officers were competent technicians rather than gentlemen of fortune and character, or more simply put, men with whom he did not sup.

Silas Deane was a Connecticut delegate to the Second Continental Congress. Like Franklin and Adams, his office found him deeply ensconced in military affairs, Congress having selected him for the Marine Committee in May. Like Adams, he described the Associator infantry battalions of Colonels John Dickinson, Daniel Roberdeau, and John Cadwalader in great detail in a letter to his wife, Elizabeth, their smart uniforms representing the latest trends in military wear. Like Franklin and Adams, Deane, an attorney and thus exempt from militia service, likely had little or no military experience. Consequently, neither Deane nor Adams mentioned the leaders of the Philadelphia Artillery, despite the fact that elements of the Artillery Battalion drilled daily outside the State House.[12]

In contrast to the novelty of riflemen in their fringed hunting shirts, and the infantry's innovative uniform, trains of artillery were relatively common in other American seaport cities, including Boston, Providence, New York, and Charleston. The Philadelphia Artillery Battalion's blue and red uniform differed little from artillery uniforms elsewhere. In a city buzzing with military activity, the Philadelphia Artillery Battalion's technical proficiency vied with the smart appearance of the infantry and the eclectic activities of the riflemen in Deane's and Adams's letters home.

The artillery also lacked access to the commander. Shortly before his departure to take command of the Continental Army, escorted as far as Kingston, New York, by troopers of the Philadelphia Light Horse, George Washington reviewed the Associators, including the artillery, yet neglected to record any comments on them.[13] His omission almost certainly stemmed from the use of artillery in battle. During the 1776 campaign, artillery was usually attached to an infantry brigade commanded by a colonel or a brigadier general. Those officers in turn met or corresponded with the commanding general at his headquarters, while lower ranking captains and lieutenants actually commanded gun crews. Artillerists were military specialists who performed a service in battle, usually in detachments consisting of one or two guns, led by captains or subalterns. Regimental and brigade commanders maneuvered these detachments around the battlefield. In early 1777, Washington organized specialist troops such as riflemen, artillery, and artificers that fought or supported the army in a similar fashion, into administrative corps under a colonel or a general. Artillerists below the rank of colonel therefore had few direct encounters with general officers, so they did not normally appear in Washington's letters. Members of the light horse, on the other hand, had frequent contact with the commander in chief in their security and reconnaissance role, as well as access to high-ranking congressmen. In addition to famous actions at Trenton, Princeton, and with Reed on his daring reconnaissance, the Philadelphia Light Horse provided no fewer than four official escorts to the commander in chief, and one to his wife, Martha.

The omission of the artillery from the letters of such prominent Revolutionary leaders illustrates the character of the Associator Artillery and the paradox of the Association itself. Neither represented anything new or remarkable to anyone outside of Pennsylvania. Artillery service required considerable skill, mental fortitude, and technical aptitude. Artillerists performed a vital function but were not part of the decision-making inner circle in colonial Pennsylvania.

Associators were insurgents. The Philadelphia artillerists had always represented a distinctly different outlook from that of Pennsylvania's established leadership; battalions of foot and the light horse echoed their outlook in word and deed. From 1729 to 1747, the artillery defended Philadelphia's harbor while Philadelphia's leadership focused on the loftier goals of land acquisition and westward expansion. During the War of Austrian Succession, the Associator Artillery, along with the rest of the Philadelphia Associators, protested a legislative logjam triggered by squabbles between the proprietor and the Pennsylvania Assembly. The Associators established themselves as an independent entity from 1748 to 1754. By 1754 they were a well-trained, well-equipped force. During the Seven Years' War, the Associator Artillery continued to demonstrate its independence, parading, training, and lobbying before military and political leaders, including William Denny, General Forbes, and Franklin. When the Paxton Boys threatened the city, members of the train of artillery stood shoulder to shoulder with British Army regulars and civilian volunteers to defend their homes and businesses. During the Revolution, the technically adept members of the Philadelphia Artillery, many of them staunch Whigs, manned city defenses. On every occasion, the Philadelphia Artillery defended its interests and its city.

On March 17, 1777, the Military Association passed into history when Pennsylvania enacted a true militia law. For the first time since its founding, Pennsylvania made military service compulsory for free men eighteen to fifty-three years old. The Associators fused into the militia. Some members of the Philadelphia Artillery would see combat again as soldiers in the Continental or State Artillery, but not as Associators.

The Philadelphia Artillery Battalion's organizational lineage transferred to two commands. During winter and spring 1777, Pennsylvania expanded the State Artillery Battalion into a regiment containing eight companies. Thomas Procter was promoted to colonel.[14] Procter's command, renamed the 4th Regiment, Continental Artillery, constituted Pennsylvania's artillery quota for the Continental Army. The 4th Continental Artillery saw extensive service during the Battles of Brandywine, Germantown, and Monmouth, the 1779 Wyoming Valley campaign, Greene's Southern campaign, and Yorktown.[15] On September 11, 1777, at the Battle of Brandywine, Edward Hector, an African-American wagoner serving with the regiment, risked his life and the lives of his horses to retrieve one of the regiment's guns, which had been left behind by its crew in their retreat.[16] At the Battle of Monmouth, Joseph Plumb Martin, who fought with a Connecticut regiment, saw a ball shoot away part of the petticoats of a woman serving a gun crew.[17] Most historians agree that this woman was Mary Ludwig Hays, the famed "Molly Pitcher." Congress disbanded Procter's regiment on November 15, 1783.[18]

The artillery remaining in Philadelphia was reorganized as the 1st Pennsylvania Artillery Battalion on August 16, 1777. Jehu Eyre assumed command, with the rank of colonel. The

1st Pennsylvania Artillery fought at the Battles of Brandywine, Germantown, and Whitemarsh, and manned the Delaware River defenses at Billingsport.[19] Benjamin Loxley returned to duty during the Philadelphia campaign. The war was hard on Loxley. During the war, he claimed nearly six thousand pounds in damages resulting from the British occupation. In 1779, his son Abram, who had been a commissioned officer in the artillery, came home from war to die, arduous campaigning having wrecked his health.

Of course, the war was hard on other Associators as well. Paroled a year after his capture at Fort Washington in 1776, John Adlum, having suffered the hardships of soldiering, the trauma of the British assault, and the degradation of internment, never returned to service. After the war, Adlum relocated to Havre de Grace, Maryland, where he pioneered viticulture. Margaret Corbin became a prisoner with the rest of Fort Washington's garrison upon its surrender on November 16, 1776. Because of her wounds, her British captors released her. She eventually found her way back to Philadelphia to recuperate. As a tribute to Corbin's bravery, the Continental Army assigned her to the Invalid Corps, an organization normally reserved for male soldiers to garrison military sites.[20] On July 6, 1779, Congress voted her a private's half-pay for life in recognition of her heroism.[21] Tradition holds that Corbin lived her remaining days in the village of Highland Falls, New York. She is buried at the Chapel of the United States Military Academy, at West Point.

In 1779, the same year Congress voted Corbin her pension, the 1st Company, 1st Pennsylvania Artillery, petitioned Pennsylvania president Joseph Reed for relief from repeated deployments. They reminded Reed that in July 1776, the artillery had defended Amboy, Elizabeth, and other Jersey shore points "to endeavor to repel the force of a considerable British and Hessian Army then landed, or landing, on Staten Island," and also defended Philadelphia's river defenses during the 1777 campaign "while many of our wives and families were in this City, then in possession of the Enemy."[22] That year, another band of artillerists agitated over perceived price fixing. Congressional authorities, aided by the artillerists' erstwhile comrades, the Philadelphia Light Horse, crushed them in what came to be known as the Fort Wilson riot.

After the war, Pennsylvania reorganized the 1st Pennsylvania Artillery as the Regiment of Artillery of the City of Philadelphia.[23] Thomas Procter commanded the regiment.[24] The perpetuation of the Philadelphia Artillery Regiment following the Revolutionary War continued the lineage and tradition of the old Military Association, as did other organizations, including the old Philadelphia Light Horse, now designated as the First Troop Philadelphia City Cavalry. During the 1800s, the former artillerists reorganized as the 1st Regiment of Infantry and went on to serve with distinction in the Civil War. In December 1944, their lineal descendents, now organized as the 103d Engineer Combat Battalion, defended the town of Hosingen, Luxembourg, during the Battle of the Bulge, using .50-caliber machine guns salvaged from downed aircraft. Benjamin Loxley, who had once modified ship's guns to make field pieces, and Joseph Moulder, who had stemmed the rout of the Continental Line at Princeton, might have nodded in approval.

Though rendered obsolete by Pennsylvania's 1777 Militia Act and often confused with the militia and Continental battalions that developed out of it, the Associator Artillery was respected by those who remembered it. Alexander Graydon, who fought alongside the Associator Artillery at Fort Washington, recalled its service during the Paxton Boys' march. Artists Charles Willson Peale, his brother James Peale, and William Mercer memorialized the Associators' participation in the Battle of Princeton on canvas. To Philadelphians who remembered it, the Association had been a prominent aspect of city life.

Following service in Canada, Colonel John Philip de Haas returned to the Philadelphia barracks with a cadre from the old 1st Pennsylvania Battalion. As Associators returned in triumph from service with the main army, the regiment, reorganized and designated the 2nd Pennsylvania, accepted veterans and new recruits to its ranks. Colonel Edward Hand's regiment, now designated as the 1st Regiment, stayed with the main army throughout the war, its legendary marksmen trading their rifles for muskets and serving with distinction alongside the 2nd Pennsylvania and other regiments as part of General Anthony Wayne's famed brigade of the Pennsylvania Line.

Edward Hand became one of Washington's most trusted advisers on light infantry tactics, a mode of warfare at which the 1st Pennsylvania and later the entire army excelled.

Hard service in the army, the uncertain terms of enlistment, and the unfulfilled promises of an ungrateful country eventually proved unbearable for the Pennsylvania soldiers. In January 1781, the entire Pennsylvania Line mutinied at Morristown. Reorganized into three provisional regiments and promised legal recourse to civil authorities by Generals Wayne and Washington, the Pennsylvania Line fought on with steadfast valor to the end of the war.

The remaining infantry regiments in the city organized as the city brigade on March 17, 1777, and the 1st Brigade, 1st Division, Pennsylvania Militia before finally consolidating into a single regiment in 1858. During the Civil War, that regiment expanded, first to form the 18th Infantry and later the 72nd Pennsylvania Volunteer Infantry (Fire Zouaves), which, as part of the Philadelphia Brigade, fought with distinction at Gettysburg, where it helped throw back Pickett's Charge on July 3, 1863. Still later, as the 3rd Infantry, it answered the call during the Spanish American War, and, in 1917, reorganized as the 111th Infantry and fought through the bloody Meuse-Argonne offensive of World War I with the 28th Division.

Following the Revolutionary War, prestigious militia units, such as the First Troop Philadelphia City Cavalry, served the needs of ambitious young Philadelphia men or high-ranking veterans looking for a military family with which to serve. Thomas Procter enlisted as a private in the troop before assuming command of the Philadelphia Artillery Regiment in 1794.[25] William Browne, who had been a captain of a Pennsylvania Navy detachment at Trenton and Princeton, did likewise, as did Samuel Miles, formerly of the State Rifle Regiment, and Jacob Morgan, late of the 3rd Battalion, Philadelphia Associators.[26]

Elsewhere, former Associator commands survived as flank companies under the new federal militia system. In 1792, the Reading Artillerists organized in their namesake city, where in 1775 rifle and foot battalions had organized. Veterans of York County's battalions may have organized the York Rifles in the 1790s. Perhaps as a tribute to its heritage, the uniform of the

Fig. 20. Camp Lafayette at York, Pennsylvania, by Huddy and Duval, show-ing a typical muster of elements of the mid-nineteenth century Pennsylvania militia. A member of the York Rangers stands in the foreground, wearing an anachronistic rifle shirt. Note the range of hills in the background that less than a century prior had concealed enemy war parties. (*Author's Collection*)

York Rangers by 1841 consisted of a somewhat old-fashioned hunting frock and tomahawk, reminiscent of the uniforms and equipment worn by Pennsylvania riflemen in 1775 (fig. 20).

Like antiquarian John Fanning Watson, Pennsylvania militia companies reached back to their Revolutionary roots. In 1823, Captain John Rhea Clarendon Smith of the First City Troop recognized that the "Troop is identified with the revolutionary history of our country & was at all times conspicuously useful in the arduous struggle to establish our Liberty & Rights." He sought to capture the troop's history using the few surviving documents then known to exist.[27] Smith contacted John Donnaldson, who fought at the Battle of Princeton, and asked him to compile an account using some of the original docu-ments. Donnaldson finished his work on April 3, 1824, laying the groundwork for the troop history that Captain Smith and others eventually compiled.

With the frontier now hundreds of miles to the west, policed by the tiny regular army, Pennsylvanians no longer needed to lobby their government for military funding.

Because Pennsylvanians made up the bulk of the soldiers recruited into the army's only regiment, Josiah Harmar became its first commander in 1784. Harmar had commanded a company in the 1st Pennsylvania Battalion under John Philip de Haas in 1775. David Ziegler, who had served as a junior officer in the same regiment throughout the war, now commanded one of Harmar's companies. Benjamin Franklin was the state's chief executive. As communities grew and became more complex, as social lines stratified, and as military needs changed, Pennsylvania militia companies changed as well, with the men who served in them becoming, in many ways, the small, volunteer trainbands they had been under the Penns.

Although eclipsed by intervening events and overshadowed by the achievements of personages such as Benjamin Franklin and John Dickinson, the Association was never completely forgotten. The First City Troop still carries a copy of the standard that Captain Markoe paid John Folwell and James Claypoole to design and make in 1775. On April 15, 1922, the Pennsylvania National Guard adopted a crest consisting of a rampant lion holding a naked scimitar in its right paw and the shield of the Penn family in its left. The inspiration for this crest first flew on the color of one of the Associator regiments organized in 1748. Since 1929, soldiers of the 111th Infantry Regiment have worn an insignia bearing the likeness of Benjamin Franklin on their uniforms. In anticipation of the 250th anniversary of the founding of the Military Association, the Pennsylvania Army National Guard's history detachment initiated extensive research into its origins.[28] On December 7, 1997, 250 years to the day after the first formation of the Associators, the Pennsylvania Army National Guard dedicated a granite monument on the approximate site of the first Associator fort at Atwood's Wharf, in Philadelphia. A few months later, the Commonwealth of Pennsylvania placed a historical marker at the site of the Grand Battery.

In spring 2002, famed historical artist Don Troiani executed a painting for the 103d Engineer Battalion, Pennsylvania Army National Guard. Troiani's rendering reconstructs two members of the Philadelphia Artillery Battalion as they might have appeared in spring 1775.[29] They are dressed in blue coats trimmed in red, the uniform worn by most eighteenth century artillerists. In 1756, Philadelphia artillerists paraded in uniform under their own standards. In 1764, Benjamin Loxley donned his old uniform to defend Philadelphia from the Paxton Boys. The uniform reflected the relative affluence of its members, but more than that, the uniform signified the artillerists' organizational integrity, technical proficiency, and membership in a military corps.

Troiani's artillerists stand in the State House yard close to the wooden storerooms Loxley built in 1756. During the French War, the Philadelphia Artillery helped turn the State House into an arsenal. The train of artillery's demonstrations and frequent training epitomized imperial solidarity and defense of a land regarded by Associators as their home and birthright. Early in the Revolution, the men of the Philadelphia Artillery often drilled behind the State House; at other times artillerists and other Associators guarded the building while the Second Continental Congress deliberated inside. Here, joiner Robert Jewell lost his hand loading one of the brass six-pounders, "on a public occasion." The Revolution gave the artillery its first real chance to defend the city and country.

The subjects of Troiani's picture are shown with one of the "neatly painted" field pieces that the train of artillery purchased in 1755. Cannon were the train's principal tools. Loxley used the four cannon to train his gun crews through the French and Indian War. At the approach of the Paxton Boys, Associators dragged them out of storage as a show of force. Loxley rescued them from the British Army during the nonimportation crisis. The Philadelphia Artillery Battalion hauled them all through the Revolutionary War. Those four cannon were the pride of the Philadelphia Artillery. More important, the cannon symbolized the Philadelphia Artillery's independent stand on defense. As often as the Philadelphia Artillery trained with those guns, it used them to demonstrate against entrenched powers and salute its champions.

Men like Benjamin Loxley; Richard Nixon, an officer in the 1747 Association; and James Biddle, captain of one of the artillery companies in 1775, were almost certainly deeply religious. Many who promoted defense were, nevertheless, members of sects that professed pacifism. Samuel Mifflin, Thomas

Mifflin, and Samuel Morris were or had been members of the Friends, in some cases at least until they took commissions with the Associators. The Associators were a diverse group, but despite their heterogeneous demographics, the Association exhibited a remarkably consistent set of values over thirty years of service. Its members considered themselves "mighty men of valour" who would pass before their "brethren armed" and protect those who could not help themselves.

In the course of the thirty years' service, Associators achieved increasing levels of legitimacy within Pennsylvania's military infrastructure–as local defenders, as training cadres, and ultimately reaching their peak through participation in Revolutionary committees. Associators shared the drive to resist and the means to execute that resistance, and their inclusion in the Revolutionary committees of 1775 and 1776 enabled Pennsylvania to be among the first and most successful of the states to send troops to the field. In a colony founded on religious exceptionalism, Associators saw themselves not only as loyal subjects of the king but as active participants in a contest against arbitrary rule. Associators from all regions considered military service in defense of their religious and civil liberty as a natural right.

As much as cannon were the tools of the artillery, the train of artillery was the tool of a distinct group of Philadelphians who saw themselves as members of a larger world. In 1748, Philadelphians used cannon to protest Pennsylvania's pacifist, expansionist policy. In 1756, they used cannon to show imperial solidarity. In 1764, artillerists turned out to defend their city against equally marginalized frontiersmen. In 1775, the Associators helped mobilize the city for war against an oppressive regime. Many by that time sat on Revolutionary subcommittees or in city government. In 1776, the Associators fought for independence. For thirty years, the Associator Artillery was a political tool. Like any tool, it was laid aside when no longer useful. By 1777, Philadelphia was part of a republic, and a militia law was on the books. The artillerists had at last achieved their goal. The days of the Associators had ended.

Appendix

ASSOCIATOR AND STATE REGIMENTS, 1747–1777
Except where otherwise noted, sources for the names listed below are cited in the main text, or can be found in the published *Pennsylvania Archives*, or the *Pennsylvania Gazette*. Associators' full names, where available, are listed.

NOVEMBER 21, 1747
Military Association of the City of Philadelphia chartered.

DECEMBER 3, 1747
Associator companies recruited along geographical rather than class lines.

DECEMBER 7, 1747
Associated Regiment of Foot of the City of Philadelphia organized.

JANUARY 1, 1748
Associator Commissions:

Officers of the Associated Regiment of Foot of the City of Philadelphia:

Colonel Abraham Taylor
Lieutenant Colonel Thomas Lawrence
Major Samuel McCall

1ST COMPANY
  Captain Charles Willing
  Lieutenant Atwood Shute
  Ensign James Claypoole

2ND COMPANY
  Captain Thomas Bond
  Lieutenant Richard Farmer
  Ensign Plunkett Fleeson[1]

3RD COMPANY
  Captain John Inglis
  Lieutenant Lynford Lardner
  Ensign Thomas Lawrence Jr.

4TH COMPANY
Captain James Polegreen
Lieutenant William Bradford
Ensign William Bingham

5TH COMPANY
Captain Peacock Bigger
Lieutenant Joseph Redman
Ensign Joseph Wood

6TH COMPANY
Captain Thomas Bourne
Lieutenant Robert Owen
Ensign Peter Etter

7TH COMPANY
Captain William Cuzzins
Lieutenant George Spafford
Ensign Abraham Mason

8TH COMPANY
Captain Septimus Robinson
Lieutenant William Klemm
Ensign William Rush

9TH COMPANY
Captain James Coultas
Lieutenant George Gray Jr.
Ensign Abraham Jones

10TH COMPANY
Captain John Ross
Lieutenant Richard Swann
Ensign Philip Benezet

11TH COMPANY
Captain Richard Nixon
Lieutenant Richard Renshaw
Ensign Francis Garrigues (Garrique)

ARTILLERY COMPANY AT FORT
Captain George Noarth

ARTILLERY COMPANY AT GRAND BATTERY
Captain John Sibbald

Officers of the Associated Regiment of Foot Philadelphia County:
Colonel Edward Jones
Lieutenant Colonel Yorke
Major Shaw
Captain De Haven
Captain Jacob Hale
Captain John Hall
Captain Hughes
Captain Pawling
Captain Robins

Officers of the Associated Regiment of Foot Bucks County:
Captain Alexander Graydon
Lieutenant Anthony De Normandie
Ensign James Barber

Officers of the Associated Regiment of Foot Chester County:
Major John Mathers
Captain George Aston
Captain Moses Dickie
Captain Robert Grace
Captain James Graham
Captain Roger Hunt
Captain James Hunter
Captain Hugh Kirkpatrick
Captain John Mather
Captain William McCoull
Captain Andrew McDowell
Captain William McKnight
Captain David Parry
Captain Richard Richison
Captain George Taylor
Captain John Williamson
Lieutenant Robert Anderson
Lieutenant John Boyd
Lieutenant William Buchanan
Lieutenant John Culbertson
Lieutenant John Cunningham

Lieutenant John Cuthbert
Lieutenant William Darlington
Lieutenant Isaac Davy
Lieutenant John Kent
Lieutenant James Mather
Lieutenant James McMaken
Lieutenant Charles Moore
Lieutenant Guyon Moore
Lieutenant Robert Morrell
Lieutenant John Vaughn
Ensign Nathaniel Davies
Ensign James Scoot
Ensign William Littler
Ensign Robert Aull
Ensign Edward Pearce
Ensign Francis Garmer
Ensign Samuel Love
Ensign Jacob Free
Ensign James Montgomery
Ensign William Cumming
Ensign John Hambrith
Ensign John Johnson
Ensign George McCullough
Ensign Joseph Talbert
Ensign Benjamin Weatherby

Officers of the Associated Regiment of Foot of New Castle County:
Colonel William Armstrong[2]
Lieutenant Colonel William Patterson
Major William McCrea
Captain Evan Rice
Captain John Allmond
Captain Grey
Captain McMechan
Captain David Bush
Captain Crow
Captain Dabford
Captain Reese
Captain Potter

Lieutenant William Patterson
Lieutenant James Walker
Lieutenant Lulof Peterson
Ensign William McCrea
Ensign Charles Bryan Sr.

NOVEMBER 1755
Various Associator companies organized along the line of Blue Mountain:
Hance Hamilton's Company, York
Berks County ranging company[3]
Conrad Weiser's guards, Berks County
John Steel's Company
Andrew Bay's Company
Thomas Barton's Company
John Elder's Company[4]

1756
Associated Regiment of Foot of the City of Philadelphia:
Honorary Colonel Benjamin Franklin
Lieutenant Colonel Jacob Duché[5]
Major Daniel Piles[6]
Regimental staff
Regimental band

CAPTAIN WILLIAM VANDERSPIEGLE'S COMPANY[7]
  First Lieutenant William Henry
  Second Lieutenant Joseph Wood
  Ensign John Blackwood
  Three sergeants
  One hundred privates

CAPTAIN JOHN KIDD'S COMPANY[8]
  Lieutenant Walter Shea
  Ensign Joseph Stamper
  Two sergeants
  Eighty privates

CAPTAIN CHARLES BATHO'S COMPANY[9]
  Lieutenant Buckridge Sims[10]
  Ensign Peter Turner
  Two sergeants
  Eighty privates

Five companies of foot (commander's names not known)
Other officers:
  Lieutenant Thomas Willing (until March 1756)
  Lieutenant John Nixon (after March 1756)
GRENADIER COMPANY
  Captain
  First Lieutenant
  Second Lieutenant
  120 grenadiers

PIONEER DETACHMENT

TRAIN OF ARTILLERY ASSOCIATION BATTERY AT WICCACOE
  Captain Samuel Mifflin
  Lieutenant Oswell Eve[11]
  Ensign William Moore[12]
  Private John Anderson
  Private Adam Blake
  Private Joseph Brown
  Private Richard Budden
  Private Andrew Carson
  Private Samuel Carson
  Private Samuel Chancellor
  Private James Craig
  Private William Dowell
  Private John Gass
  Private William Green
  Private Francis Grice
  Private George Houston
  Private John Inglis
  Private Alexander Kennedy
  Private Archibald McCall
  Private George McCalla
  Private Evan Morris
  Private William Plumsted
  Private Robert Ragg
  Private George Rankin
  Private Joseph Redman
  Private John Searle
  Private John Sibbald
  Private Archibald Stewart
  Private Charles Stedman

Private George Stephenson
Private Peter Suff
Private David Thompson
Private William Wallace

ARTILLERY COMPANY
Captain George Noarth
First Lieutenant Benjamin Loxley
Second Lieutenant John Goodwin

TROOP OF LIGHT HORSE
Captain Edward Jones
Lieutenant Lynford Lardner
Cornet John Taylor
Quartermaster George Adam Gaab
Quartermaster Leonard Melchior
John Ableron[13]
Michael Age
Alexander Alexander
Alexander Barclay
Jacob Bender
Jacob Bransed
Jacob Brich
John Butler
Thomas Donner
Adam Fraiss
David Franks
Casper Fretter
Jacob Froufalt
Matthias Gensal
Thomas Gordon
Moses Hartman
Abel Hess
Michael Hurton
Alexander Huston
John Kearsley, Jr.
Abraham Kendy
Conrad Kumly
John Kuntz
Jacob Maag
Adam Marshall
Moses Mordecai

Jacob Phisler
John Rower
George Sarley
Frans Senner
John Shillberger
Henry Shineberg
Edward Shippen Jr.
Peter Signar
John Simon
Christian Snyder
Lorentz Sportz
Alexander Stedman
Joseph Swift
Peter Turner
John Whiler
John Wolpp

MAY 8, 1756
St. Vincent and Pikesland Township Company organized.

JUNE–JULY 1763
James Smith's Company organized.

1764
Associated Regiment of Foot of the City of Philadelphia[14]
Storekeeper of the Province, Benjamin Loxley
Six Companies of Foot
Train of Artillery
Troop of Horse

NOVEMBER 17, 1774
Light Horse of the City of Philadelphia organized.

1775
Existing Commands:

TRAIN OF ARTILLERY
Major Samuel Mifflin
Captain Benjamin Loxley
Private Robert Jewell

LIGHT HORSE
Captain Abraham Markoe
First Lieutenant Andrew Allen
Second Lieutenant Samuel Morris
Cornet James Mease

Treasurer/First Sergeant Thomas Leiper
Sergeant William Hall
Corporal Samuel Howell Jr.
Corporal James Hunter
Quartermaster Levi Hollingsworth
Trooper John Boyle
Trooper James Budden
Trooper Samuel Caldwell
Trooper Andrew Caldwell
Trooper George Campbell
Trooper John Dunlap
Trooper George Fullerton
Trooper George Graff
Trooper Robert Hare
Trooper Henry Hill
Trooper Blair McClenachan
Trooper John Mease
Trooper John Mitchell
Trooper Samuel Penrose
Trooper Thomas Peters
Trooper William Pollard
Trooper Benjamin Randolph
Trooper William Tod
Trooper William West Jr.

PHILADELPHIA GREENS
Captain John Cadwalader
Seventy-six men
Identified members:
Private Alexander Graydon
Private John Lardner
Private Thomas Peters
Private Samuel Howell Jr.
Private John Maxwell Nesbitt
Private David Conyngham

QUAKER BLUES
Captain Joseph Cowperthwaite
Identified members:
Private Clement Biddle

RICHARD HUMPHREYS'S COMPANY[15]

APRIL 26, 1775
Two companies organized at Reading:
Captain George Nagel
Captain John Spohn

MAY 1775
Philadelphia Associators organized into three infantry battalions numbered 1st through 3rd, one rifle battalion, and one artillery battalion:

1ST BATTALION
  Colonel John Dickinson
  Major Jacob Morgan
  Major William Coats
  Captain William Will
  Captain Smythers
  Captain James Irvine

2ND BATTALION
  Colonel Daniel Roberdeau
  Captain Francis Wade
  Captain Peters
  Captain William Bradford
  Adjutant Thomas Hanson

3RD BATTALION
  Colonel John Cadwalader
  Lieutenant Colonel John Nixon
  Major Thomas Mifflin
  Major Samuel Meredith
  Captain Lambert Cadwalader, Light Company
  First Lieutenant George Morgan
  Captain John Shee
  Captain Francis Gurney
  Captain George Clymer
  Captain James Guy[16]
  Captain Thomas Wharton
  Captain Henderson
  Captain Richard Peters
  Captain John Wilcocks
  Captain Jacob Morgan
  Captain Little
  Captain Richard Willing

Captain Richard Humphreys
Captain Moore Furman
Captain Francis C. Hassenclever[17]
Captain Christopher Kucher[18]
Captain McElwain[19]
Captain John Lord[20]
Captain Boyer[21]
Captain Sharp Delany[22]
Captain Thomas Fitzsimmons[23]
Captain Joseph Cowperthwaite

MAY 1775
Philadelphia Artillery Battalion organized.

Major Samuel Mifflin
Captain Benjamin Loxley
Captain Joseph Moulder
Captain James Biddle
Captain Thomas Procter

RIFLE BATTALION
Colonel Timothy Matlack

Philadelphia County organized into four battalions:

6TH BATTALION[24]
Colonel William Hamilton

7TH BATTALION
Colonel Robert Lewis
Major John Moore

8TH BATTALION
Colonel Thomas Potts

9TH BATTALION[25]
Colonel Samuel Miles

Berks County Association

BATTALION OF FOOT
Colonel John Patton
Captain John Lesher
Captain Michael Furrer
Captain George Miller
Captain Michael Wolf

LANCASTER COUNTY ASSOCIATION

BATTALION OF FOOT (FOUR COMPANIES)

BATTALION OF RIFLEMEN (HANOVER TOWNSHIP)

York County Association:

1ST BATTALION
  Colonel James Smith
  Major Michael Swope

Cumberland County Association:

1ST BATTALION (LOWER DISTRICT)
  Colonel Robert Callender

2D BATTALION (UPPER DISTRICT)
  Colonel William Thompson (commanded Upper and Middle Districts)
  Colonel John Montgomery
  Colonel James Wilson (district west of Kittatinny Mountain)

MAY 16, 1775
Westmoreland Battalions associated:

1ST BATTALION
  Colonel John Proctor

2ND BATTALION
  Colonel John Carnahan
  Major James Smith

JUNE 3, 1775
Thirty Associator companies organized and exercising.[26]
Officers, battalion assignment not yet known:
Captain John Mifflin[27]
Lieutenant Wyckoff[28]
Ensign John Mifflin[29]

JUNE 14, 1775
Congress authorizes ten companies of Pennsylvania, Maryland, and Virginia riflemen for service in the newly declared Continental Army surrounding Boston.

JUNE 20, 1775
General George Washington reviews the Philadelphia Associator commands.[30]

AUGUST 10, 1775
Bucks County Association:[31]

1ST BATTALION
  Colonel Joseph Kirkbride
  Lieutenant Colonel Alexander Anderson
  First Major Joseph Penrose
  Second Major Joseph McIlvain

2ND BATTALION
  Colonel John Beatty
  Lieutenant Colonel Robert Shewell
  First Major James McMaster
  Second Major William Roberts

3RD BATTALION
  Colonel George Taylor
  Lieutenant Colonel Robert Robinson
  First Major John Tenbrook
  Second Major John Heany

AUGUST 11, 1775
Pennsylvania Committee of Safety names Robert Towers commissary of the magazine and military stores.[32]

OCTOBER 12, 1775
Pennsylvania authorizes the 1st State Battalion, consisting of eight companies, for Continental service.

OCTOBER 16, 1775
Fort Mud garrison organized:
  Captain Thomas Procter
Philadelphia Light Horse engaged delivering payroll to Continental Army in northern New York and Canada.[33]

FEBRUARY 12, 1776
Pennsylvania orders the city battalions to furnish the equivalent of a battalion for service in New York; rifle battalion to furnish an attached company.[34]

AUGUST 1775–JUNE 1776
4th Battalion, Philadelphia Associators organized:[35]
  Colonel Thomas McKean
  Captain Charles Willson Peale
  Captain John Barker[36]

Philadelphia County:
11TH BATTALION
  Colonel Hill

JUNE 1776
Tench Francis's Ranger Company expanded to nine compa-
nies, reorganized as the Rifle Battalion, Philadelphia County
Associators.[37]
Colonel Tench Francis

AUGUST 9–20, 1776
Philadelphia Light Horse ordered into Continental service for
New York campaign[38]

DECEMBER 20, 1776
Colonel John Cadwalader musters one thousand six hundred
Philadelphia Associators

CADWALADER'S BRIGADE
  Colonel John Cadwalader
  Lieutenant Colonel William Coates[39]
  Captain Francis Wade, Brigade Quartermaster[40]
Three provisional battalions under the command of the follow-
ing:[41]
Colonel John Nixon
Colonel Jacob Morgan
Colonel Paul Cox
Colonel William Bradford
Major Robert Knox
Major Joseph Cowperthwaite
Major Samuel Meredith
Captain Charles Willson Peale
Captain John Barker[42]

Light Infantry Battalion (provisional), consisting of four
Pennsylvania companies:[43]
Captain George Henry

DOVER LIGHT INFANTRY (ATTACHED)[44]
  Captain Thomas Rodney
  Sergeant McKnatt[45]

ARTILLERY COMPANY OF THE NORTHERN LIBERTIES
  Captain Jehu Eyre

First Lieutenant William Brown
Second Lieutenant John Brown
Second Lieutenant Samuel Williams

ARTILLERY COMPANY
   Captain Wingate Newman
   Captain Lieutenant William Baxter
   Second Lieutenant Nathaniel Wallace
   Second Lieutenant John Sober

Pennsylvania State Artillery Battalion

2ND COMPANY
   Captain Thomas Forrest
   First Lieutenant Worley Emes
   Third Lieutenant Patrick Duffy

Pennsylvania Navy and Marines (including Continental Marines) serving as artillery:
Captain Isaac Craig's Company
Captain William Shippen's Company
Putnam Battery, Pennsylvania Navy
Captain William Brown's Company
Captain Andrew Porter's Company
Captain Thomas Read's Company

Notes

INTRODUCTION

1. Donald W. Holst, "A Portrait of the Battle of Princeton," *Military Collector and Historian* 37 (Fall 1985): 146-52.

2. Ibid. See also Samuel J. Newland, *The Pennsylvania Militia: The Early Years, 1669-1792* (Annville, PA: Commonwealth of Pennsylvania, Department of Military and Veterans Affairs, 1997), color plate 14. The ancestor units of no fewer than three currently active Pennsylvania Army National Guard elements are represented in the painting: Troop A, 1st Squadron, 104th Cavalry Regiment (First Troop Philadelphia City Cavalry), the 111th Infantry Regiment (Associators), and the 103d Engineer Battalion (Dandy First).

3. Russell F. Weigley, "The Colonial Militia," in Uzal W. Ent, ed., *The First Century: A History of the 28th Infantry Division* (Harrisburg, PA: Stackpole, 1979), 18. See also Newland, *Pennsylvania Militia: Defending the Commonwealth*, 13-14.

4. *Pennsylvania Gazette*, May 14, 1741. As grantee of a royal charter, William Penn virtually owned Pennsylvania and administered it on the king's behalf, as lord proprietor. As such, he could choose to rule the colony himself or through a lieutenant governor. The proprietorship was hereditary and passed to Penn's heirs upon his death.

5. Fairfax Downey, *Sound of the Guns: The Story of American Artillery from the Ancient and Honourable Company to the Atom Cannon and Guided Missile* (New York: David McKay, 1955), 4.

6. See also *Pennsylvania Gazette*, March 3, 1729; March 4, 1731; August 14, 1732; and March 6 and September 25, 1734.

7. John R. Elting, ed., *Military Uniforms in America: The Era of the American Revolution, 1755-1795* (San Rafael, CA: Presidio, 1974), 12.

8. The four colonial wars fought in North America between 1689 and 1763 are traditionally known in the United States as the French and Indian Wars. King William's War (1689-1697) is also known as the War of the League of Augsburg. Queen Ann's War (1702-1713) is called the War of Spanish Succession. The maritime phase of King George's War (1744-1748), better known as Europe's War of Austrian Succession, was known to American colonists as the War of Jenkins' Ear (1739-1742) or simply the "Spanish War." The Seven Years' War (1756-1763), Third Silesian War, the French and Indian War (1754-1761) or the Great War for Empire, was known to American colonists as the French War. The overlap in dates and the disparity in names reflect the disparate outlook of American colonists and subsequent generations of historians.

9. *Pennsylvania Gazette*, March 3, 1729; March 4, 1731; August 14, 1732; March 6, 1734; September 25, 1734; July 3, 1740; and May 14, 1741.

10. Benjamin Franklin, *Benjamin Franklin's Autobiography*, ed. J. A. Leo LeMay and P. M. Zall (New York: W. W. Norton, 1986), 92.

11. Franklin, *Autobiography*, 96.

12. Newland, *Pennsylvania Militia: The Early Years*, 47.

13. Benjamin Loxley, "Benjamin Loxley's Account of his Ancestors, of his Parents, and of Himself and Family, Dated June 20, 1789," Manuscript Collection, Historical Society of Pennsylvania, Philadelphia.

14. Alexander Graydon, *Memoirs of a Life, Chiefly Passed in Pennsylvania, Within the Last Sixty Years* (Edinburgh: William Bradford and T. Cadell, 1822), 40-41.

15. See Robert L. D. Davidson, *War Comes to Quaker Pennsylvania, 1682-1756* (New York: Columbia University Press, 1957), for a general discussion of the decline of Pennsylvania's pacifist policy. See also John W. Jackson, *Fort Mifflin: Valiant Defender of the Delaware* (Philadelphia: Old Fort Mifflin Historical Society Committee, 1986), 1, and Jeffery M. Dorwart, *Fort Mifflin of Philadelphia: An Illustrated History* (Philadelphia: University of Pennsylvania Press, 1998), 11-12.

16. See Emory Upton, *The Military Policy of the United States* (Washington, DC: Government Printing Office, 1904) for a discourse on the need for a professional American military, and John McAuley Palmer, *America in Arms: The Experience of the United States with Military Organization* (New Haven, CT: Yale University Press, 1941) for a counterpoint to Upton's argument and a defense of the volunteer system. Matthew C. Ward argues on behalf of the British Army establishment in *Breaking the Backcountry: The Seven Years' War in Virginia and Pennsylvania, 1754-1765* (Pittsburgh: University of Pittsburgh Press, 2003).

17. Fred Anderson, *A People's Army: Massachusetts Soldiers and Society in the Seven Years War* (New York: W. W. Norton, 1984), vii.

18. Newland, *Pennsylvania Militia: The Early Years*, 47.

19. Robert K. Wright Jr., *The Continental Army* (Washington, DC: United States Army Center of Military History, 1983), xi.

20. George Smith, *An Universal Military Dictionary: A Copious Explanation of the Technical Terms &c. Used in the Equipment, Machinery, Movements, and Military Operations of an Army* (London: J. Millan, 1779; repr., Ottawa, ON: Museum Restoration Service, 1969). See also John B. B. Trussell, *The Pennsylvania Line: Regimental Organization and Operations, 1775-1783* (Harrisburg: Commonwealth of Pennsylvania, Pennsylvania Historical and Museum Commission, 1993), iii, iv.

21. Trussell, *Pennsylvania Line*, iii, v.

22. Ibid.

23. Lawrence Stone, "Prosopography," *Historical Studies Today* (Winter 1971): 46.

CHAPTER ONE: PENNSYLVANIA BEFORE THE MILITARY ASSOCIATION

1. William Penn, "To the Free Society of Traders," August 16, 1683, in Mary Maples Dunn et al., eds., *The Papers of William Penn*, 5 vols. (Philadelphia: University of Pennsylvania Press, 1981), 2:445.
2. Ibid.
3. Ibid.
4. Ibid., 455.
5. Ibid., 442.
6. Ibid.
7. Ibid., 442-43.
8. *Colonial Records*, 1:44.
9. Sir William Petty to William Penn, London, August 14, 1682, in *Colonial Records*, 1:49.
10. William Penn to William Crispin, John Bezar, and Nathaniel Allen, London, September 30, 1681, in *Papers of William Penn*, 1:121.
11. Ibid.
12. *Colonial Records*, 1:40-46.
13. Samuel Kelly, *Samuel Kelly: An Eighteenth Century Seaman, Whose Days Have Been Few and Evil, to Which Is Added Remarks, etc., on Places He Visited during His Pilgrimage in This Wilderness*, ed. Crosbie Garstin (New York: Frederick A. Stokes, 1925), 140.
14. Ibid.
15. Ibid.
16. "Charter of the Province of Pennsylvania, 1681," in Slaughton George, Benjamin M. Nead, and Thomas McCamant, eds., *Charter to William Penn and the Laws of the Province of Pennsylvania, Passed Between the Years 1682 and 1700* (Harrisburg, PA: Lane S. Hart, 1879), 82.
17. "Charter of the Province of Pennsylvania, 1681," 87.
18. Ibid., 88.
19. John K. Mahon, *History of the Militia and the National Guard* (New York: Macmillan, 1983), 7, 262.
20. William Lambard, *Eirenarcha: Or of the Office of the Justices of Peace* (London: 1581; repr., New York: Da Capo, 1970), 378. Kyle F. Zelner, *A Rabble in Arms: Massachusetts Towns and Militiamen during King Philip's War* (New York: New York University Press, 2009), 19-28.
21. Lambard, *Eirenarcha*, 378.
22. Ibid., 380.
23. Ibid., 378, 380.
24. Ibid., 379.
25. Nathaniel B. Shurtleff, ed., *Records of the Governor and Company of Massachusetts Bay in New England*, 5 vols. (Boston: William White, Printer to the Commonwealth, 1853-54), 1:85.
26. George et al., *Charter To William Penn*, 38-44. See also John Shy, *Toward*

Lexington: The Role of the British Army in the Coming of the American Revolution (Princeton, NJ: Princeton University Press, 1965), 4.

27. "Wm. Penn to the Council, 1685," Kensington, June 19, 1685, in *Colonial Records*, 1:94.

28. Donald H. Kent, *The French Invasion of Western Pennsylvania, 1753* (Harrisburg: Pennsylvania Historical and Museum Commission, 1991), 3.

29. Penn, "To the Free Society of Traders," 2:448. See also Velma Thorne Carter, *Penn's Manor of Springfield: An Historical Presentation Written under the Auspices of the Bicentennial Committee* (Springfield Township, PA: Springfield Township Bicentennial Committee, 1976), 9-12.

30. Penn, "To the Free Society of Traders," 2:448.

31. Ibid.

32. Ibid.

33. Ibid., 449.

34. Ibid., 450.

35. "Charter of the Province of Pennsylvania, 1681," 81. See also Penn, "To the Free Society of Traders," 2:451.

36. Melvyn P. Leffler, "National Security," in Michael J. Hogan and Thomas G. Paterson, eds., *Explaining the History of American Foreign Relations* (Cambridge: Cambridge University Press, 1991), 202. According to diplomatic historian Leffler, "national security policy encompasses the decisions and actions deemed imperative to protect domestic core values from external threats."

37. "Wm. Penn to the Governor and Council of West Jersey," Philadelphia, April 11, 1683, in *Colonial Records*, 1:60.

38. Ibid.

39. Ibid.

40. Graham Evans and Jeffrey Newnham, *The Penguin Dictionary of International Relations* (London: Penguin, 1998), 504-5.

41. "Lawes Established by the Authority of his Majesties Letters Patents, Granted to his Royall Highness James Duke of Yorke and Albany; Bearing the Date the 12th Day of March in the Sixteenth Year of the Raigne of Our Soveraigne Lord Kinge Charles the Second," in George et al., *Charter to William Penn*, 42.

42. Shy, *Toward Lexington*, 4.

43. William L. Shea, *The Virginia Militia in the Seventeenth Century* (Baton Rouge: Louisiana State University Press, 1983), 21.

44. Ibid., 41-42.

45. Ibid. 43.

46. Ibid., 51, 52.

47. Ibid., 57.

48. Ibid., 63.

49. Ibid., 73.

50. Robert K. Wright Jr., "Massachusetts Militia Roots: A Bibliographic Study" (1986), Massachusetts National Guard Museum and Archives, Worcester, MA.

51. Ibid.

52. Ibid.

53. Ibid.

54. Susan Hardman Moore, *Pilgrims: New World Settlers and the Call of Home* (New Haven, CT: Yale University Press, 2007), 109-117.

55. Thomas Copley to Lord Baltimore, April 3, 1638, in *Calvert Papers Number One* (Baltimore: Peabody Publication Fund, 1889), 159-164. See also Newton D. Mereness, *Maryland as a Proprietary Province* (London: Macmillan, 1901), 96.

56. "An act for military discipline, 1638," in William Hand Browne, ed., *Archives of Maryland*, 66 vols. (Baltimore: Maryland Historical Society, 1883-1954), 1:609.

57. Ibid., 610.

58. Ibid., 609.

59. M. L. Brown, *Firearms in Colonial America: The Impact on History and Technology, 1492-1792* (Washington, DC: Smithsonian Institution Press, 1980), 85-86.

60. Paul A. W. Wallace, *Indians in Pennsylvania* (Harrisburg: Pennsylvania Historical and Museum Commission, 1961), 99-100.

61. Mereness, *Maryland as a Proprietary Province*, 307. See also *Archives of Maryland*, 1:461-478.

62. James H. Merrell, *Into the American Woods: Negotiators on the Pennsylvania Frontier* (New York: W. W. Norton, 1999), 35. See also Russell F. Weigley, "The Colonial Militia," in Robert Grant Crist, ed., *The First Century: A History of the 28th Infantry Division* (Harrisburg, PA: Stackpole, 1979), 17.

63. Merrell, *Into the American Woods*, 129.

64. *Colonial Records*, 1:47.

65. *Colonial Records*, 1:48-49.

66. *Colonial Records*, 5:2.

67. John Mack Faragher, *Daniel Boone: The Life and Legend of an American Pioneer* (New York: Henry Holt, 1992), 18.

68. Merrell, *Into the American Woods*, 35.

69. George et al., *Charter to William Penn*, 157.

70. Donald G. Shomette, *Pirates on the Chesapeake: Being a True History of Pirates, Picaroons, and Raiders on Chesapeake Bay, 1610-1807* (Centreville, MD: Tidewater, 1985), 96-99.

71. William S. Hanna, *Benjamin Franklin and Pennsylvania Politics* (Palo Alto, CA: Stanford University Press, 1964), 7.

72. James H. Hutson, *Pennsylvania Politics, 1746-1770: The Movement for Royal Government and Its Consequences* (Princeton, NJ: Princeton University Press, 1972), 66.

73. Hanna, *Benjamin Franklin and Pennsylvania Politics*, viii.

74. Ibid.

75. Carl Van Doren, *Benjamin Franklin* (Garden City, NY: Garden City Publishing, 1941), 101.

76. Ibid., 102.

77. Hutson, *Pennsylvania Politics*, 64, 67.

78. Ibid., viii.

79. Ibid., 3-4.

80. Ibid.

81. Ibid., 10-11.

82. Sam Bass Warner Jr., *The Private City: Philadelphia in Three Periods of Its Growth* (Philadelphia: University of Pennsylvania Press, 1968), 9.

83. *Colonial Records*, 1:47-48.

84. Wallace, *Indians in Pennsylvania*, 133.

85. George et al., *Charter To William Penn*, 107.

86. Francis Jennings, *The Ambiguous Iroquois Empire: The Covenant Chain Confederation of Indian Tribes with the English Colonies from Its Beginnings to the Lancaster Treaty of 1744* (New York: W. W. Norton, 1984), xvii.

87. Ibid.

88. See also Francis Jennings's influential *Invasions of America* (Syracuse, NY: Syracuse University Press, 1975); *The History and Culture of Iroquois Diplomacy: An Interdisciplinary Guide to the Treaties of the Six Nations and Their League* (Syracuse, NY: Syracuse University Press, 1985); and *Empire of Fortune: Crowns, Colonies, and Tribes in the Seven Years War in America* (New York: W.W. Norton, 1988).

89. John Bartram, *Observations on the Inhabitants, Climate, Soil, Rivers, Productions, Animals, and other matters worthy of Notice Made By Mr. John Bartram in his Travels from Pensilvania to Onondago, Oswego, and Lake Ontario, in Canada To which is annex'd, a curious Account of the Cataracts at Niagara, by Mr. Peter Kalm, A Swedish Gentleman who travelled there* (London: J. Whiston and B. White, 1751), 14.

90. Ibid. See also Jennings, *Ambiguous Iroquois Empire*, 51.

91. "Message Shawnee Chiefs to Gov. Gordon, 1732," in *Colonial Records*, 1:329.

92. Jennings, *Ambiguous Iroquois Empire*, 176.

93. Kent, *French Invasion*, 5.

94. Jennings, *Ambiguous Iroquois Empire*, 174.

95. Ibid., 204

96. Ibid., 266.

97. John R. Stilgoe, *Common Landscape of America, 1580 to 1845* (New Haven, CT: Yale University Press, 1982), 180-81.

98. Samuel Pennypacker, "The Settlement of Germantown, PA and the Causes Which Led to It," *Pennsylvania Magazine of History and Biography* 4 (1880): 39.

99. Stilgoe, *Common Landscape*, 79-80.

100. Ibid., 170-77.

101. Bartram, *Observations*, 12-13. See also *Colonial Records*, 5:452. For a discussion of Jacobitism and its impact on the Pennsylvania backcountry, see Bruce Lenman, *The Jacobite Clans of the Great Glen, 1650-1784* (Aberdeen: Scottish Cultural Press, 1995), and Ward, *Breaking the Backcountry*.

102. For a discussion of Jacobitism and its effect on the American Revolution, see Lenman, *Jacobite Clans.*

103. Stilgoe, *Common Landscape,* 79.

104. *Colonial Records,* 4:639, 5:440-49. Lieutenant Governor George Thomas appointed Richard Peters (1704-1744) provincial secretary and clerk of the council on February 14, 1742.

105. Merrell, *Into the American Woods,* 176.

106. Warner, *Private City,* 12.

107. Billy G. Smith, *The "Lower Sort": Philadelphia's Laboring People, 1750-1800* (Ithaca, NY: Cornell University Press, 1990), 14-16, 39.

108. Warner, *Private City,* 13.

109. Smith, *"Lower Sort,"* 76-77. See also Marcus Rediker, *Between the Devil and the Deep Blue Sea: Merchant Seamen, Pirates, and the Anglo-American Maritime World, 1700-1750* (Cambridge: Cambridge University Press, 1987), 82-83.

110. Smith, *"Lower Sort,"* 81.

111. Ibid., 89, 154.

112. Carl E. Swanson, *Predators and Prizes: American Privateering and Imperial Warfare, 1739-1748* (Columbia: University of South Carolina Press, 1991), 119.

113. *Pennsylvania Gazette,* March 3, 1729. See also Watson, *Annals of Philadelphia,* 1:325, 344-45.

114. *Pennsylvania Gazette,* March 4, 1731; August 14, 1732; March 6 and September 25, 1734; April 17 and July 3, 1740; and May 14, 1741.

115. Samuel J. Newland, *The Pennsylvania Militia: Defending the Commonwealth and the Nation, 1669-1870* (Annville, PA: Commonwealth of Pennsylvania, Department of Military and Veterans Affairs, 2002), 15-16.

116. Merrell, *Into the American Woods,* 35. See also *Plain Truth: Or Serious Considerations on the Present State of the City of Philadelphia and Province of Pennsylvania,* in Benjamin Franklin, *The Papers of Benjamin Franklin,* Leonard W. Labaree et al., eds., 28 vols. (New Haven, CT: Yale University Press, 1960), 3:191.

117. *Pennsylvania Gazette,* March 4, 1731.

118. Ibid., August 14, 1732.

119. Ibid., March 6, 1734.

120. Ibid., September 25, 1734.

121. The term used for enlisted soldiers through most of the eighteenth century was "matross." Later in the century, "gunner" came into general usage.

122. Ibid., July 3, 1740.

123. Ibid., May 14, 1741.

Chapter Two: Founding the Association, 1740–1748

1. Loxley, "Benjamin Loxley's Account," 2.

2. See Smith, *The "Lower Sort,"* for a discussion of Philadelphia's poor population.

3. Hanna, *Benjamin Franklin and Pennsylvania Politics,* 22.

4. Anderson, *People's Army*, 26.

5. Zelner, *Rabble in Arms*, 207-211.

6. *Pennsylvania Gazette*, April 17, 1740..

7 Ibid.

8. Douglas Edward Leach, *Roots of Conflict: British Armed Forces and Colonial Americans, 1677-1763* (Chapel Hill: University of North Carolina Press, 1986), 50. See also Lee Offen, *America's First Marines: Gooch's American Regiment, 1740-1742* (Jacksonville, FL: Fortis, 2010).

9. Offen, *America's First Marines*, i.

10. Ibid., iv, 1.

11. Ibid., 1.

12. *Pennsylvania Gazette*, May 22, 1740. See also Offen, *America's First Marines*, 1-5.

13. Leach, *Roots of Conflict*, 52.

14. *Pennsylvania Gazette*, July 23, 1740; April 8, 1742; April 22, 1742; and September 2, 1742. See also *Murtie June Clark, Colonial Soldiers of the South, 1732-1774* (Baltimore: Genealogical Publishing, 1983), 125-258, and Offen, *America's First Marines*, 9-10.

15. Charles P. Keith, *Chronicles of Pennsylvania from the English Revolution to the Peace Aix-la-Chapelle, 1688-1748*, 2 vols. (Philadelphia: privately printed, 1917), 2:806. See also *Pennsylvania Gazette*, August 7, 1740.

16. John A. Houlding, *Fit for Service: The Training of the British Army, 1715-1795* (Oxford: Clarendon, 1981), 188-89.

17. Ibid., 92.

18. Loxley, "Benjamin Loxley's Account," 10.

19. Ibid., 3.

20. Ibid., 2.

21. *Pennsylvania Gazette*, May 22, 1740, and November 5, 1744.

22. Charles Patrick Neimeyer, *America Goes to War: A Social History of the Continental Army* (New York: New York University Press, 1996), 12.

23. *Pennsylvania Gazette*, July 24, 1740, September 2, 1742, and July 31, 1746.

24. Anderson, *People's Army*, 26-27.

25. DeWitt Bailey, "British Military Small Arms in North America, 1755-1783," *American Society of Arms Collectors Bulletin* 71 (1994): 4.

26. *Pennsylvania Gazette*, July 23, 1740.

27. Ibid.

28. Keith, *Chronicles of Pennsylvania*, 1:806.

29. Ibid.

30. *Pennsylvania Gazette*, September 8, 1740.

31. *Pennsylvania Gazette*, August 7, 1740, and September 8, 1740.

32. Howard Henry Peckham, *The Colonial Wars, 1689-1762* (Chicago: University of Chicago Press, 1964), 91.

33. Leach, *Roots of Conflict*, 61.

34. *Pennsylvania Gazette*, November 5, 1744.

35. Leach, *Roots of Conflict*, 61, 63.

36. *Pennsylvania Gazette,* July 31, 1746.

37. Loxley, "Benjamin Loxley's Account," 10.

38. *Colonial Records,* 5:38.

39. Peckham, *Colonial Wars,* 110.

40. *Colonial Records,* 1:6-17.

41. *Colonial Records,* 5:38.

42. Keith, *Chronicles of Pennsylvania,* 2:883.

43. William Trent to Governor George Thomas, Albany, October 21, 1746, in John Blair Sinn, ed., *Record of Pennsylvania Marriages,* 3 vols. (Harrisburg, PA: E. K. Meyers, 1890), 3:450. See also Newland, *Pennsylvania Militia: Defending the Commonwealth,* 31.

44. *Pennsylvania Gazette,* July 24, 1746.

45. *Colonial Records,* 5:38.

46. Newland, *Pennsylvania Militia: The Early Years,* 33.

47. *Pennsylvania Gazette,* July 31, August 7; September 4, 1746; April 16, 1747; and July 19, 1750.

48. Ibid., September 11 and October 30, 1746; and May 7, 1747.

49. Ibid., July 31 and August 4, 1746.

50. *Colonial Records,* 1:8-11.

51. Ibid.

52. *Pennsylvania Gazette,* September 4 and 11, 1746; and August 19, 1750.

53. *Colonial Records,* 1:6-8.

54. Ibid.

55. *Pennsylvania Gazette,* April 5, 1750.

56. Ibid., April 5 and August 19, 1750.

57. Leach, *Roots of Conflict,* 63, 75. See also Swanson, *Predators,* 2.

58. *Pennsylvania Gazette,* June 18, 1741.

59. Swanson, *Predators,* 2.

60. Newland, *Pennsylvania Militia: Defending the Commonwealth,* 33.

61. Hanna, *Benjamin Franklin and Pennsylvania Politics,* 11.

62. Ibid., 12.

63. Ibid.

64. Ibid., 13.

65. Ibid., 17-21.

66. Ibid., 15.

67. Franklin, *Autobiography,* 84.

68. *Virginia Gazette,* January 9, 1746.

69. Ibid., January 16, 1746.

70. Franklin, *Autobiography,* 92.

71. Franklin, *Papers,* 3:191.

72. Ibid., 3:199.

73. Ibid., 3:195.

74. Ibid., 3:195-96.

75. Ibid., 3:196.

76. Ibid., 3:197.

77. Ibid., 3:191.
78. Ibid.
79 Ibid.
80. Ibid.
81. Ibid., 3:194.
82. Ibid., 3:201.
83. Ibid., 3:202.
84. Ibid., 3:203.
85. "Articles of Association," in Franklin, *Papers*, 3:205-12.
86. Ibid., 3:205.
87. Ibid. See also Swanson, *Predators*, 220.
88. "Articles of Association," in Franklin, *Papers*, 3:205.
89. Ibid., 3: 206.
90. John Locke, *Two Treatises of Government and a Letter Concerning Toleration*, ed. Ian Shapiro, (New Haven, CT: Yale University Press, 2003), 177.
91. *Pennsylvania Gazette*, April 17, 1740.
92. Barbara A. Gannon, "The Lord is a Man of War, The God of Love and Peace: The Association Debate, Philadelphia, 1747-1748," *Pennsylvania History* 65 (Winter 1998): 61.
93. "Articles of Association," in Franklin, *Papers*, 3:206.
94. Ibid.
95. Ibid.
96. Ibid., 206-07.
97. Ibid., 207.
98. Ibid.
99. Ibid. See also, *Colonial Records*, 5:319, 321.
100. Ibid., 3:207-208.
101. Albert W. Haarmann and Eric I. Manders, "Pennsylvania Associators 1747-1748," *Military Collector and Historian* 33 (Fall 1981): 100.
102. Richard Peters to Thomas Penn, November 29, 1747, in Franklin, *Papers*, 3:216.
103. Franklin, *Autobiography*, 87-88.
104. John Swift to John White, November 29, 1747, in Thomas Balch, ed., *Letters and Papers Relating Chiefly to the Provincial History of Pennsylvania, With Some Notices of the Writers* (Philadelphia: Crissy and Markley, 1855), 10-11.
105. *Pennsylvania Gazette*, December 3, 1747.
106. Loxley, "Benjamin Loxley's Account," 2. See also Smith, *The "Lower Sort,"* for a discussion of the urban poor who made up a majority of Philadelphia's population.
107. *Colonial Records*, 5:174-75. See also Craig Horle, Joseph S. Foster, and Laurie M. Wolfe, eds., *Lawmaking and Legislators in Pennsylvania: A Biographical Dictionary*, 2 vols. (Philadelphia: University of Pennsylvania Press, 1997), 2:907.
108. Horle et al., *Lawmaking*, 2:905-907.
109. *Pennsylvania Gazette*, October 18, November 1, and December 6, 1733;

December 24, 1735; and December 8, 1757. See also *Pennsylvania Archives*, 9 series, 119 vols. (Harrisburg, PA: Theo. Fenn, 1852-1935), 6th ser., 1:466, and *Colonial Records*, 5:267.

110. *Pennsylvania Gazette*, October 18, November 1, and December 6, 1733; December 24, 1735; May 28, 1741; May 17, 1744; and December 8, 1757. See also *Pennsylvania Archives*, 6th ser., 1:466.

111. *Colonial Records*, 5:249. See also K. Alonzo Brock, ed., "The Journal of William Black, 1744," *Pennsylvania Magazine of History and Biography* 1 (1877): 247; and Howard I. Chapelle, *The History of American Sailing Ships* (New York: Bonanza, 1935), 297-98.

112. *An Authentic Historical Memoir of the Schuylkill Fishing Company of the State in Schuylkill from its Establishment on that Romantic Stream, Near Philadelphia, in the Year 1732, to the Present Time, By a Member* (Philadelphia: Judah Dobson, 1830), 13.

113. *Pennsylvania Gazette*, December 10, 1747.

114. *Pennsylvania Archives*, 4th ser., 3:1003. Pennsylvania's taxable population in 1760 was 31,667.

115. James H. Hutson, "An Investigation of the Inarticulate: Philadelphia's White Oaks." *William and Mary Quarterly: A Magazine of Early American History* 28 (January 1971): 15.

116. *Colonial Records*, 5:158.

117. *Pennsylvania Gazette*, December 10, 1747.

118. *Colonial Records*, 5:174-75. See also *Pennsylvania Gazette*, January 5, 1748.

119. Horle et al., *Lawmaking*, 2:907.

120. *Colonial Records*, 5:185-94. See also Newland, *Pennsylvania Militia: The Early Years*, 42.

121. *Colonial Records*, 5:185-94. See also *Pennsylvania Gazette*, January 26, February 9, April 16, June 9, and September 1, 1748.

122. Sally F. Griffith, "Order, Discipline, and a few Cannon: Benjamin Franklin, the Association, and the Rhetoric and Practice of Boosterism," *Pennsylvania Magazine of History & Biography* 116 (April 1992): 152.

123. George D. Moller, *American Military Shoulder Arms: Colonial and Revolutionary War Arms* (Boulder: University of Colorado Press, 1991), 117, 124, 133, 233-34. The cost of firearms varied. Muskets cost between two and eight pounds, rifles cost roughly twice as much. See also John Folwell, "Mr. Marchoo Dr. to John Folwell, £1.15." and Abraham Markoe, "To James Claypoole, Dr. £8.00," First Troop, Philadelphia City Cavalry Museum, Philadelphia. Captain Abraham Markoe of the Philadelphia Light Horse Troop paid nine pounds fifteen shillings for an embroidered silk standard in 1775. See also Rediker, *Between the Devil*, 305. The average merchant seaman's wage was one pound sixty-six shillings per month. See also Anthony D. Darling, *Redcoat and Brown Bess* (Alexandria Bay, NY: Museum Restoration Service, 1971), 9. A British Army soldier earned eight pence per day.

124. Franklin, *Autobiography*, 92.

125. *Pennsylvania Gazette,* January 12, 1748. See also Franklin, *Autobiography,* 92.

126. Pole arms were weapons that included pikes, spontoons, and halberds. Pikes and spontoons were spearlike, while a halberd resembled an elaborate battle-ax.

127. John Swift to John White, November 29, 1747, in Balch, *Letters and Papers,* 10-11.

128. Franklin, *Autobiography,* 92.

129. Loxley, "Benjamin Loxley's Account," 3. See also John Swift to John White, April 12, 1748, in Balch, *Letters and Papers,* 15-16.

130. Brock, "The Journal of William Black, 1744," 247. See also Chapelle, *History of American Sailing Ships,* 297-98. *Le Trembleur* cost eight hundred pounds.

131. *Colonial Records,* 5:249.

132. Dorwart, *Fort Mifflin,* 11, 14.

133. *Colonial Records,* 5:172-73.

134. *Colonial Records,* 5:187.

135. Franklin, *Autobiography,* 93. See also Davidson, *War Comes,* 54.

136. *Colonial Records,* 5:228.

137. Griffith, "Order," 151.

138. *Pennsylvania Gazette,* April 28, 1748.

139. Ibid., April 28, 1748; March 12, 1767; and May 16, 1771.

140. *Colonial Records,* 5:249. See also John Swift to John White, April 12, 1748, in Balch, *Letters and Papers,* 15-16.

141. Ibid.

142. John Swift to John White, April 12, 1748, in Balch, *Letters and Papers,* 15-16.

143. Gunther E. Rothenberg, *The Art of Warfare in the Age of Napoleon* (Bloomington: Indiana University Press, 1978), 76.

144. Van Doren, *Benjamin Franklin,* 200.

145. Ibid.

146. *Colonial Records,* 5:261.

147. D. Bush, &c., to President Palmer, Wilmington, July 6, 1748, in *Colonial Records,* 2:6.

148. *Pennsylvania Gazette,* May 26, 1748.

149. James Logan to Benjamin Franklin, Philadelphia, December 7, 1747, in Franklin, *Papers,* 3:219-20.

150. Newland, *Pennsylvania Militia: The Early Years,* 73.

151. *Pennsylvania Gazette,* July 18, 1745.

152. John Swift to John White, April 12, 1748, in Balch, *Letters and Papers,* 15-16.

153. *Pennsylvania Gazette,* May 21, 1748. See also *Colonial Records,* 5:249, 251.

154. *Colonial Records,* 5:250.

155. *Pennsylvania Gazette,* May 26, 1748.

156. *Pennsylvania Gazette,* June 23, 1748.

157. *Colonial Records*, 5:267.

158. *Pennsylvania Gazette*, May 28, 1741, and May 17, 1744.

159. Thomas Penn to Richard Peters, March 30, 1748, in Franklin, *Papers*, 3:186.

160. Hanna, *Benjamin Franklin and Pennsylvania Politics*, 65.

161. *Pennsylvania Gazette*, September 1, 1748.

162. Ibid., November 21, 1751.

163. Loxley, "Benjamin Loxley's Account," 3.

164. "Restoration of the Schuylkill Gun to the 'State in Schuylkill,' April 23d, 1884," *Pennsylvania Magazine of History and Biography* 8 (1884): 199.

165. Rediker, *Between the Devil*, 82-83.

166. Ibid., 122.

167. Ibid.

168. Ibid., 121-22.

169. Swanson, *Predators*, 118.

170. Jean Appier Hanzelet Lorrain, *La Pyrotechnie de Hanzelet Lorrain* (Grenoble: Edition des 4 Siegneurs, 1971). See also Thomas Hanson, *The Prussian Evolutions in Actual Engagements; Both in Platoons, Sub, and Grand-Divisions; Explaining All the different Evolutions and Manœuvres, in Firing, Standing, Advancing, and Retreating, . . . to Which Is Added, The Prussian Manual Exercise: Also The Theory and some Practices of Gunnery* (Philadelphia: J. Douglas McDougall, 1775).

171. Brigadier O. F. G. Hogg, *Artillery: Its Origin, Heyday, and Decline* (Hamden, CT: Archon, 1970), 274.

172. Hanson, *Prussian Evolutions*, 21.

173. Ibid.

174. Kent, *French Invasion*, 5-6. See also Francis Parkman, *Montcalm and Wolfe: The French and Indian War* (Boston: Little, Brown, 1884; repr., New York: Da Capo, 1995), 6-10, 12, 21-22.

CHAPTER THREE: WAR IN PENNSYLVANIA, 1754–1760

1. Fred Anderson, *Crucible of War: The Seven Years' War and the Fate of Empire in British North America, 1754-1766* (New York: Knopf, 2000), 28-29. Jesuit-educated Charles-Michel Mouet de Langlade (1728-9-1800-1), the son of Augustin Mouet de Langlade and Ottawa Domitilde, would gain prominence in the service of New France during the Seven Years' War, and later under the British during the Revolutionary War.

2. *Pennsylvania Gazette*, October 27, 1752. Black (actually blue) wampum passed between tribes was, along with the tomahawk, the symbol of war and death. White wampum signified peace.

3. *Colonial Records*, 2:16, 50.

4. William Trent's Journal, cited in Mary Carson Darlington, ed., *History of Colonel Henry Bouquet and the Western Frontiers of Pennsylvania, 1747-1764* (Pittsburgh: privately printed, 1920), 17-40.

5. Alfred Procter James and Charles Morse Stotz, *Drums in the Forest*

(Pittsburgh: Historical Society of Western Pennsylvania, 1958), 21. See also Anderson, *Crucible of War*, 11-32, 124, 134, 158-167.

6. Ensign Ward's Deposition, cited in Darlington, ed., *History of Colonel Henry Bouquet*, 41-47.

7. James and Stotz, *Drums in the Forest*, 124.

8. Anderson, *Crucible of War*, 5-7.

9. *Pennsylvania Gazette*, October 15, 1754.

10. Loxley, "Benjamin Loxley's Account," 6.

11. *Pennsylvania Gazette*, October 18, November 1, and December 6, 1733; December 24, 1735; December 8, 1757. See also *Pennsylvania Archives*, 6th ser., 1:466.

12. Dorwart, *Fort Mifflin*, 23.

13. Loxley, "Benjamin Loxley's Account," 6. See also F. Edward Wright, *Abstracts of Philadelphia County Wills*, 4 vols. (Westminster, MD: Family Line Publications, 1998), 3:213.

14. Houlding, *Fit for Service*, 183. Benjamin Franklin published *Blakeney's Exercise* in 1746, 1747, and 1755. It was published in New York in 1754 and 1756.

15. Anderson, *Crucible of War*, 88.

16. Ibid., 87.

17. Ibid., 87-88.

18. General Edward Braddock to Robert Napier, Fort Cumberland, Wills Creek, June 8, 1755, in Stanley Pargellis, *Military Affairs in North America, 1748-1765: Selected Documents from the Cumberland Papers in Windsor Castle* (New York: D. Appleton-Century Company, 1936), 85.

19. Anderson, *Crucible of War*, 92-93. See also Franklin, *Autobiography*, 117-18.

20. *Pennsylvania Gazette*, July 17, 1755.

21. Ibid.

22. James Smith, *An Account of the Remarkable Occurrences in the Life and Travels of Col. James Smith*, ed. William M. Darlington (Cincinnati: Robert Clark, 1907), 9.

23. *Pennsylvania Gazette*, July 18 and July 24, 1755.

24. Loxley, "Benjamin Loxley's Account," 7.

25. *Pennsylvania Gazette*, August 21, 1755.

26. Loxley, "Benjamin Loxley's Account," 6. See also James and Stotz, *Drums in the Forest*, 87.

27. Loxley, "Benjamin Loxley's Account," 7.

28. Ibid.

29. Ibid. A fusil was a light musket, like a carbine. It was shorter than the standard infantry musket and had a smaller bore.

30. Ibid. See also *Pennsylvania Gazette*, March 25, 1756.

31. *Pennsylvania Gazette*, November 6, 1755. See also John Potter to Richard Peters, November 3 1755, in *Colonial Records*, 6:673-77, and Louis M. Waddell and Bruce D. Bomberger, *The French and Indian War in Pennsylvania, 1753-1763: Fortification and Struggle during the War for Empire* (Harrisburg: Pennsylvania Historical and Museum Commission, 1996), 15.

32. *Pennsylvania Gazette*, November 6, 1755. See also Benjamin Chambers, Falling Spring, "To the Inhabitants of the lower part of the County of Cumberland," *Colonial Records*, 6:675-76.

33. *Colonial Records*, 6:675. See also Waddell and Bomberger, *French and Indian War*, 82.

34. John Armstrong to Robert Hunter Morris, Carlisle, November 3, 1755, in *Colonial Records*, 6:676.

35. *Pennsylvania Archives*, 1st ser., 2:448-49.

36. Ibid., 2:1148-49. See also *Pennsylvania Archives*, Second Ser., 9: 781.

37. John Potter to Richard Peters, November 3, 1755, in *Colonial Records*, 6:674.

38. *Colonial Records*, 5:467-68. See also *Pennsylvania Archives*, 3rd ser., 9:193.

39. John Potter to Richard Peters, November 3, 1755, in *Colonial Records*, 6:674.

40. "A List of Things Sent to General Braddock," June 9, 1755," in *Colonial Records* 6:415. See also "A Letter to Governor Morris from Mr. Conrad Weiser," Heidelberg, June 12, 1755, in *Colonial Records*, 6:443, and Robert Strettell, "To the Gentlemen of the Council," Philadelphia, January 24, 1756, in *Colonial Records*, 6:778.

41. George Croghan, "Memorandum," December 23 1754, in *Colonial Records*, 6:219.

42. "Governor Morris to Governor of Virginia," in *Pennsylvania Archives*, 1st ser., 2:454. See also Governor Morris to General Shirley, in *Pennsylvania Archives*, 1st ser., 2:457.

43. Governor Morris to Conrad Weiser, 1755, in *Pennsylvania Archives*, 1st ser., 2:461-462. See also *Pennsylvania Gazette*, August 7, August 14, and August 31, 1755.

44. *Colonial Records*, 2:392.

45. John Armstrong to Robert Hunter Morris, Carlisle, November 2, 1755, in *Colonial Records*, 6:676.

46. James Burd to Edward Shippen, Shippensburg, November 2, 1755, in *Pennsylvania Archives*, 1st ser., 2:455.

47. *Pennsylvania Archives*, 5th ser., 1:23. See also Waddell and Bomberger, *French and Indian War*, 77.

48. *Pennsylvania Gazette*, June 5, 1761.

49. *Pennsylvania Archives*, 1st ser., 2:511.

50. George Stevenson to Rev. Mr. Smith, York, November 5, 1755, in *Pennsylvania Archives*, 1st ser., 2:466.

51. *Pennsylvania Gazette*, November 6, 1755.

52. *Pennsylvania Archives*, 5th ser., 1:23.

53. Franklin, *Autobiography*, 123.

54. Robert K. Wright Jr., "Nor Is Their Standing Army to Be Despised: The Emergence of the Continental Army as a Military Institution," in Ronald Hoffman and Peter J. Albert, eds., *Arms and Independence: The Military Character of the American Revolution* (Charlottesville: University Press of Virginia, 1984), 167-68. See also John Grenier, *The First Way of War: American*

War Making on the Frontier, 1607-1814 (Cambridge: Cambridge University Press, 2005), 102-14.

55. *Colonial Records*, 6:769.

56. Ibid., 79, 275.

57. Ibid., 275.

58. Ibid.

59. Ibid., 79.

60. Ibid.

61. *Pennsylvania Archives*, 2nd ser., 2:598

62. Hutson, *Pennsylvania Politics*, 25.

63. Ibid., 24-25.

64. Ibid. See also *Pennsylvania Archives*, 5th ser., 1:132.

65. Brooke Hindle, "The March of the Paxton Boys," *William and Mary Quarterly* 3 (October 1946): 479.

66. George Dallas Albert, *Report of the Commission to Locate the Site of the Frontier Forts of Pennsylvania*. 2 vols. (Harrisburg, PA: Clarence M. Busch, 1896), 1:16.

67. *Colonial Records*, 2:392.

68. Ibid.

69. Davidson, *War Comes*, 168-69.

70. Franklin, *Autobiography*, 124. See also "Petition of Inhabitants of Northampton County, October 5 1757," in *Pennsylvania Archives*, 1st ser., 3:284-86.

71. Benjamin Franklin to Governor Robert Hunter Morris, Gnadenhutten, January 25-26, 1756, in *Colonial Records*, 7:15-17.

72. *Colonial Records*, 6:773-74.

73. Smith, *Military Dictionary*, 192.

74. *Colonial Records*, 7:78-79.

75. *Pennsylvania Gazette*, April 29, 1756. See also "Instructions of Captain Dumas, 1756," in *Colonial Records*, 2:600.

76. Edward Shippen to Governor Robert Hunter Morris, Lancaster, April 24, 1756, in *Colonial Records*, 2:642-43. See also *South Carolina Gazette*, June 17, 1756.

77. Edward Shippen to Governor Robert Hunter Morris, Lancaster, April 24, 1756, in *Colonial Records*, 2:643.

78. "A List of Officers in the Province Pay, with the Dates of their Commissions," in *Pennsylvania Archives*, 1st ser., 3:88-89.

79. Newland, *Pennsylvania Militia: Defending the Commonwealth*, 79-80.

80. Ibid.

81. *Pennsylvania Gazette*, August 19, 1756.

82. "Orders and Instructions to E. Saltar, 1756," in *Colonial Records*, 2:604-05.

83. James Young, "A Journal from Reading to the Sundry Forts and Garrisons Along the Northern Frontiers of this Province," in *Pennsylvania Archives*, 1st ser., 2:675-81.

84. Ibid.

85. *Colonial Records*, 7:153, 161.

86. Hutson, *Pennsylvania Politics*, 17-18.

87. Van Doren, *Benjamin Franklin*, 244.

88. Ibid.

89. Ibid., 26.

90. Ibid.

91. Stanley Pargellis, ed., *Military Affairs in North America, 1748-1765: Selected Documents from the Cumberland Papers at Windsor Castle* (New York: D. Appleton–Century, 1936), 263-86.

92. *Pennsylvania Gazette*, June 24, 1756.

93. Joan Pinkerton Gordon, "Barracks in Lancaster: The First Ten Years," *Journal of the Lancaster County Historical Society* 99 (Summer 1997): 82-83.

94. Leach, *Roots*, 92.

95. Ibid.

96. Ibid., 93.

97. Ibid.

98. Watson, *Annals*, 1:415-16. See also Joseph Plumb Martin, *Private Yankee Doodle: Being a Narrative of Some of the Adventures, Dangers and Sufferings of a Revolutionary Soldier* (Hallowell, ME: Glazier, Masters, 1830; repr. Conshohocken, PA: Eastern Acorn, 1998), 246-47.

99. Henry Bouquet, *The Papers of Henry Bouquet*, 19 vols., ed. S. K. Stevens and D. H. Kent (Harrisburg: Pennsylvania Historical and Museum Commission, 1941), 4:146-47. See also *Pennsylvania Gazette*, March 25, 1756.

100. *Colonial Records*, 6:770.

101. Benjamin Loxley, "Bill for Work on Battery, 1756," and "to 54 carriages for Cannon–67.10," Manuscript Collection, Historical Society of Pennsylvania, Philadelphia.

102. Edward Shippen to Joseph Shippen, September 14, 1756, in Balch, *Letters and Papers*, 63.

103. *Colonial Records*, 10:301. See also *Pennsylvania Gazette* May 23, 1751, and August 21, 1766.

104. *Colonial Records*, 10:301. See also *Pennsylvania Gazette*, May 14, 1752.

105. *Colonial Records*, 5:62. See also *Pennsylvania Archives*, 2nd ser., 2:631, 648.

106. "Restoration of the Schuylkill Gun," 199.

107. Wright, *Abstracts of Philadelphia County Wills*, 1:22, 2:81, 3:25, 68, 129. See also *Pennsylvania Archives*, 2nd ser., 2:629, 631, 635, 648-49; *A History of the Schuylkill Fishing Company of the State in Schuylkill, 1732-1788* (Philadelphia: privately printed, 1889), 362; Townsend Ward, "South Second Street and Its Associations," *Pennsylvania Magazine of History & Biography* 5 (1881): 48; and Swanson, *Predators*, 92, 94.

108. Howard I. Chapelle, *The History of the American Sailing Navy: The Ships and Their Development* (New York: Bonanza, 1949), 60.

109. *An Historical Catalogue of the St. Andrew's Society of Philadelphia, With Biographical Sketches of Deceased Members, 1749-1907* (Philadelphia: privately printed, 1907), 209.

110. *History of the Schuylkill Fishing Company*, 358, 361.

111. Horle et al., *Lawmaking and Legislators in Pennsylvania*, 2:73.

112. Loxley, "to 54 carriages for Cannon–67.10."

113. *Pennsylvania Gazette*, November 4, 1756. See also *Colonial Records*, 6:770.

114. Franklin, *Autobiography*, 128.

115. Ibid., 128-29.

116. *Pennsylvania Gazette*, March 4, 1756.

117. Franklin, *Autobiography*, 129.

118. Isaac Norris to Charles Norris, Philadelphia, April 29, 1755, in Hanna, *Benjamin Franklin and Pennsylvania Politics*, 104.

119. *Pennsylvania Gazette*, March 25, 1756. See also Isaac Norris to Charles Norris, Philadelphia, April 29, 1755, in Hanna, *Benjamin Franklin and Pennsylvania Politics*, 104; and Raoul F. Camus, *Military Music of the American Revolution* (Chapel Hill: University of North Carolina Press, 1976), 43.

120. Loxley, "Benjamin Loxley's Account," 1. See also Benjamin Loxley, "The Journal of Benjamin Loxley, 1771-1785," 67, 80, Manuscript Collection, Historical Society of Pennsylvania, Philadelphia. See also Houlding, *Fit for Service*, 183.

121. *Pennsylvania Gazette*, April 8, 1756. See also Franklin, *Autobiography*, 128.

122. *Pennsylvania Gazette*, March 4, 1756.

123. Ibid., August 26, 1756.

124. *Pennsylvania Gazette*, March 17, 1756.

125. Haarmann and Manders, "Pennsylvania Associators," 102.

126. *Pennsylvania Gazette*, March 25, 1756.

127. *Pennsylvania Archives*, 1st ser., 3:19. See also *Pennsylvania Gazette*, May 6, 1756.

128. Colonial Records, 7:64, 70.

129. *Pennsylvania Gazette*, April 1, 1756.

130. Ibid., May 20, 1756.

131. Ibid., August 26, 1756.

132. Ibid.

133. Ibid.

134. Franklin, *Autobiography*, 134.

135. Hutson, *Pennsylvania Politics*, 28.

136. Ibid., 27.

137. Ibid.

138. *Pennsylvania Gazette*, April 8, 1756. See also Franklin, *Autobiography*, 128.

139. Henry Ward to Catherine Johnson, June 28, 1758, in Henry Ward, "Papers," Manuscript Collection, Historical Society of Pennsylvania, Philadelphia. See also Hogg, *Artillery*, 142-43.

140. The worm was a corkscrew-shaped tool used to scour the inside of a cannon barrel. The sponge was a large swab that was dipped in a bucket of water and likewise rammed down the barrel to douse burning cartridge residue.

141. Joseph Moulder, "To John Nixon, Order to Pay Capt. Jos. Moulder 25

pounds for his Purchase of Tin for the Use of the Province, July 10, 1776," Manuscript Collection, Historical Society of Pennsylvania, Philadelphia.

142. Watson, *Annals*, 1:401-02.

143. Benjamin Loxley, "A Return of Artillery, Small Arms & Sundry Stores belonging to this Province Delivered by me, to the Provincial Commissioners on Account of George North, Capt. of our Pennsylvania Artillery Company, Philadelphia, May the 4th 1758," Manuscript Collection, Historical Society of Pennsylvania, Philadelphia.

144. *Colonial Records*, 3:19.

145. Ibid., 19-20. See also "Gov. Morris' Order Y't The Companies Raised On The 1st March 1756 Be Regimented," in *Pennsylvania Archives*, 2nd ser., 2:599-600.

146. "Richard Baird's Deposition, 1758." In *Colonial Records*, 3:396-97.

147. Phillip Davies, "Plan For The Defence of Cumberland Co., 1754," in *Pennsylvania Archives*, 1st ser., 2:289. See also "Distances of Philip Davies From Harris's," in *Pennsylvania Archives*, 1st ser., 2:134; and Waddell and Bomberger, *French and Indian War*, 17, 81.

148. Davies, "Plan," in *Pennsylvania Archives*, 1st ser., 2:289.

149. Ibid.

150. "Distances of Philip Davies From Harris's," in *Pennsylvania Archives*, 1st ser., 2:134.

151. Davies, "Plan," in *Pennsylvania Archives*, 1st ser., 2:289.

152. Ibid.

153. *Pennsylvania Gazette*, May 6, 1756.

154. *Colonial Records*, 2:656-57.

155. Ibid. See also "Petition of Inhabitants of Northampton County, October 5, 1757," in *Pennsylvania Archives*, 1st ser., 3:284-86. A year later, German-speaking inhabitants of Lehigh Township, Northampton County, north of Allentown, petitioned the governor and assembly to "grant us Men and Ammunition, that we may thereby be enabled to defend our selves, our Properties, and the Lives of our Wifes and Children."

156. *Pennsylvania Archives*, 1st ser., 2:757.

157. Ibid.

158. Ibid.

159. George Stevenson to (unknown), 1756, in *Pennsylvania Archives*, 1st ser. 2:775-76.

160. Ibid.

161. Sinn, ed., *Record of Pennsylvania Marriages*, 3:540-43.

162. For a history of the siege of Fort William Henry and the subsequent controversy surrounding its capitulation, see Ian K. Steele, *Betrayals: Fort William Henry & the "Massacre"* (New York: Oxford University Press, 1990).

163. Steele, *Betrayals*, 145.

164. Graydon, *Memoirs*, 22.

165. *Pennsylvania Archives*, 1st ser., 3:120-136.

166. Ibid., 120.

167. Ibid.

168. Ibid., 125.

169. Ibid., 127.

170. Ibid., 128.

171. Ibid.

172. Ibid.

173. Ibid., 132.

174. Ibid., 121.

175. Ibid., 128-9.

176. Ibid., 123.

177. Ibid.

178. Ibid., 126.

179. Ibid., 126-7.

180. Ibid., 126.

181. Ibid., 125.

182. Ibid., 136.

183. *Pennsylvania Gazette*, October 7, 1756.

184. Hutson, *Pennsylvania Politics*, 38.

185. Ibid., 41.

186. *Pennsylvania Gazette*, December 8, 1757.

187. Jenny West, *Gunpowder, Government, and War in the Mid-Eighteenth Century* (Woodbridge, England: Royal Historical Society, Boydell Press, 1991), 114.

188. *Colonial Records*, 8:39.

189. Ibid.

190. John Forbes to James Abercromby, April 20, 1758, in John Forbes, *Writings of General John Forbes Relating to Service in North America*, ed. Alfred Procter James (Menasha, WI: Collegiate Press, 1938), 65.

191. John Forbes to William Denny, Philadelphia, April 20, 1758, in Forbes, *Writings*, 66-67.

192. Ibid.

193. Loxley, "Benjamin Loxley's Account," 7.

194. Ibid.

195. Ibid.

196. Ibid. See also "3 Battalion, Vol. 1," W. O. 54/681, National Archives, Kew, England.

197. Loxley, "Benjamin Loxley's Account," 7.

198. Leach, *Roots*, 122. The issue of rank between regular army officers and provincials was hotly contested throughout the French and Indian War. By 1758, the rule had been amended to accommodate colonial concerns, but in such a way as to cause continued friction between colonists and regulars. On February 6, 1758, General Abercromby made it clear that the most junior major in the British Army outranked any general officer in the provincial service.

199. "3 Battalion."

200. John Forbes to James Abercromby, April 22, 1758, in Forbes, *Writings*, 69.

201. Loxley, "Return of Artillery."

202. George Stevenson to Richard Peters, York, April 30, 1758, in *Pennsylvania Archives*, 1st ser., 3:384.

203. Ibid. See also "Major Burd's Proposal for Protection, 1757," in *Pennsylvania Archives*, 1st ser., 3:101.

204. George Stevenson to Richard Peters, York, May 8, 1758, in *Pennsylvania Archives*, 1st ser., 3:392.

205. George Stevenson to Richard Peters, York, May 15, 1758, in *Pennsylvania Archives*, 1st ser., 3:394. See also "Major Burd's Proposal for Protection, 1757," in *Pennsylvania Archives*, 1st ser., 3:101.

206. "Return of Officers, 6 June 1758," in *Pennsylvania Archives*, 1st ser., 3:410-11.

207. David Jameson to Governor William Denny, York, June 6, 1758, *Pennsylvania Archives*, 1st ser., 3:412.

208. George Stevenson to Richard Peters, York, May 21, 1758, in *Colonial Records*, 3:400.

209. George Stevenson to Richard Peters, York, May 15, 1758, in *Colonial Records*, 3:395.

210. George Stevenson to Richard Peters, York, May 21, 1758, in *Colonial Records*, 3:400.

211. Richard Peters to George Stevenson, Philadelphia, May 3, 1758, in *Pennsylvania Archives*, 1st ser., 3:386. See also George Stevenson to Richard Peters, York, May 15, 1758. *Colonial Records*, 3:395. See also "Petition of Inhabitants of Northampton County, October 5 1757," in *Pennsylvania Archives*, 1st ser., 3:284-86.

212. Anderson, *Crucible of War*, 282.

213. Loxley, "Benjamin Loxley's Account," 14.

CHAPTER FOUR: THE PHILADELPHIA ASSOCIATORS AND THE PAXTON BOYS

1. Bouquet, *Papers*, 4:146.

2. Anderson, *Crucible*, 307-8.

3. James and Stotz, *Drums in the Forest*, 166.

4. Loxley, "Benjamin Loxley's Account," 14. See also James and Stotz, *Drums in the Forest*, 87.

5. Peter D. Keyser, "Memorials of Col. Jehu Eyre," *Pennsylvania Magazine of History and Biography* 3 (1879): 296.

6. Ibid., 296-97.

7. Ibid., 299.

8. Ibid.

9. Ibid.

10. Ibid.

11. Ibid., 300. See also Waddell and Bomberger, *French and Indian War*, 43, 91.

12. Ibid.

13. Smith, *Account of the Remarkable Occurrences,* 5.

14. Ibid., 8-9.

15. Ibid., 16.

16. Ibid., 107.

17. Ibid., 304.

18. Keyser, "Memorials," 306.

19. Ibid.

20. See Peter Silver, *Our Savage Neighbors: How Indian War Transformed Early America* (New York: W. W. Norton, 2008), and Ward, *Breaking the Backcountry,* for a discussion of the impact of the Seven Years' War on eastern Pennsylvania.

21. Keyser, "Memorials," 306.

22. Ibid., 305.

23. Ibid. See also Colin G. Calloway, *The American Revolution in Indian Country: Crisis and Diversity in Native American Communities* (Cambridge: Cambridge University Press, 1995), 5, and Silver, *Our Savage Neighbors.*

24. Keyser, "Memorials," 412.

25. Wilbur R. Jacobs, *The Paxton Riots and the Frontier Theory* (Chicago: Rand McNally, 1967), 2.

26. Hutson, *Pennsylvania Politics,* 94-95.

27. Ibid., 95.

28. Ibid., 66.

29. *Pennsylvania Gazette,* October 7, 1756, and May 30, 1763.

30. Loxley, "Journal of Benjamin Loxley," 22. See also Loxley, "Benjamin Loxley's Account," 4-5.

31. Hutson, *Pennsylvania Politics,* 58-72.

32. Jacob L. Grimm, "Archaeological Investigation of Fort Ligonier, 1960-1965," *Annals of the Carnegie Museum* 42 (1970): 185-86. See also Darlington, *History of Colonel Henry Bouquet,* 142.

33. Albert, *Frontier Forts,* 1:22.

34. James and Stotz, *Drums in the Forest,* 87.

35. Louis Ourry to Henry Bouquet, June 1, 1763, in Darlington, *History of Colonel Henry Bouquet,* 136-38.

36. John Shy, *Toward Lexington: The Role of the British Army in the Coming of the American Revolution* (Princeton, NJ: Princeton University Press, 1965), 114.

37. Darlington, *History of Colonel Henry Bouquet,* 140.

38. Ibid., 142-43.

39. Jennings, *Empire of Fortune,* 446.

40. Henry Bouquet to Captain Ecuyer, June 5, 1763, Bouquet, *Papers,* 148.

41. George Croghan to Henry Bouquet, June 8, 1763, Bouquet, *Papers,* 150-51.

42. Newland, *Defending the Commonwealth,* 94.

43. *Pennsylvania Gazette,* February 9, 1764; May 22 and June 12, 1766; March 31, 1768; and November 21, 1771. See also "3 Battalion, Vol. 1," W. O. 54/681,

National Archives, Kew, England. Hay was promoted to captain on January 1, 1759.

44. Smith, *Account of the Remarkable Occurrences*, 108.

45. Ibid.

46. Hindle, "March of the Paxton Boys," 466.

47. Ibid.

48. Ibid.

49. Ibid., 467.

50. Ibid.

51. Ibid.

52. William Henry to the Reverend John Heckwelder, Lancaster, 1763, in William Henry Egle, ed., *Notes and Queries: Historical Biographical, and Genealogical: Relating Chiefly to Interior Pennsylvania*, 4th ser. (Harrisburg, PA: Harrisburg Publishing, 1895), 2:90-91.

53. Hutson, *Pennsylvania Politics*, 80.

54. Ibid.

55. Ibid., 82.

56. Ibid., 80-81.

57. Hindle, "March of the Paxton Boys," 468.

58. Hutson, *Pennsylvania Politics*, 84.

59. Hindle, "March of the Paxton Boys," 468-69.

60. Ibid., 469.

61. Ibid., 471.

62. Ibid., 472.

63. Ibid.

64. Ibid., 473.

65. Moravian Indian diary, Philadelphia Barracks, January 24, 1764, accessed October 4, 2011, at http://bdhp.moravian.edu/community_records/chris-tianindians/diaires/barracks/1764/translation64.html. See also Watson, *Annals*, 1:416.

66. Moravian Indian diary, January 27, 1764.

67. Moravian Indian diary, January 28, 1764.

68. Hindle, "March of the Paxton Boys," 474.

69. Ibid.

70. Ibid.

71. Ibid.

72. Moravian Indian diary, February 2, 1764.

73. Hindle, "March of the Paxton Boys," 474.

74. Ibid., 475.

75. Moravian Indian diary, February 4, 1764.

76. *Pennsylvania Gazette*, February 9, 1764.

77. Hindle, "March of the Paxton Boys," 475. See also Graydon, *Memoirs*, 40.

78. Haarmann and Manders, "Pennsylvania Associators 1747-1748," 102.

79. Hindle, "March of the Paxton Boys," 476.

80. Graydon, *Memoirs*, 40. "Firedrake" is another term for a fire-breathing dragon. Graydon could also have been engaging in wordplay, because "fire-

drake" also referred to an andiron, a possible allusion to Loxley's pragmatic nature and community-focused lifestyle.

81. Moravian Indian diary, February 4, 1764. See also *Pennsylvania Gazette*, February 9, 1774, and Hindle, "March of the Paxton Boys," 476.

82. Hindle, "March of the Paxton Boys," 475.

83. Ibid.

84. Moravian Indian diary, February 5, 1764.

85. Ibid.

86. Hindle, "March of the Paxton Boys," 476.

87. Ibid., 478.

88. Ibid. The rioters who marched on Philadelphia in 1764 were soon known collectively as the Paxton Boys, after Paxton Township, in western Lancaster County, where many of them lived.

89. Ibid., 480.

90. Ibid., 481.

91. Moravian Indian diary, February 9, 1764.

92. For an account of the aftermath of the Paxton affair, see Alison Olson, "The Pamphlet War over the Paxton Boys," *Pennsylvania Magazine of History and Biography* 123 (January/April 1999): 31-53.

93. Hindle, "March of the Paxton Boys," 482.

94. Smith, *Account of the Remarkable Occurrences*, 109-114. See also *Pennsylvania Gazette*, August 17, 1769.

95. *Pennsylvania Gazette*, October 5, 1769.

96. Hindle, "March of the Paxton Boys," 485.

97. Hutson, "Investigation," 15.

98. Hindle, "March of the Paxton Boys," 478.

99. Gregory T. Knouff, "'An Arduous Service': The Pennsylvania Backcountry Soldiers' Revolution," *Pennsylvania History* 61 (January 1994), 69.

100. Carl Bridenbaugh, *Cities in Revolt: Urban Life in America, 1743-1776* (New York: Capricorn, 1955), 43.

101. Hutson, *Pennsylvania Politics*, 4.

102. Watson, *Annals*, 1:410-12. Watson describes Loxley as "a military chieftain of an earlier day."

103. Hindle, "March of the Paxton Boys," 485.

104. Ibid., 483. See also "George Roberts to Samuel Powel, Philadelphia, May 21, 1765," in "Powel-Roberts Correspondence, 1761-1765," *Pennsylvania Magazine of History and Biography* 18 (1894): 41.

CHAPTER FIVE: THE ASSOCIATORS AND THE MAKING OF REVOLUTION

1. *Pennsylvania Gazette*, June 12, 1766.

2. Pauline Maier, *From Resistance to Revolution: Colonial Radicals and the Development of American Opposition to Britain, 1765-1776* (New York: W. W. Norton, 1991), xviii. See also Edmund S. Morgan, *Benjamin Franklin* (New Haven, CT: Yale University Press, 2002), 92-96, 147-48.

3. "From the Merchants and Traders of Philadelphia, in the Province of Pennsylvania, to the Merchants and Manufacturers of Great Britain (Undated)," Manuscript Collection, Historical Society of Pennsylvania, Philadelphia. See also *Pennsylvania Gazette*, November 7, 1765.

4. Richard Alan Ryerson, *The Revolution Is Now Begun: The Radical Committees of Philadelphia, 1765-1776* (Philadelphia: University of Pennsylvania Press, 1978), 72.

5. "Philadelphia Tea Commissioners, December 2, 1773," Pennsylvania Stamp Act and Non-Importation Resolutions Collection, American Philosophical Society, Philadelphia.

6. *Pennsylvania Gazette*, May 22, 1766.

7. Ibid., March 31, 1768.

8. Loxley, "Benjamin Loxley's Account," 4. See also Loxley, "Journal of Benjamin Loxley," 73.

9. Loxley, "Benjamin Loxley's Account," 3-4.

10. Watson, *Annals of Philadelphia*, 1:411.

11. Loxley, "Benjamin Loxley's Account," 4-5. See also *Pennsylvania Archives*, 2nd ser., 2:155, and Watson, *Annals*, 1:411.

12. *Pennsylvania Gazette*, July 25, 1751. See also Loxley, "Journal of Benjamin Loxley, 36."

13. Loxley, "Benjamin Loxley's Account," 1. See also Loxley, "Journal of Benjamin Loxley," 67, 80.

14. *Pennsylvania Gazette*, May 29, 1755.

15. Loxley, "Benjamin Loxley's Account," 9.

16. Watson, *Annals*, 1:411. See also John W. Jackson, *With the British Army in Philadelphia, 1777-1778* (San Rafael, CA: Presidio, 1979), 109.

17. Franklin, *Autobiography*, 87-88. See also Watson, *Annals*, 1:411.

18. Loxley, "Benjamin Loxley's Account," 14. See also Loxley, "Journal of Benjamin Loxley," 103, and *Pennsylvania Gazette*, May 22 and June 12, 1766.

19. Loxley, "Benjamin Loxley's Account," 6, 14.

20. Ibid., 6.

21. Loxley, "Journal of Benjamin Loxley," 51.

22. Ibid., 97.

23. Ibid.

24. Ibid., 103.

25. Van Doren, *Benjamin Franklin*, 315-16.

26. Ibid., 316-17.

27. Hanna, *Pennsylvania Politics*, 189-91.

28. Van Doren, *Benjamin Franklin*, 527-28.

29. Loxley, "Benjamin Loxley's Account," 4.

30. Watson, *Annals*, 1:416.

31. Shy, *Toward Lexington*, 391.

32. Dorwart, *Fort Mifflin*, 14.

33. Shy, *Toward Lexington*, 391.

34. Maier, *Resistance to Revolution*, 267.

35. Ryerson, *Revolution*, 4.

36. Ibid., 4-5. According to Richard Alan Ryerson, "these legions of political novices formed the first wave of a new kind of political leadership in Pennsylvania, one based less upon inherited wealth and status than upon the driving ambition of self-made men."

37. Fairman Rogers et al., *History of the First Troop Philadelphia City Cavalry from Its Organization November 17, 1774, to Its Centennial Anniversary, November 17, 1874* (Philadelphia: Hallowell, 1909), 305. Committees of Correspondence convened to share information between colonies in order to coordinate organized resistance to Crown policies.

38. *Colonial Records*, 1:598-99.

39. Rogers, *History*, 4-5. See also John Donnaldson, "Donnaldson Narrative," First Troop Philadelphia City Cavalry, Philadelphia.

40. David Conyingham, *The Reminiscences of David Hayfield Conyngham, 1750-1834: A Hero of the Revolution and the Head of the Revolutionary House of Conyngham and Nesbitt* (Wilkes-Barre, PA: Wyoming Historical and Geological Society, 1904), 18. See also John Lardner to Captain R. C. Smith, July 31, 1824, in William S. Stryker, *The Battles of Trenton and Princeton* (Boston: Houghton and Mifflin, 1898), 443.

41. John Lardner to Captain R. C. Smith, July 31, 1824, in Stryker, *Battles of Trenton and Princeton*, 443.

42. William Henry Rawle, "Col. Lambert Cadwalader: A Sketch," *Pennsylvania Magazine of History and Biography* 10 (1886): 3-4.

43. Graydon, *Memoirs*, 118-21.

44. Ibid., 118.

45. John Adams to Isaac Smith Sr., Philadelphia, June 7, 1775, in Lyman H. Butterfield, Wendell D. Garrett, and Marjorie E. Sprague, eds., *Adams Family Correspondence*, 5 vols. (Cambridge, MA: Belknap Press of Harvard University Press, 1963), 1:213.

46. John Adlum, *Memoirs of the Life of John Adlum in the Revolutionary War*, ed. Howard H. Peckham (Chicago: Caxton Club, 1968), vii, 2-4.

47. Adlum, *Memoirs*, vii, 2-4.

48. Ibid., 2-4.

49. Ibid., vii, 2-4.

50. *Pennsylvania Archives*, 2nd ser., 15:344-45.

51. Ibid., 345.

52. Ibid., 14, 238.

53. William Henry Egle, ed., *Pennsylvania in the War of the Revolution: Associated Battalions and Militia, 1775-1783*, 2 vols. (Harrisburg, PA: E. K. Meyers, 1890, 1892), 271-75. See also *Pennsylvania Gazette*, August 28, 1776.

54. Smith, *Military Dictionary*, 66. See also Wright, *Continental Army*, 48.

55. Adlum, *Memoirs*, 3.

56. Whitfield J. Bell Jr., ed., "Addenda to Watson's Annals of Philadelphia: Notes by Jacob Mordecai, 1836," *Pennsylvania Magazine of History and Biography* 98 (April 1974): 146. See also Christopher Marshall, *Extracts from*

the Diary of Christopher Marshall, Kept in Philadelphia and Lancaster, during the American Revolution, 1774-1781, ed. William Duane (Albany, NY: Joel Munsell, 1877), 22.

57. Loxley, "Benjamin Loxley's Account," 1. See also *Pennsylvania Archives*, 2nd ser., 13:559-60.

58. Loxley, "Benjamin Loxley's Account," 9. See also *Pennsylvania Archives*, 2nd ser., 13:559-60.

59. Loxley, "Journal of Benjamin Loxley," 180.

60. Loxley, "Benjamin Loxley's Account," 9.

61. Ryerson, *Revolution*, 124, 233, 268.

62. Ibid.

63. Keyser, "Memorials," 72, 86. See also *Pennsylvania Gazette*, October 10, 1771.

64. *Pennsylvania Gazette*, September 8, 1773.

65. *Pennsylvania Archives*, 6th ser., 1:466.

66. Ryerson, *Revolution*, 272.

67. *Pennsylvania Gazette*, April 12, 1770.

68. Ibid., October 5, 1774.

69. Edward Duffield Neill, "Rev. Jacob Duché: The First Chaplain of Congress," *Pennsylvania Magazine of History and Biography* 2 (1878): 67.

70. *Pennsylvania Archives*, 6th ser., 1:466-71. See also Loxley, "Journal of Benjamin Loxley," 37, 60, 104.

71. Loxley, "Journal of Benjamin Loxley," 104, 161, 194.

72. Peter Force, *American Archives: Fifth Series, Containing a Documentary History of the United States of America from the Declaration of Independence, July 4th 1776, to the Definitive Treaty of Peace with Great Britain, September 3, 1783*, 3 vols. (Washington, DC: M. St. Clair and Peter Force, 1848), 1:787-88.

73. Ibid.

74. Ibid.

75. Loxley, "Journal of Benjamin Loxley," 80. See also Rogers, *History*, 4.

76. Loxley, "Journal of Benjamin Loxley," 80.

77. Ibid., 181. See also *Pennsylvania Gazette*, May 9, 1751, and Bell, "Addenda," 154-55.

78. *Pennsylvania Gazette*, October 3, 1754, October 14, 1756, and June 6, 1757.

79. Loxley, "Journal of Benjamin Loxley," 80.

80. *Pennsylvania Gazette*, January 16, 1772.

81. Egle, ed., *Pennsylvania in the War*, 772.

82. Chapelle, *History of the American Sailing Navy*, 60.

83. Ryerson, *Revolution*, 133. See also Keyser, "Memorials," 418.

84. Loxley, "Journal of Benjamin Loxley," 80.

85. Ryerson, *Revolution*, 133.

86. *Pennsylvania Archives*, 6th ser., 1:466-71. See also *Pennsylvania Gazette*, December 29, 1778.

87. James Lovell to Captain Thomas Procter, Philadelphia, dated November 5, 1776, in William Bell Clark, William James Morgan, and Michael Crawford,

eds., *Naval Documents of the American Revolution*, 11 vols. (Washington, DC: Government Printing Office, 1964-2005), 7:52. See also *Naval Documents of the American Revolution*, 5:673, and Benjamin M. Nead, "A Sketch of General Thomas Procter, with Some Account of the First Pennsylvania Artillery in the Revolution," *Pennsylvania Magazine of History and Biography* 4 (1880): 454.

88. Keyser, "Memorials," 413-14.

89. Loxley, "Journal of Benjamin Loxley," 98. See also Loxley, "Benjamin Loxley's Account," 8.

90. Loxley, "Journal of Benjamin Loxley," 23-25.

91. Ibid., 36.

92. Ibid., 37-42, 44, 45, 47.

93. Loxley, "Benjamin Loxley's Account," 8. See also Keyser, "Memorials," 413-14.

94. Silas Deane to Elizabeth Deane, Philadelphia, June 3, 1775, in *Collections of the New York Historical Society*, 5 vols. (New York: privately printed, 1887-91), 1:54. See also Rawle, "Col. Lambert Cadwalader: A Sketch," *Pennsylvania Magazine of History and Biography* 10 (1886), 4.

95. Elting, ed., *Military Uniforms*, 104.

96. Silas Deane to Elizabeth Deane, Philadelphia, June 3, 1775, in *Collections of the New York Historical Society*, 1:48, 53. See also John Adams to Isaac Smith Sr., Philadelphia, June 7, 1775, in Butterfield et al., eds., *Adams Family Correspondence*, 1:212.

97. "General Bradstreet's Statement December 17, 1764," in Franklin B. Hough, ed., Diary of the Siege of Detroit in the War with Pontiac, Also a Narrative of the Principal Events of the Siege, by Major Robert Rogers; A Plan for Conducting Indian Affairs, by Colonel Bradstreet; and other Authentick Documents, never before printed (Albany, NY: J. Munsell, 1860), 152.

98. Elting, *Military Uniforms*, 104.

99. Hanson, *Prussian Evolutions*, title page.

100. *Pennsylvania Archives*, 6th ser., 1:183. See also Silas Deane to Elizabeth Deane, Philadelphia, June 3, 1775, in *Collections of the New York Historical Society*, 1:53.

101. *Pennsylvania Archives*, 6th ser., 1:183. See also *Pennsylvania Archives*, 6th ser., 1:8-9 for a list of members of the company who were absent as of December 19, 1776. See also John Adams to Isaac Smith Sr., Philadelphia, June 7, 1775, in Butterfield et al., eds., *Adams Family Correspondence*, 1:213.

102. Charles Henry Hart, *Memoir of the Life and Services of Colonel John Nixon 1733-1808* (Philadelphia: Collins, Printer, 1877), 2.

103. Sharp Delany, "Orderly Book of Captain Sharp Delany, Third Battalion Pennsylvania Militia, July 16-25, 1776," *Pennsylvania Magazine of History and Biography* 32 (1908), 302.

104. Elting, *Military Uniforms*, 104.

105. Charles Willson Peale, Philadelphia, August 9, 1775, in Lillian B. Miller,

ed., *The Selected Papers of Charles Willson Peale and His Family*, 3 vols. (New Haven, CT: Yale University Press, 1983), 1:192.

106. *Colonial Records*, 10:315. See also *Virginia Gazette*, June 14, 1776.

107. *Colonial Records*, 10:315-22.

108. *Pennsylvania Archives*, 5th ser., 5:148-54.

109. *Pennsylvania Archives*, 5th ser., 7:4-10. See also *Pennsylvania Gazette*, May 21, 1783; Francis B. Heitman, *Historical Register of Officers of the Continental Army during the War of the Revolution, April 1775 to December 1783* (Washington, DC: Rare Book Shop Publishing, 1914); and Trussell, *Pennsylvania Line*, 148, 150.

110. "Minutes of the Convention of Delegates from the Associated Battalions Held at Lancaster, July 4, 1776," in *Pennsylvania Archives*, 2nd ser., 13:263. See also *Pennsylvania Gazette*, August 22, 1776. Green's was one of two rifle battalions organized in Lancaster County, the other commanded by Colonel John Ferree. Numbered the 10th and 11th in the minutes of the convention, they appear to have also been designated as the 1st and 2nd Battalions of Riflemen of Lancaster County.

111. *Pennsylvania Archives*, 6th ser., 2:618-19. See also Adlum, *Memoirs*, 4-5, 13.

112. Thomas G. Tousey, *Military History of Carlisle and Carlisle Barracks* (Richmond, VA: Dietz, 1939), 62.

113. Ibid., 62-63.

114. *Pennsylvania Archives*, 2nd ser., 14:689-90. See also Smith, *Account of the Remarkable Occurrences*, 132.

115. *Colonial Records*, 10:315-22.

116. Ibid., 10:315-16.

117. *Pennsylvania Gazette*, September 6, 1775.

118. "Accident Report, State House Yard, 1774" Independence National Historical Park Collection, Independence National Historical Park, Philadelphia.

119. Worthington C. Ford, Gaillard Hunt, John C. Fitzpatrick, and Roscoe R. Hill, eds., *Journals of the Continental Congress, 1774-1789* (Washington, DC: Government Printing Office, 1904-1937), 2:156.

120. Loxley, "Benjamin Loxley's Account," 8.

121. Ibid.

122. Frank Moore, *Songs and Ballads of the American Revolution: With Notes and Illustrations* (New York: D. Appleton, 1856), 90-91.

123. *Pennsylvania Archives*, 2nd ser., 13:292, 300, 304. See also *Pennsylvania Archives*, 2nd ser., 13:271-75, and 5th ser., 7:4-10.

124. *Pennsylvania Archives*, 6th ser., 2:262.

125. Charles Henry Hart, "Colonel Robert Lettis Hooper: Deputy Quartermaster General in the Continental Army and Vice President of New Jersey," *Pennsylvania Magazine of History and Biography* 36 (1912), 66-67; and James Armstrong to James Wilson, Carlisle, May 26, 1775, cited in Tousey, *Military History*, 62-63. See also Deuteronomy 34:1-4 (King James Bible).

126. Loxley, "Benjamin Loxley's Account," 9.

127. Ibid., 8.

128. Ibid., 9.

129. Ibid.

130. *Colonial Records,* 10:285.

131. Ibid., 500, 626.

132. *Pennsylvania Gazette,* July 19, 1775.

133. *Colonial Records,* 10:301.

134. Ibid., 285, 296.

135. Ibid., 409.

136. Loxley, "Journal of Benjamin Loxley," 180. See also *Colonial Records,* 10:629-630.

137. *Colonial Records,* 10:327.

138. Ibid.

139. Dorwart, *Fort Mifflin,* 21.

140. *Pennsylvania Gazette,* August 2, 1775.

141. Hanson, *Prussian Evolutions,* frontispiece.

142. Ibid. See also *Pennsylvania Gazette,* December 6, 1775, and John Beatty to William Bradford, Warwick, Bucks County, May 16, 1775, in John William Wallace, *An Old Philadelphian: Colonel William Bradford, the Patriot Printer of 1776: Sketches of His Life* (Philadelphia: Sherman, 1884), 112.

143. Egle, ed., *Pennsylvania in the War,* 1:254-57.

144. *Colonial Records,* 10:321.

145. Ibid., 282.

146. Ibid.

147. Ibid., 279, 282, 358, 399, 420-22, 458, 461, 493, 495, 650.

148. Ibid., 333, 335, 346.

149. Hart, "Colonel Robert Lettis Hooper," 66.

150. *Colonial Records,* 10:506, 650, 761.

151. Ibid., 586-89. See also Delany, "Orderly Book," 303.

152. *Colonial Records,* 10:586-89.

153. Ibid., 626.

154. Ibid., 550.

155. Ibid., 581. See also *Pennsylvania Archives,* 2nd ser., 13:250-51.

156. *Pennsylvania Archives,* 2nd ser., 13:251.

157. Steven Rosswurm, *Arms, Country, and Class: The Philadelphia Militia and the "Lower Sort" during the American Revolution, 1775-1783* (New Brunswick, NJ: Rutgers University Press, 1987), 166-71.

158. Ibid., 94. See also *Pennsylvania Archives,* 2nd ser., 3:135, and *Pennsylvania Archives,* 3rd ser., 14:392.

159. *Pennsylvania Archives,* 2nd ser., 13:505-6.

160. Rosswurm, *Arms, Country,* 66-68.

161. Aaron Wright, "Revolutionary Journal of Aaron Wright, 1775," *Historical Magazine of America* 5 (July 1861): 211.

162. Smith, *Military Dictionary,* 193.

163. *Colonial Records,* 10:406, 416, 466.

164. Wright, *Continental Army,* 259-64.

165. *Colonial Records,* 10:454

166. Wright, *Continental Army,* 57.

167. Ibid., 79.

168. *Pennsylvania Archives,* 2nd ser., 2:57-61.

169. *Colonial Records,* 10:483.

170. William Henry Egle, ed., *Pennsylvania Archives: Journals and Diaries of the War of the Revolution with Lists of Officers and Soldiers, 1775-1783* (Harrisburg, PA: E. K. Meyers, 1893), 943.

171. Egle, ed., *Pennsylvania in the War,* 943.

172. Nead, "Sketch of General Thomas Procter," 455.

173. Trussell, *Pennsylvania Line,* 190.

174. Ibid., 192.

175. Ibid.

176. Ibid., 191-92.

177. *Pennsylvania Archives,* 1st ser., 6:26.

CHAPTER SIX: TO TRENTON AND PRINCETON

1. *Pennsylvania Archives,* 2nd ser., 14:154-64.

2. John Beatty to William Bradford, Warwick, Bucks County, May 16, 1775, in John William Wallace, *An Old Philadelphian, Colonel William Bradford, the Patriot Printer of 1776: Sketches of His Life* (Philadelphia: Sherman, 1884), 112.

3. General George Washington to Major General Artemas Ward, New York, June 16, 1776, in Philander D. Chase et al., eds., *The Papers of George Washington: Revolutionary War Series,* 12 vols. (Charlottesville: University Press of Virginia, 1993), 5:15. See also *Colonial Records,* 10:470, 479, and Wright, *Continental Army,* 341.

4. *Pennsylvania Archives,* 5th ser., 5:843-46. See also Force, *American Archives,* 5th ser., 1:474-75, 600-601, 788. See also Benjamin Loxley, "A Journal of the Campaign to Amboy and Other Parts of the Jersies, 1776," 13, 42, Historical Society of Pennsylvania Manuscript Collection, Philadelphia.

5. *Pennsylvania Archives,* 2nd ser., 10:50.

6. Ibid., 52.

7. Ibid.

8. Rogers, *History,* 5-6.

9. Revolutionary War Pension Files, M-804, roll 858, page 528, National Archives and Records Administration, Washington, DC. See also "Quarter-Master George Lewis Leffler's Unpublished Diary," in Edward W. Spengler, *The Annals of the Families of Caspar, Henry, Baltzer, and George Spengler, Who Settled in York County Respectively in 1729, 1732, 1732, and 1751, With Biographical and Historical Sketches, and Memorabilia of Contemporaneous Local Events* (York, PA: York Daily Publishing, 1896), 298, and Philip J. Schlegel, *Recruits to Continentals: A History of the York County Rifle Company, June 1775-January 1777* (York, PA: York County Historical Society, 1979), 29, 32.

238 + *Notes to Pages 147–153*

10. *Pennsylvania Archives*, 2nd ser., 14:303.

11. Loxley, "Benjamin Loxley's Account," 9.

12. Dorwart, *Fort Mifflin*, 22; see also Loxley, "Benjamin Loxley's Account," 9.

13. Lancelot Théodore Turpin de Crisse, *An Essay on the Art of War: Translated from the French of Count Turpin By Joseph Otway*, 2 vols. (London: A. Hamilton, 1761; repr., Toronto, ON: Gale Eighteenth Century Collections Online, Print Editions, 2011), 1:52, 53.

14. Ibid., 52, 53. See also George Washington to Jonathan Trumbull Sr., Headquarters, New York, July 9, 1776, and George Washington to Colonel Thomas Seymour, New York, July 8, 1776, in Chase et al., eds., *Papers of George Washington*, 5:244, 253, and Oliver L. Spaulding Sr., "The Military Studies of George Washington," *The American Historical* Review (July 1924): 678.

15. Trussell, *Pennsylvania Line*, 165-67. See also *Pennsylvania Archives*, 5th ser., 2:257. The Pennsylvania State Rifle Regiment and the Battalion of Musketry consolidated March 13, 1776, to form the Pennsylvania State Rifle Battalion.

16. Force, *American Archives*, 5th ser., 1:15.

17. *Pennsylvania Archives*, 2nd ser., 13:267.

18. Ibid., 268.

19. Force, *American Archives*, 5th ser., 1:884.

20. Ibid.

21. Wallace, *An Old Philadelphian*, 250-51.

22. *Pennsylvania Archives*, 5th ser., 5:447.

23. Ibid., 844-45.

24. Darlington, *Account of the Remarkable Occurrences*, 132.

25. Richard M. Ketchum, *The Winter Soldiers* (Garden City, NY: Doubleday, 1973), 177-78.

26. *Colonial Records*, 10:626.

27. Benjamin Loxley, "Return of Stores Ordinance, etc. to Complete 1st Co. of Artillery." Manuscript Collection, Historical Society of Pennsylvania, Philadelphia.

28. Loxley, "Journal of the Campaign," 1.

29. Ibid.

30. Force, *American Archives*, 5th ser., 1:787-88.

31. Keyser, *Memorials*, 414-15.

32. Force, *American Archives*, 5th ser., 1:474-75, 600-1, 788. See also Loxley, "Journal of the Campaign," 13, 42.

33. Loxley, "Journal of the Campaign," 5.

34. Loxley, "Journal of Benjamin Loxley," 180.

35. Force, *American Archives*, 5th ser., 1:474-75.

36. Ibid. See also Eric I. Manders, "Notes on Troop Units in the Flying Camp, 1776," *Military Collector and Historian* 26 (Spring 1974): 12.

37. *Colonial Records*, 10:712, 724.

38. Force, *American Archives*, 5th ser., 1:474-75.

39. Loxley, "Journal of the Campaign," 1.

40. Ibid., 4.

41. *Colonial Records*, 11:77.

42. Force, *American Archives*, 5th ser., 1:474-75.

43. Loxley, "Journal of Benjamin Loxley," 207.

44. Loxley, "Benjamin Loxley's Account," 12.

45. Ibid.

46. *Pennsylvania Archives*, 5th ser., 3:943.

47. Nead, "Sketch of General Thomas Procter," 456.

48. Ibid.

49. Egle, ed., *Pennsylvania in the War*, 2:773-76. See also Manders, "Notes," 12.

50. Schlegel, *Recruits to Continentals*, 16-18.

51. Wright, "Revolutionary Journal of Aaron Wright, 1775," 209.

52. Ibid.

53. Ibid.

54. *Pennsylvania Archives*, 2nd ser., 2:248-49.

55. Ibid.

56. General William Livingston to William Hooper, "Camp at Elizabeth Town point 29 August 1776," in Carl E. Prince et al., eds., *The Papers of William Livingston*, 5 vols. (Trenton: New Jersey Historical Commission, 1979-1988), 1:128-129.

57. Rawle, "Col. Lambert Cadwalader," 5.

58. Ketchum, *Winter Soldiers*, 132, 158.

59. Rawle, "Col. Lambert Cadwalader," 10. See also Andreas Wiederhold, "The Capture of Fort Washington, New York, Described by Captain Wiederhold, of the Hessian 'Regiment Knyphausen,'" *Pennsylvania Magazine of History and Biography* 23 (1899): 95.

60. Lambert Cadwalader, "Letter of Lambert Cadwalader to Timothy Pickering on the Capture of Fort Washington," *Pennsylvania Magazine of History and Biography* 25 (1901): 260.

61. Ibid.

62. Wiederhold, "Capture of Fort Washington," 97.

63. Christopher Ward, *The War of the Revolution*, 2 vols. (New York: Macmillan, 1952), 1:269.

64. Cadwalader, "Letter of Lambert Cadwalader," 259-60.

65. Rawle, "Col. Lambert Cadwalader," 6.

66. Ibid., 9. See also *Pennsylvania Archives*, 5th ser., 3:943, Nead, "Sketch of General Thomas Procter," 456, Egle, *Pennsylvania in the War*, 2:773, and Adlum, *Memoirs*, 60.

67. Adlum, *Memoirs*, 53.

68. Rawle, "Col. Lambert Cadwalader," 10.

69. Ward, *War of the Revolution*, 1:271. See also *Adlum, Memoirs*, 66.

70. Ward, *War of the Revolution*, 1:271.

71. Ibid. See also Chadwick Allen Harp, "Remember the Ladies: Women and the American Revolution," *Pennsylvania Heritage Quarterly of the Pennsylvania Historical and Museum Commission* 20 (Spring 1994): 34. See also Adlum, *Memoirs*, 56.

72. Ward, *War of the Revolution*, 1:272.

73. Wiederhold, "Capture of Fort Washington," 95. See also Robert K. Wright Jr., "'Spark of Genius': Bernhard Wilhelm von Wiederhold and His Maps," *The Hessians: Journal of the Johannes Schwalm Historical Association* 12 (2009): 7, 9.

74. William W. Burke and Linnea M. Bass, "Preparing a British Unit for Service in America: The Brigade of Foot Guards, 1776," *Military Collector and Historian* 47, no. 1 (Spring 1995): 2.

75. Ibid., 4.

76. Ibid., 4-6.

77. Wiederhold, "Capture of Fort Washington," 96.

78. Cadwalader, "Letter of Lambert Cadwalader," 260. See also Wright, "Spark of Genius," 9.

79. Wright, "Spark of Genius," 9.

80. Ibid.

81. Ibid.

82. *Pennsylvania Archives*, 5th ser., 3:948.

83. Wright, "Spark of Genius," 9.

84. Wiederhold, "Capture of Fort Washington," 96-97.

85. Ketchum, *Winter Soldiers*, 157. See also Wiederhold, "Capture of Fort Washington," 97.

86. Wiederhold, "Capture of Fort Washington," 97.

87. Ward, *War of the Revolution*, 1:289.

88. Ibid. The strength of Washington's main army at this time fluctuated daily.

89. Ibid., 289-90.

90. Brigadier General James Grant to General Edward Harvey, Brunswick, New Jersey, December 26, 1776, in James Grant, *James Grant of Ballindalloch Papers*, Edinburgh: National Archives of Scotland.

91. Thomas Rodney, *Diary of Captain Thomas Rodney, 1776-1777, with an Introduction by Caesar A. Rodney, His Great-Grandson* (Wilmington: Historical Society of Delaware, 1888), 11.

92. Ibid., 14.

93. Brigadier General James Grant to General Edward Harvey, Brunswick, New Jersey, December 26, 1776, in Grant, *Papers*. See also Ward, *War of the Revolution*, 1:284.

94. Ward, *War of the Revolution*, 1:291.

95. Ibid., 292.

96. Ibid., 291.

97. *Pennsylvania Archives*, 5th ser., 5:16-25. See also "Pennsylvania Committee of Safety Broadside, November 24, 1776." Manuscript Collection, Library of Congress, Washington, DC.

98. Revolutionary War Pension Files, M-804, roll 858, page 528. See also *Pennsylvania Archives*, 6th ser., 2:618-19; George R. Prowell, *History of York County, Pennsylvania*, 2 vols. (Chicago: J. H. Beers, 1907), 1:184; and Adlum, *Memoirs*, 4.

99. William A. Porter, "A Sketch of the Life of General Andrew Porter," *Pennsylvania Magazine of History and Biography* 4 (1880): 263-64. See also Isaac Craig, "Muster-Rolls of Marines and Artillery Commanded by Capt. Isaac Craig, of Pennsylvania, in 1775 and 1778," *Pennsylvania Magazine of History and Biography* 8 (1884): 350; Rogers, *History*, 180; and *Colonial Records*, 10:605.

100. Horace Wells Sellers, "Charles Willson Peale, Artist-Soldier," *Pennsylvania Magazine of History and Biography* 38 (1914): 271.

101. Ibid., 273.

102. Ibid., 271, 273. On December 7, Peale noted that each man had "received his complement of cartridges."

103. Ibid., 273-74.

104. Ibid., 276-77.

105. Ibid., 273, 275, 276.

106. Donnaldson, "Narrative," 7.

107. Rodney, *Diary*, 17.

108. Ward, *War of the Revolution*, 1:292-93.

109. Rodney, *Diary*, 20, 24. See also Chase et al., eds., *Papers of George Washington*, 7:425.

110. *Colonial Records*, 10:605.

111. Keyser, "Memorials," 416.

112. Stryker, *Battles of Trenton and Princeton*, 136.

113. Ward, *War of the Revolution*, 1:294.

114. Rodney, *Diary*, 23.

115. Colonel John Cadwalader to General George Washington, Bristol, Pennsylvania, December 26, 1776, in Chase et al., eds., *Papers of George Washington*, 7:442. See also William Young, "Journal of Sergeant William Young: Written during the Jersey Campaign in the Winter of 1776-7," *Pennsylvania Magazine of History and Biography* 8 (1884): 258-59; and Sellers, "Charles Willson Peale," 276.

116. Sellers, "Charles Willson Peale," 276.

117. George Washington, General Orders, Bucks County, Pennsylvania, December 25, 1776, in Chase et al., eds., *Papers of George Washington*, 7:434.

118. Ibid.

119. Donnaldson, "Narrative," 8.

120. George Washington, General Orders, Bucks County, Pennsylvania, December 25, 1776, in Chase et al., eds., *Papers of George Washington*, 7:404.

121. "Indent of Stores for two Six pounders Sent under the command of Cap. Thomas Forrest To Join the Grand Army at Trentown, Philadelphia December 4th 1776," in Nead, "Sketch of General Thomas Procter," 470.

122. George Washington, General Orders, Bucks County, Pennsylvania, December 25, 1776, in Chase et al., eds., *Papers of George Washington*, 7:434.

123. Ward, *War of the Revolution*, 1:296.

124. Ibid., 1:298.

125. Ibid.

126. Sellers, "Charles Willson Peale," 276.

127. Ward, *War of the Revolution*, 1:300.

128. Ibid.

129. Ketchum, *Winter Soldiers*, 304.

130. Ward, *War of the Revolution*, 1:295.

131. Ibid., 295, 301.

132. Ketchum, *Winter Soldiers*, 311-12.

133. Ward, *War of the Revolution*, 1:300.

134. Ketchum, *Winter Soldiers*, 312.

135. Ward, *War of the Revolution*, 1:300.

136. Ibid., 301.

137. Lieutenant Patrick Duffy to Colonel Thomas Procter, McConkey's Ferry, Pennsylvania, December 28, 1776, in Stryker, *Battles of Trenton and Princeton*, 370.

138. Joseph Reed, "General Joseph Reed's Narrative of the Movements of the American Army in the Neighborhood of Trenton in the Winter of 1776-77," *Pennsylvania Magazine of History and Biography* 8 (1884): 391.

139. Ward, *War of the Revolution*, 1:308.

140. Reed, "General Joseph Reed's Narrative," 399-400.

141. "Annotations by Thomas Peters, 1815." Maryland Historical Society, Baltimore.

142. Ibid.

143. Reed, "General Joseph Reed's Narrative," 399-400.

144. Thomas Sullivan, "The Battle of Princeton," *Pennsylvania Magazine of History and Biography* 32 (1908): 55.

145. Ibid.

146. Ward, *War of the Revolution*, 1:308.

147. Reed, "General Joseph Reed's Narrative," 402.

148. Ibid. See also Young, "Journal of Sergeant William Young," 264.

149. Rodney, *Diary*, 32.

150. Young, "Journal of Sergeant William Young," 263-64. See also "An Account of the Battle of Princeton: From the Pennsylvania Evening Post, Jan. 16, 1777," *Pennsylvania Magazine of History and Biography* 8 (1884): 310.

151. "Account of the Battle of Princeton," 310.

152. Rodney, *Diary*, 33.

153. "Account of the Battle of Princeton," 310.

154. Sullivan, "Battle of Princeton," 55.

155. Rodney, *Diary*, 36.

156. Ibid., 34.

157. Ibid., 36. See also Sullivan, "Battle of Princeton," 55.

158. Rodney, *Diary*, 36. See also Donnaldson, "Narrative," 13-14.

159. Sullivan, "Battle of Princeton," 56.

160. Donnaldson, "Narrative," 13-14. See also Rodney, *Diary*, 37, and Rogers, *History*, 10.

161. George Washington to John Hancock, Pluckamin, New Jersey, January 5, 1777, in Chase et al., eds., *Papers of George Washington*, 7:521.

162. "Account of the Battle of Princeton," 312.

163. Ibid., 274. See also Brigadier General James Grant to Richard Rigby, Brunswick, New Jersey, January 15, 1777, in Grant, *Papers*.

164. Young, "Journal of Sergeant William Young," 266, 269-70.

165. Ketchum, *Winter Soldiers*, 360.

166. Lieutenant Patrick Duffy to Colonel Thomas Procter, McConkey's Ferry, Pennsylvania, December 28, 1776, in Stryker, *Battles of Trenton and Princeton*, 370.

167. "Letter from the American Army," January 7, 1777, in Stryker, *Battles of Trenton and Princeton*, 466.

168. Donnaldson, "Narrative," 8.

169. "George Washington to Captain Samuel Morris, Morristown, New Jersey, 23 January 1777," Independence National Historical Park Collection, Independence National Historical Park, Philadelphia.

170. Rodney, *Diary*, 42, 48. See also Joseph Reed to Thomas Bradford, Morristown, January 24, 1777, in William B. Reed, *President Reed of Pennsylvania: A Reply to Mr. George Bancroft and Others* (Philadelphia: Howard Challen, 1867), 109.

171. Joseph Reed to Thomas Bradford, Morristown, January 24, 1777, in Reed, *President Reed*, 109-10.

CONCLUSION

1. Watson, *Annals of Philadelphia*, 1:401-2.

2. Ibid., x.

3. Lewis Clark Walkinshaw, *Annals of Southwestern Pennsylvania* (New York: Lewis Historical Publishing, 1939), 2:315.

4. Watson, *Annals of Philadelphia*, 1:411-12. See also Loxley, "Journal of Benjamin Loxley," 246.

5. Silas Deane to Elizabeth Deane, Philadelphia, June 3, 1775, in *Collections of the New York Historical Society*, 1:48, 53.

6. Ibid., 29, 54, 55.

7. Ibid., 54.

8. Ibid.

9. John Adams to Isaac Smith Sr., Philadelphia, June 7, 1775, in Butterfield et al., eds., *Adams Family Correspondence*, 1:212.

10. John Adams to Abigail Adams, Philadelphia, June 10, 1775, in Butterfield et al., eds., *Adams Family Correspondence*, 1: 213-14.

11. Ibid.

12. Silas Deane to Elizabeth Deane, Philadelphia, June 3, 1775, 1:53. See also Loxley, "Benjamin Loxley's Account," 9.

13. *Pennsylvania Evening Post*, June 22, 1775.

14. Nead, "Sketch of General Thomas Procter," 458.

15. Wright, *Continental Army*, 341.

16. Trussell, *Pennsylvania Line*, 206.

17. Martin, *Private Yankee Doodle*, 132-33.

18. Wright, *Continental Army*, 340.

19. Keyser, "Memorials," 420-21.

20. Trussell, *Pennsylvania Line*, vii.

21. Ibid., 203.

22. "Memorial of the First Company of Militia Artillery, 1779," in *Pennsylvania Archives*, 1st ser., 7:392-93.

23. "103d Engineer Battalion Unit History Worksheet," United States Army Center of Military History, Fort Lesley J. McNair, Washington, DC.

24. Newland, *Pennsylvania Militia: Defending the Commonwealth*, 162.

25. Rogers, *History*, 180.

26. Ibid.

27. Donnaldson, "Narrative," 1.

28. Newland, *Pennsylvania Militia: Defending the Commonwealth*, vi.

29. Holst, "Portrait of the Battle of Princeton," 146. See also Loxley, "Journal of Benjamin Loxley," 51, 173, and Loxley, "Benjamin Loxley's Account," 9.

APPENDIX

1. Wright, *Abstracts of Philadelphia County Wills*, 4:17.

2. This regiment had ten companies. Colonel Armstrong raised a company that was commanded by a lieutenant when the regiment took to the field.

3. *Pennsylvania Gazette*, June 5, 1761.

4. George Stevenson to Rev. Mr. Smith, York, November 5, 1755, in *Pennsylvania Archives*, 1st ser., 2:466.

5. *Pennsylvania Archives*, 2nd ser., 2:521. See also *Pennsylvania Gazette*, April 8, 1756.

6. *Pennsylvania Gazette*, April 8, 1756.

7. *Pennsylvania Archives*, 1st ser., 3:19.

8. Ibid.

9. Ibid.

10. Ibid.

11. *Colonial Records*, 10:301.

12. *Pennsylvania Gazette*, March 25, 1756. See also *Colonial Records*, 7:62.

13. The enlisted men's ranks are unknown. Following the conventions of the time, at least one man might have been a sergeant, and two might have been corporals.

14. *Pennsylvania Gazette*, February 9, 1764.

15. Bell, ed., "Addenda," 146. See also Marshall, *Extracts from the Diary*, 22.

16. Delany, "Orderly Book," 302.

17. *Pennsylvania Archives*, 6th ser., 1:9-10.

18. Ibid., 11.

19. Delany, "Orderly Book," 302.

20. Ibid.

21. Ibid., 305.

22. Ibid., 302.

23. Ibid.

24. *Pennsylvania Archives*, 2nd ser., 13:257-58.

25. Trussell, *Pennsylvania Line*, 165-67. See also *Pennsylvania Archives*, 5th ser., 2:257.

26. Silas Deane to Elizabeth Deane, Philadelphia, June 3, 1775, 1:53.

27. Ibid., 48.

28. Ibid.

29. Ibid.

30. *Pennsylvania Evening Post*, June 22, 1775.

31. *Pennsylvania Gazette*, July 26, 1775.

32. *Colonial Records*, 10:301.

33. Rogers, *History*, 5.

34. *Colonial Records*, 10:483.

35. Ibid., 315. See also *Virginia Gazette*, June 14, 1776.

36. *Colonial Records*, 10:649. See also Bell, ed., "Addenda," 147.

37. Elting, ed., *Military Uniforms*, 104.

38. Hugh Mercer to Benjamin Randolph, John Dunlap, James Hunter, John Lardner, Thomas Peters, Thomas Leiper, Amboy, New Jersey, August 26, 1776, First Troop Philadelphia City Cavalry, Philadelphia. See also Payroll, Light Horse of Philadelphia, August 9–August 20, 1776, First Troop Philadelphia City Cavalry, Philadelphia.

39. *Pennsylvania Archives*, 1st ser., 5:528.

40. Rodney, *Diary*, 28.

41. *Pennsylvania Archives*, 1st ser., 5:159-60.

42. Bell, ed., "Addenda," 147.

43. Rodney, *Diary*, 22, 23, 32, 39.

44. Ibid., 22.

45. Ibid., 33, 35, 39.

Bibliography

MANUSCRIPTS, LETTERS, AND UNPUBLISHED TRACTS

Biddle Family Papers. University of Delaware Library, Special Collections Department, Newark.

First Troop Philadelphia City Cavalry, Philadelphia, Pennsylvania.

"From the Merchants and Traders of Philadelphia, in the Province of Pennsylvania, to the Merchants and Manufacturers of Great Britain (Undated)." Historical Society of Pennsylvania Manuscript Collection, Philadelphia.

Grant, James. "James Grant of Ballindalloch Papers." National Archives of Scotland, Edinburgh.

Independence National Historical Park Collection, Independence National Historical Park, Philadelphia.

Loxley, Benjamin. Correspondence and papers. Manuscript Collection. Historical Society of Pennsylvania, Philadelphia.

Moulder, Joseph. "To John Nixon, Order to Pay Capt. Jos. Moulder 25 pounds for his Purchase of Tin for the Use of the Province, July 10, 1776." Manuscript Collection. Historical Society of Pennsylvania, Philadelphia.

"Pennsylvania Committee of Safety Broadside, November 24, 1776." Manuscript Collection. Library of Congress, Washington, DC.

Pennsylvania Stamp Act and Non-Importation Resolutions Collection. American Philosophical Society, Philadelphia.

Peters, Thomas. "Annotations by Thomas Peters, 1815." Maryland Historical Society, Baltimore.

Read, Joseph. "To Joseph Stiles for 750 Arms from Board of War, September 15, 1779." Manuscript Collection. Historical Society of Pennsylvania, Philadelphia.

Revolutionary War Pension Files, Roll 858. National Archives and Records Administration, Washington, DC.

"3 Battalion, Vol. 1," W. O. 54/681, National Archives, Kew, England.

Wright, Robert K., Jr. "Massachusetts Militia Roots: A Bibliographic Study," 1986. Massachusetts National Guard Museum and Archives, Worcester.

PUBLISHED PRIMARY SOURCES

Adlum, John. *Memoirs of the Life of John Adlum in the Revolutionary War*. Edited by Howard H. Peckham. Chicago: Caxton Club, 1968.

"An Account of the Battle of Princeton: From the Pennsylvania Evening Post, Jan. 16, 1777." *Pennsylvania Magazine of History and Biography* 8 (1884): 310-12.

Archives of Maryland. 66 vols. Baltimore: Maryland Historical Society, 1883-1954.

Balch, Thomas, ed. *Letters and Papers Relating Chiefly to the Provincial History of Pennsylvania, With Some Notices of the Writers*. Philadelphia: Crissy and Markley, 1855.

Bartram, John. *Observations on the Inhabitants, Climate, Soil, Rivers, Productions, Animals, and other matters worthy of Notice Made By Mr. John Bartram in his Travels from Pensilvania to Onondago, Oswego, and Lake Ontario, in Canada To which is annex'd, a curious Account of the Cataracts at Niagara, by Mr. Peter Kalm, A Swedish Gentleman who travelled there*. London: J. Whiston and B. White, 1751.

Bell, Whitfield J., Jr., ed. "Addenda to Watson's Annals of Philadelphia: Notes by Jacob Mordecai, 1836." *Pennsylvania Magazine of History and Biography* 98 (April 1974): 131-70.

Bouquet, Henry. *The Papers of Henry Bouquet*. 19 vols. Edited by S. K. Stevens and D. H. Kent. Harrisburg: Pennsylvania Historical and Museum Commission, 1941.

Brock, K. Alonzo, ed. "The Journal of William Black, 1744." *Pennsylvania Magazine of History and Biography* 1 (1877): 233-49.

Butterfield, Lyman H., Wendell D. Garrett, and Marjorie E. Sprague, eds. *Adams Family Correspondence*. 5 vols. Cambridge, MA: Belknap Press of Harvard University Press, 1963.

Cadwalader, Lambert. "Letter of Lambert Cadwalader to Timothy Pickering on the Capture of Fort Washington." *Pennsylvania Magazine of History and Biography* 25 (1901): 259-62.

Calvert Papers Number One. Baltimore: Peabody Publication Fund, 1889.

Chase, Philander D., W. W. Abbot, Dorothy Twohig, Beverly H. Runge, Beverly S. Kirsch, Debra B. Kessler, Frank E. Grizzard Jr., et al., eds. *The Papers of George Washington: Revolutionary War Series*. 12 vols. Charlottesville: University Press of Virginia, 1993.

Clark, William Bell, William James Morgan, and Michael Crawford, eds. *Naval Documents of the American Revolution.* 11 vols. Washington, DC: Government Printing Office, 1964-2005.

Collections of the New York Historical Society. 5 vols. New York: privately printed, 1887-91.

Colonial Records of Pennsylvania, The Minutes of the Provincial Council of Pennsylvania, From the Organization to the Termination of the Proprietary Government. 16 Vols. Harrisburg, PA: Theo. Fenn, 1851.

Conyingham, David. *The Reminiscences of David Hayfield Conyngham, 1750-1834: A Hero of the Revolution and the Head of the Revolutionary House of Conyngham and Nesbitt.* Wilkes-Barre, PA: Wyoming Historical and Geological Society, 1904.

Craig, Isaac. "Muster-Rolls of Marines and Artillery Commanded by Capt. Isaac Craig, of Pennsylvania, in 1775 and 1778." *Pennsylvania Magazine of History and Biography* 8 (1884): 350-54.

Crisse, Lancelot Théodore Turpin de. *An Essay on the Art of War: Translated from the French of Count Turpin By Joseph Otway.* 2 vols. London: A. Hamilton, 1761. Reprint, Toronto, ON: Gale Eighteenth Century Collections Online, Print Editions, 2011.

Delany, Sharp. "Orderly Book of Captain Sharp Delany, Third Battalion Pennsylvania Militia, July 16-25, 1776." *Pennsylvania Magazine of History and Biography* 32 (1908): 302-08.

Egle, William Henry. *Notes and Queries: Historical Biographical, and Genealogical: Relating Chiefly to Interior Pennsylvania.* 4th ser. Harrisburg, PA: Harrisburg Publishing (1895).

———, ed. *Pennsylvania Archives: Journals and Diaries of the War of the Revolution with Lists of Officers and Soldiers, 1775-1783.* Harrisburg, PA: E. K. Meyers, 1893.

———. *Pennsylvania in the War of the Revolution: Associated Battalions and Militia, 1775-1783.* 2 vols. Harrisburg, PA: E. K. Meyers, 1890, 1892.

Forbes. John. *Writings of General John Forbes Relating to Service in North America.* Edited by Alfred Procter James. Menasha, WI: Collegiate Press, 1938.

Force, Peter. *American Archives: Fifth Series, Containing a Documentary History of the United States of America from the Declaration of Independence, July 4th 1776, to the Definitive Treaty of Peace with Great Britain, September 3, 1783.* 3 vols. Washington, DC: M. St. Clair and Peter Force, 1848.

Ford, Worthington C., Gaillard Hunt, John C. Fitzpatrick, and Roscoe R. Hill, eds. *Journals of the Continental Congress, 1774-1789.* Washington, DC: Government Printing Office, 1904-1937.

Franklin, Benjamin. *Benjamin Franklin's Autobiography.* Edited by J. A. Leo LeMay and P. M. Zall. New York: W. W. Norton, 1986.

———. *The Papers of Benjamin Franklin.* Edited by Leonard W. Labaree, Whitfield J. Bell, Helen C. Boatfield, Helene H. Fineman, Ralph L. Ketcham, James H. Hutson, William B. Willcox, et al. eds. 28 vols. New Haven, CT: Yale University Press, 1960.

George, Slaughton, Benjamin M. Nead, and Thomas McCamant, eds. *Charter to William Penn and the Laws of the Province of Pennsylvania, Passed Between the Years 1682 and 1700.* Harrisburg, PA: Lane S. Hart, 1879.

Graydon, Alexander. *Memoirs of a Life, Chiefly Passed in Pennsylvania, Within the Last Sixty Years.* Edinburgh: privately printed, 1822.

Hanson, Thomas. *The Prussian Evolutions in Actual Engagements; Both in Platoons, Sub, and Grand-Divisions; Explaining All the different Evolutions and Manœuvres, in Firing, Standing, Advancing, and Retreating, . . . to Which Is Added, The Prussian Manual Exercise: Also The Theory and some Practices of Gunnery.* Philadelphia: J. Douglas McDougall, 1775.

Hanzelet Lorrain, Jean Appier. *La Pyrotechnie de Hanzelet Lorrain.* Grenoble: Edition des 4 Siegneurs, 1971.

Hough, Franklin B., ed. *Diary of the Siege of Detroit in the War with Pontiac, Also a Narrative of the Principal Events of the Siege, by Major Robert Rogers; A Plan for Conducting Indian Affairs, by Colonel Bradstreet; and other Authentick Documents, never before printed.* Albany, NY: J. Munsell, 1860.

Humphrey, John T. *Pennsylvania Births: Philadelphia County, 1766-1780.* Washington, DC: Humphrey, 1995.

Kelly, Samuel. *Samuel Kelly: An Eighteenth Century Seaman Whose Days Have Been Few and Evil, to Which Is Added Remarks, etc., on Places He Visited during His Pilgrimage in This Wilderness.* Edited by Crosbie Garstin. New York: Frederick A. Stokes, 1925.

Klepp, Susan E., and Billy G. Smith, eds. *The Infortunate: The Voyage and Adventures of William Moraley, an Indentured Servant.* University Park: Pennsylvania State University Press, 1992.

Marshall, Christopher. *Extracts from the Diary of Christopher Marshall, Kept in Philadelphia and Lancaster, during the American Revolution, 1774-1781.* Edited by William Duane. Albany, NY: Joel Munsell, 1877.

Martin, Joseph Plumb. *Private Yankee Doodle: Being a Narrative of Some of the Adventures, Dangers and Sufferings of a Revolutionary Soldier.* Hallowell, ME: Glazier, Masters, 1830. Reprint, Conshohocken, PA: Eastern Acorn, 1998.

McCrea, Kenneth D., ed. *Pennsylvania Land Applications.* 2 vols. Philadelphia: Genealogical Society of Pennsylvania, 2003.

Miller, Lillian B., ed. *The Selected Papers of Charles Willson Peale and His Family.* 3 vols. New Haven, CT: Yale University Press, 1983.

Müller, John. *A Treatise of Artillery, 1780.* London: 1780. Reprint, Bloomfield, ON: Museum Restoration Service, 1977.

Pargellis, Stanley. *Military Affairs in North America, 1748-1765: Selected Documents from the Cumberland Papers in Windsor Castle.* New York: D. Appleton-Century Company, 1936.

Parsons, Jacob Coxe, ed. *Extracts from the Diary of Jacob Hiltzheimer of Philadelphia 1765-1798.* Philadelphia: William Fell, 1893.

Penn, William. *The Papers of William Penn.* Edited by Richard S. Dunn, Mary Maples Dunn, Scott M. Wilds, Richard A. Ryerson, Jean R. Soderland, and Ned C. Landsman. 5 vols. Philadelphia: University of Pennsylvania Press, 1981.

Pennsylvania Archives. 9 series, 119 vols. Harrisburg, PA: Theo. Fenn, 1852-1935.

"Powel-Roberts Correspondence, 1761-1765." *Pennsylvania Magazine of History and Biography* 18 (1894): 35-42.

Prince, Carl E., Dennis P. Ryan, Pamela B. Schafler, and Donald W. White, eds. *The Papers of William Livingston.* 5 vols. Trenton: New Jersey Historical Commission, 1979-1988.

R., Sergeant. "The Battle of Princeton." *Pennsylvania Magazine of History and Biography* 20 (1896): 515-19.

Reed, Joseph. "General Joseph Reed's Narrative of the Movements of the American Army in the Neighborhood of Trenton in the Winter of 1776-77." *Pennsylvania Magazine of History and Biography* 8 (1884): 391-402.

Regulations for the Prussian Infantry, Translated from the Original, With Augmentations and Alterations made by the King of Prussia Since the Publication of the Last Edition, To Which is Added the

Prussian Tactick; Being a Detail of the Grand Manoeuvre As Performed by the Prussian Armies. J. Nourse, 1759. Reprint, New York: Greenwood, 1968.

Rodney, Thomas. *Diary of Captain Thomas Rodney, 1776-1777, with an Introduction by Caesar A. Rodney, His Great-Grandson.* Wilmington: Historical Society of Delaware, 1888.

Sinn, John Blair, ed. *Record of Pennsylvania Marriages.* 3 vols. Harrisburg, PA: E. K. Meyers, 1890.

Smith, George. *An Universal Military Dictionary: A Copious Explanation of the Technical Terms &c. Used in the Equipment, Machinery, Movements, and Military Operations of an Army.* London: J. Millan, 1779. Reprint, Ottawa, ON: Museum Restoration Service, 1969.

Smith, James. *An Account of the Remarkable Occurrences in the Life and Travels of Col. James Smith.* Edited by William M. Darlington. Cincinnati: Robert Clark, 1907.

Sullivan, Thomas. "The Battle of Princeton." *Pennsylvania Magazine of History and Biography* 32 (1908): 54-57.

Wiederhold, Andreas. "The Capture of Fort Washington, New York, Described by Captain Wiederhold, of the Hessian 'Regiment Knyphausen.'" *Pennsylvania Magazine of History and Biography* 23 (1899): 95-97.

Wright, Aaron. "Revolutionary Journal of Aaron Wright, 1775." *Historical Magazine of America* 5 (July 1861): 208-12.

Young, William. "Journal of Sergeant William Young: Written during the Jersey Campaign in the Winter of 1776-7." *Pennsylvania Magazine of History and Biography* 8 (1884): 255-78.

SECONDARY SOURCES

Albert, George Dallas. *Report of the Commission to Locate the Site of the Frontier Forts of Pennsylvania.* 2 vols. Harrisburg, PA: Clarence M. Busch, 1896.

Anderson, Fred. *Crucible of War: The Seven Years' War and the Fate of Empire in British North America, 1754-1766.* New York: Knopf, 2000.

———. *A People's Army: Massachusetts Soldiers and Society in the Seven Years War.* New York: W. W. Norton, 1984.

An Authentic Historical Memoir of the Schuylkill Fishing Company of the State in Schuylkill from its Establishment on that Romantic Stream, Near Philadelphia, in the Year 1732, to the Present Time, By a Member. Philadelphia: Judah Dobson, 1830.

Bailey, DeWitt. "British Military Small Arms in North America, 1755-1783." *American Society of Arms Collectors Bulletin* 71 (1994): 3-14.

Bakeless, John. *Turncoats, Traitors, and Heroes.* Philadelphia: J. B. Lippincott, 1959.

Blumin, Stuart M. *The Emergence of the Middle Class: Social Experience in the American City, 1760-1900.* Cambridge: Cambridge University Press, 1989.

Boatner, Mark M. *Encyclopedia of the American Revolution.* Mechanicsburg, PA: Stackpole, 1994.

Bridenbaugh, Carl. *Cities in Revolt: Urban Life in America, 1743-1776.* New York: Capricorn, 1955.

Brown, M. L. *Firearms in Colonial America: The Impact on History and Technology, 1492–1792.* Washington, DC: Smithsonian Institution Press, 1980.

Brumwell, Stephen. *Redcoats: The British Soldier and the War in the Americas, 1755-1763.* Cambridge: Cambridge University Press, 2002.

Burke, William W., and Linnea M. Bass. "Preparing a British Unit for Service in America: The Brigade of Foot Guards, 1776." *Military Collector and Historian* 47, No. 1 (Spring 1995): 2-11.

Calloway, Colin G. *The American Revolution in Indian Country: Crisis and Diversity in Native American Communities.* Cambridge: Cambridge University Press, 1995.

Camus, Raoul F. *Military Music of the American Revolution.* Chapel Hill: University of North Carolina Press, 1976.

Carter, Velma Thorne. *Penn's Manor of Springfield: An Historical Presentation Written under the Auspices of the Bicentennial Committee.* Springfield Township, PA: Springfield Township Bicentennial Committee, 1976.

Chapelle, Howard I. *The History of American Sailing Ships.* New York: Bonanza, 1935.

———. *The History of the American Sailing Navy: The Ships and Their Development.* New York: Bonanza, 1949.

Clark, Murtie June. *Colonial Soldiers of the South, 1732-1774.* Baltimore: Genealogical Publishing, 1983.

Clarke, William P. *Official History of the Militia and National Guard of Pennsylvania from the Earliest Period of Record to the Present Time.* Philadelphia: Captain Charles J. Hendler, 1909.

"Contemporaneous Account of the Battle of Trenton." *Pennsylvania Magazine of History and Biography* 10 (1886): 203-4.

Coolidge, Guy Omeron. *The French Occupation of the Champlain Valley from 1609 to 1759.* Fleischmanns, NY: Purple Mountain, 1999.

Cress, Lawrence Delbert. *Citizens in Arms: The Army and the Militia in American Society to the War of 1812.* Chapel Hill: University of North Carolina Press, 1982.

Crist, Robert Grant, ed. *The First Century: A History of the 28th Infantry Division.* Harrisburg, PA: Stackpole, 1979.

Cunliffe, Marcus. *Soldiers and Civilians: The Martial Spirit in America, 1775-1865.* Boston: Little, Brown, 1968.

Darling, Anthony D. *Redcoat and Brown Bess.* Alexandria Bay, NY: Museum Restoration Service, 1971.

Darlington, Mary C., ed. *History of Colonel Henry Bouquet and the Western Frontiers of Pennsylvania, 1747–1764.* Pittsburgh: privately printed, 1920.

Davidson, Robert L. D. *War Comes to Quaker Pennsylvania, 1682-1756.* New York: Columbia University Press, 1957.

De Loria, Philip J. *Playing Indian.* New Haven, CT: Yale University Press, 1998.

Dorwart, Jeffery M. *Fort Mifflin of Philadelphia: An Illustrated History.* Philadelphia: University of Pennsylvania Press, 1998.

Downey, Fairfax. *Sound of the Guns: The Story of American Artillery from the Ancient and Honourable Company to the Atom Cannon and Guided Missile.* New York: David McKay, 1955.

Elting, John, ed. *Military Uniforms in America: The Era of the American Revolution, 1755-1795.* San Rafael, CA: Presidio, 1974.

Ent, Uzal W., ed. *The First Century: A History of the 28th Infantry Division.* Harrisburg, PA: Stackpole, 1979.

Evans, Graham, and Jeffrey Newnham. *The Penguin Dictionary of International Relations.* London: Penguin, 1998.

Faragher, John Mack. *Daniel Boone: The Life and Legend of an American Pioneer.* New York: Henry Holt, 1992.

Fischer, David Hackett. *Albion's Seed: Four British Folkways in America.* New York: Oxford University Press, 1989.

Gannon, Barbara A. "The Lord is a Man of War, The God of Love and Peace: The Association Debate, Philadelphia, 1747-1748," *Pennsylvania History* 65 (Winter 1998): 41-61.

Gipson, Lawrence Henry. *The British Empire before the American Revolution.* 14 vols. New York: Knopf, 1936-70.

Godcharles, Frederic A. *Pennsylvania: Political, Governmental, Military and Civil.* New York: American Historical Society, 1933.

Gordon, Joan Pinkerton. "Barracks in Lancaster: The First Ten Years." *Journal of the Lancaster County Historical Society* 99 (Summer 1997): 80-93.

Grenier, John. *The First Way of War: American War Making on the Frontier, 1607-1814.* Cambridge: Cambridge University Press, 2005.

Griffith, Sally F. "Order, Discipline, and a few Cannon: Benjamin Franklin, the Association, and the Rhetoric and Practice of Boosterism." *Pennsylvania Magazine of History & Biography* 116 (April 1992): 131-55.

Grimm, Jacob L. "Archaeological Investigation of Fort Ligonier, 1960-1965." *Annals of the Carnegie Museum* 42 (1970): 185-86.

Haarmann, Albert W., and Eric I. Manders. "Pennsylvania Associators 1747-1748." *Military Collector and Historian* 33 (Fall 1981): 100-102.

Hanna, Charles A. *The Wilderness Trail of the Ventures and Adventures of the Pennsylvania Traders on the Allegheny Path, With Some New Annals of the Old West, and the Records of Some Strong Men and Some Bad Ones.* 2 vols. New York: G. P. Putnam's Sons, 1911.

Hanna, William S. *Benjamin Franklin and Pennsylvania Politics.* Palo Alto, CA: Stanford University Press, 1964.

Harp, Chadwick Allen. "Remember the Ladies: Women and the American Revolution." *Pennsylvania Heritage Quarterly of the Pennsylvania Historical and Museum Commission* 20 (Spring 1994): 33-37.

Hart, Charles Henry. "Colonel Robert Lettis Hooper: Deputy Quartermaster General in the Continental Army and Vice President of New Jersey." *Pennsylvania Magazine of History and Biography* 36 (1912), 66-67.

———. *Memoir of the Life and Services of Colonel John Nixon 1733-1808.* Philadelphia: Collins, Printer, 1877.

Hassler, Warren W., Jr. *With Shield and Sword: American Military Affairs, Colonial Times to the Present.* Ames: Iowa State University Press, 1982.

Heitman, Francis B. *Historical Register of Officers of the Continental Army during the War of the Revolution, April 1775 to December 1783.* Washington, DC: Rare Book Shop Publishing, 1914.

Hindle, Brooke. "The March of the Paxton Boys." *The William and Mary Quarterly* 3 (October 1946): 461-86.

An Historical Catalogue of the St. Andrew's Society of Philadelphia, With Biographical Sketches of Deceased Members, 1749-1907. Philadelphia: privately printed, 1907.

A History of the Schuylkill Fishing Company of the State in Schuylkill, 1732-1788. Philadelphia: privately printed, 1889.

Hoffman, Ronald, and Peter J. Albert, eds. *Arms and Independence: The Military Character of the American Revolution.* Charlottesville: University Press of Virginia, 1984.

Hogan, Michael J., and Thomas G. Paterson, eds. *Explaining the History of American Foreign Relations.* Cambridge: Cambridge University Press, 1991.

Hogg, Brigadier O. F. G. *Artillery: Its Origin, Heyday, and Decline.* Hamden, CT: Archon, 1970.

Holst, Donald W. "A Portrait of the Battle of Princeton." *Military Collector and Historian* 37 (Fall 1985): 146-52.

Horle, Craig, Joseph S. Foster, and Laurie M. Wolfe, eds. *Lawmaking and Legislators in Pennsylvania: A Biographical Dictionary.* 2 vols. Philadelphia: University of Pennsylvania Press, 1997.

Houlding, John A. *Fit for Service: The Training of the British Army, 1715-1795.* Oxford: Clarendon, 1981.

Hunter, William A. "First Line of Defense, 1755-56." *Pennsylvania History* 22 (1955): 229-55.

Hutson, James H. "An Investigation of the Inarticulate: Philadelphia's White Oaks." *William and Mary Quarterly: A Magazine of Early American History* 28 (January 1971): 3-25.

———. *Pennsylvania Politics, 1746-1770: The Movement for Royal Government and Its Consequences.* Princeton, NJ: Princeton University Press, 1972.

Jackson, John W. *Fort Mifflin: Valiant Defender of the Delaware.* Philadelphia: Old Fort Mifflin Historical Society Committee, 1986.

———. *The Pennsylvania Navy, 1775-1781: The Defense of the Delaware.* New Brunswick, NJ: Rutgers University Press, 1974.

———. *With the British Army in Philadelphia, 1777-1778.* San Rafael, CA: Presidio, 1979.

Jacobs, Wilbur R. *The Paxton Riots and the Frontier Theory.* Chicago: Rand McNally, 1967.

James, Alfred Procter, and Charles Morse Stotz. *Drums in the Forest.* Pittsburgh: Historical Society of Western Pennsylvania, 1958.

Jennings, Francis. *The Ambiguous Iroquois Empire: The Covenant Chain Confederation of Indian Tribes with the English Colonies from Its Beginnings to the Lancaster Treaty of 1744.* New York: W. W. Norton, 1984.

———. *Empire of Fortune: Crowns, Colonies, and Tribes in the Seven Years War in America.* New York: W.W. Norton, 1988.

———. *The History and Culture of Iroquois Diplomacy: An Interdisciplinary Guide to the Treaties of the Six Nations and Their League.* Syracuse, NY: Syracuse University Press, 1985.

———. *Invasions of America.* Syracuse, NY: Syracuse University Press, 1975.

Jones, Sarah Eve. "Extracts From the Journal of Miss Sarah Eve." *Pennsylvania Magazine of History and Biography* 5 (1881): 19-36, 191-205.

Keen, Gregory B. "The Descendents of Jöran Kyn, the Founder of Upland." *Pennsylvania Magazine of History & Biography* 5 (1881): 85-217, 334-451.

Keith, Charles P. *Chronicles of Pennsylvania from the English Revolution to the Peace Aix-la-Chapelle, 1688-1748.* 2 vols. Philadelphia: privately printed, 1917.

Kent, Donald H. *The French Invasion of Western Pennsylvania, 1753.* Harrisburg: Pennsylvania Historical and Museum Commission, 1991.

Ketchum, Richard M. *The Winter Soldiers.* Garden City, NY: Doubleday, 1973.

Keyser, Peter D. "Memorials of Col. Jehu Eyre." *Pennsylvania Magazine of History and Biography* 3 (1879): 296-425.

Knouff, Gregory T. "'An Arduous Service': The Pennsylvania Backcountry Soldiers' Revolution." *Pennsylvania History* 61 (January 1994): 45-74.

Leach, Douglas Edward. *Roots of Conflict: British Armed Forces and Colonial Americans, 1677-1763.* Chapel Hill: University of North Carolina Press, 1986.

Lenman, Bruce. *Britain's Colonial Wars, 1688-1783.* London: Pearson Education, 2001.

———. *The Jacobite Clans of the Great Glen, 1650-1784.* Aberdeen: Scottish Cultural Press, 1995.

Mahon, John K. *History of the Militia and the National Guard.* New York: Macmillan, 1983.

Maier, Pauline. *From Resistance to Revolution: Colonial Radicals and the Development of American Opposition to Britain, 1765-1776.* New York: W. W. Norton, 1991.

Manders, Eric I. *The Battle of Long Island.* Monmouth Beach, NJ: Philip Freneau, 1978.

———. "Notes on Troop Units in the Flying Camp, 1776." *Military Collector and Historian* 26 (Spring 1974): 9-13.

McCullough, David. *1776.* New York: Simon and Schuster, 2005.

Memoirs of the Gloucester Fox Hunting Club near Philadelphia. Philadelphia: Judah Dobson, 1830.

Mereness, Newton D. *Maryland as a Proprietary Province.* London: Macmillan, 1901.

Merrell, James H. *Into the American Woods: Negotiators on the Pennsylvania Frontier.* New York: W. W. Norton, 1999.

Millett, Alan R., and Peter Maslowski. *For the Common Defense: A Military History of the United States of America.* New York: Free Press, 1984.

Moller, George D. *American Military Shoulder Arms: Colonial and Revolutionary War Arms.* Boulder: University of Colorado Press, 1991.

Moore, Frank. *Songs and Ballads of the American Revolution: With Notes and Illustrations.* New York: D. Appleton, 1856.

Moore, Susan Hardman. *Pilgrims: New World Settlers and the Call of Home.* New Haven, CT: Yale University Press, 2007.

Morgan, Edmund S. *Benjamin Franklin.* New Haven, CT: Yale University Press, 2002.

"The Mount Regale Fishing Company of Philadelphia." *Pennsylvania Magazine of History & Biography* 27 (1903): 88-90.

Nash, Gary B. *Quakers and Politics: Pennsylvania, 1681-1726.* Princeton, NJ: Princeton University Press, 1968.

———. *The Urban Crucible: Social Change, Political Consciousness, and the Origins of the American Revolution.* Cambridge, MA: Harvard University Press, 1979.

Nead, Benjamin M. "A Sketch of General Thomas Procter with Some Account of the First Pennsylvania Artillery in the Revolution." *Pennsylvania Magazine of History and Biography* 4 (1880): 454-70.

Neill, Edward Duffield. "Rev. Jacob Duché: The First Chaplain of Congress." *Pennsylvania Magazine of History and Biography* 2 (1878): 67.

Neimeyer, Charles Patrick. *America Goes to War: A Social History of the Continental Army.* New York: New York University Press, 1996.

Newland, Samuel J. *The Pennsylvania Militia: Defending the Commonwealth and the Nation, 1669-1870.* Annville, PA: Commonwealth of Pennsylvania, Department of Military and Veterans Affairs, 2002.

–––. *The Pennsylvania Militia: The Early Years, 1669-1792.* Annville, PA: Commonwealth of Pennsylvania, Department of Military and Veterans Affairs, 1997.

Offen, Lee. *America's First Marines: Gooch's American Regiment, 1740-1742.* Jacksonville, FL: Fortis, 2010.

Olson, Alison. "The Pamphlet War over the Paxton Boys." *Pennsylvania Magazine of History and Biography* 123 (January/April 1999): 31-56.

O'Meara, Walter Andrew. *Guns at the Forks.* Englewoods Cliffs, NJ: Prentice-Hall, 1965.

Palmer, John McAuley. *America in Arms: The Experience of the United States with Military Organization.* New Haven, CT: Yale University Press, 1941.

Paret, Peter. *Yorck and the Era of the Prussian Reform, 1807-1815.* Princeton, NJ: Princeton University Press, 1966.

Parkman, Francis. *Montcalm and Wolfe: The French and Indian War.* Boston: Little, Brown, 1884. Reprint, New York: Da Capo, 1995.

Peckham, Howard Henry. *The Colonial Wars, 1689-1762.* Chicago: University of Chicago Press, 1964.

Pennypacker, Samuel. "The Settlement of Germantown, PA and the Causes Which Led to It," *Pennsylvania Magazine of History and Biography* 4 (1880): 1-58.

Porter, William A. "A Sketch of the Life of General Andrew Porter." *Pennsylvania Magazine of History and Biography* 4 (1880): 263-301.

Prowell, George R. *History of York County, Pennsylvania.* 2 vols. Chicago: J. H. Beers, 1907.

Rappaport, George David. *Stability and Change in Revolutionary Pennsylvania: Banking, Politics, and Social Structure.* University Park: Pennsylvania State University Press, 1996.

Rawle, William Henry. "Col. Lambert Cadwalader: A Sketch." *Pennsylvania Magazine of History and Biography* 10 (1886): 1-14.

Rediker, Marcus. *Between the Devil and the Deep Blue Sea: Merchant Seamen, Pirates, and the Anglo-American Maritime World, 1700-1750.* Cambridge: Cambridge University Press, 1987.

Reed, William B. *President Reed of Pennsylvania: A Reply to Mr. George Bancroft and Others.* Philadelphia: Howard Challen, 1867.

"Restoration of the Schuylkill Gun to the 'State in Schuylkill,' April 23d, 1884." *Pennsylvania Magazine of History and Biography* 8 (1884): 199-215.

Richter, Daniel K. *The Ordeal of the Longhouse: The Peoples of the Iroquois League in the Era of European Colonization.* Chapel Hill: University of North Carolina Press, 1992.

Rogers, Fairman, William Camac, M. Edward Rogers, A. Loudon Snowden, Joseph R. Wilkins Jr., James M. MacDowell, Joseph Lapsley Wilson, and William D. Gemmill, eds. *History of the First Troop Philadelphia City Cavalry from Its Organization November 17, 1774, to Its Centennial Anniversary, November 17, 1874.* Philadelphia: Hallowell, 1909.

Rosswurm, Steven. *Arms, Country, and Class: The Philadelphia Militia and the "Lower Sort" during the American Revolution, 1775-1783.* New Brunswick, NJ: Rutgers University Press, 1987.

Rothenberg, Gunther E. *The Art of Warfare in the Age of Napoleon.* Bloomington: Indiana University Press, 1978.

Royster, Charles. *A Revolutionary People at War: The Continental Army and American Character, 1775-1783.* Published for the Institute of Early American History and Culture, Williamsburg, Virginia. Chapel Hill, NC: University of North Carolina Press, 1979.

Ryerson, Richard Alan. *The Revolution Is Now Begun: The Radical Committees of Philadelphia, 1765-1776.* Philadelphia: University of Pennsylvania Press, 1978.

Scharf, John Thomas, and Thompson Westcott. *History of Philadelphia.* 3 vols. Philadelphia: L. H. Everts, 1884.

Schlegel, Philip J. *Recruits to Continentals: A History of the York County Rifle Company, June 1775-January 1777.* York, PA: York County Historical Society, 1979.

Sellers, Horace Wells. "Charles Willson Peale, Artist-Soldier." *Pennsylvania Magazine of History and Biography* 38 (1914): 257-286.

Shea, William L. *The Virginia Militia in the Seventeenth Century.* Baton Rouge: Louisiana State University Press, 1983.

Shomette, Donald G. *Pirates on the Chesapeake: Being a True History of Pirates, Picaroons, and Raiders on Chesapeake Bay, 1610-1807.* Centreville, MD: Tidewater, 1985.

Shy, John. *Toward Lexington: The Role of the British Army in the Coming of the American Revolution.* Princeton, NJ: Princeton University Press, 1965.

Silver, Peter. *Our Savage Neighbors: How Indian War Transformed Early America.* New York: W. W. Norton, 2008.

Smith, Billy G. *The "Lower Sort": Philadelphia's Laboring People, 1750-1800.* Ithaca, NY: Cornell University Press, 1990.

Smith, Samuel Stelle. *The Battle of Princeton.* Monmouth Beach, NJ: Philip Freneau, 1967.

Spaulding, Oliver L., Sr. "The Military Studies of George Washington," *The American Historical Review* (July 1924): 675-680.

Spengler, Edward W. *The Annals of the Families of Caspar, Henry, Baltzer, and George Spengler, Who Settled in York County Respectively in 1729, 1732, 1732, and 1751, With Biographical and Historical Sketches, and Memorabilia of Contemporaneous Local Events.* York, PA: York Daily Publishing, 1896.

Steele, Ian. K. *Betrayals: Fort William Henry & the "Massacre."* Oxford: Oxford University Press, 1990.

Stilgoe, John R. *Common Landscape of America, 1580 to 1845.* New Haven, CT: Yale University Press, 1982.

Stone, Lawrence. "Prosopography." *Historical Studies Today* (Winter 1971): 46-79.

Stryker, William S. *The Battles of Trenton and Princeton.* Boston: Houghton and Mifflin, 1898.

Swanson, Carl E. *Predators and Prizes: American Privateering and Imperial Warfare, 1739-1748.* Columbia: University of South Carolina Press, 1991.

Swanson, Neil H. *The First Rebel.* New York: Farrar and Rinehart, 1937.

Tousey, Thomas G. *Military History of Carlisle and Carlisle Barracks.* Richmond, VA: Dietz, 1939.

Trussell, John B. B. *The Pennsylvania Line: Regimental Organization and Operations, 1775-1783.* Harrisburg: Pennsylvania Historical and Museum Commission, 1993.

Upton, Emory. *The Military Policy of the United States.* Washington, DC: Government Printing Office, 1904.

Van Doren, Carl. *Benjamin Franklin.* Garden City, NY: Garden City Publishing, 1941.

Waddell, Louis M. and Bruce D. Bomberger. *The French and Indian War in Pennsylvania, 1753-1763: Fortification and Struggle during the War for Empire.* Harrisburg: Pennsylvania Historical and Museum Commission, 1996.

Wainright, Nicholas B. *Paintings and Miniatures at the Historical Society of Pennsylvania.* Philadelphia: Winchell, 1974.

———. *A Philadelphia Story: The Philadelphia Contributionship for the Insurance of Houses from Loss by Fire.* Philadelphia: William F. Fell, 1952.

Walkinshaw, Lewis Clark. *Annals of Southwestern Pennsylvania.* New York: Lewis Historical Publishing, 1939.

Wallace, John William. *An Old Philadelphian: Colonel William Bradford, the Patriot Printer of 1776: Sketches of His Life.* Philadelphia: Sherman, 1884.

Wallace, Paul A. W. *Indians in Pennsylvania.* Harrisburg: Pennsylvania Historical and Museum Commission, 1961.

Ward, Christopher. *The War of the Revolution.* 2 vols. New York: Macmillan, 1952.

Ward, Matthew C. "An Army of Servants: The Pennsylvania Regiment during the Seven Years' War." *Pennsylvania Magazine of History & Biography* 119 (January/April 1995): 75-93.

———. *Breaking the Backcountry: The Seven Years' War in Virginia and Pennsylvania, 1754-1765.* Pittsburgh: University of Pittsburgh Press, 2003.

Ward, Townsend. "South Second Street and Its Associations." *Pennsylvania Magazine of History & Biography* 5 (1881): 42-60.

Warner, Sam Bass, Jr. *The Private City: Philadelphia in Three Periods of Its Growth.* Philadelphia: University of Pennsylvania Press, 1968.

Watson, John F. *Annals of Philadelphia and Pennsylvania, In the Olden Time; Being a Collection of Memoirs, Anecdotes, and Incidents of the City and its Inhabitants, and of the Earliest Settlements of the Inland Part of Pennsylvania, From the Days of the Founders.* 3 vols. Philadelphia: Elijah Thomas, 1860.

West, Jenny. *Gunpowder, Government, and War in the Mid-Eighteenth Century.* Woodbridge, England: Royal Historical Society, Boydell Press, 1991.

Wright, F. Edward. *Abstracts of Philadelphia County Wills.* 4 vols. Westminster, MD: Family Line Publications, 1998.

Wright, Robert K., Jr. *The Continental Army.* Washington, DC: United States Army Center of Military History, United States Army, 1983.

———. "'Spark of Genius': Bernhard Wilhelm von Wiederhold and His Maps." *The Hessians: Journal of the Johannes Schwalm Historical Association* 12 (2009): 1-28.

Zelner, Kyle F. *A Rabble in Arms: Massachusetts Towns and Militiamen during King Philip's War.* New York: New York University Press, 2009.

NEWSPAPERS

Pennsylvania Evening Post, January 24, 1775-October 26, 1784.

Pennsylvania Gazette, March 3, 1729-June 30, 1777.

South Carolina Gazette, June 17, 1756.

Virginia Gazette, January 9, 1746-June 14, 1776.

Acknowledgments

On a Monday night many years ago, a man approached me at a cocktail party in Philadelphia and asked me about my work. My interest at the time centered on Philadelphia's maritime history, and I told him as much. He then asked me many other questions, some of which I knew the answers to and many of which I did not, but all revolving around the matter of who originally manned the forts on the Delaware River prior to and during the Revolutionary War. At the end of the conversation, he asked me to find out what I could about the forts' garrisons, handed me his business card, introduced himself as the Pennsylvania Army National Guard Command historian, and bade me good evening. So began my friendship with Craig Nannos—and my study of the Philadelphia Artillery, which he has been instrumental in fostering.

What originally began as a search for those garrisons soon grew into a search for the organization of all of the Pennsylvania Associators. That investigation introduced me to author and noted collector Herman O. Benninghoff, who taught me one of the foremost principles of organizational history—that one must strive not to find the whole picture but to connect the dots with the evidence that comes to light.

At the National Guard Bureau in Washington, DC, Lieutenant Colonel Leonid Kondratiuk introduced me to the basics of army lineage, as did Dr. Robert K. Wright Jr. at the U.S. Army Center of Military History, also in the nation's capital. These two men have taught me more about the study of organizational history than anyone else, and they have provided me with innumerable tidbits of information and outright revelations about army history. Many of the insights in this book are theirs, for which I return my sincere gratitude.

Historian Dr. Samuel Newland generously shared his knowledge of Pennsylvania military history and kindly included my research in his two publications on the early history of the Pennsylvania Army National Guard. Stephen Wood at the Scottish United Services Museum at Edinburgh Castle encouraged my work and wrote me letters of introduction that provided me an internship with the Royal Scots Dragoon Guards (Carabiniers and Greys), an unforgettable experience that exposed me firsthand to the British regimental system, helped me learn about the early military career of John Forbes, and, by no means the least significant thing, taught me the importance of having fun with my studies.

At Temple University, the late Dr. Russell F. Weigley encouraged my research and graciously overlooked my bloated prose and sloppy scholarship. My thesis adviser, Dr. Gregory Urwin, did not, and in the process gave me a first-rate education in writing and scholarly research, for which I am grateful. I have found his mentorship, wisdom, and good-natured criticism invaluable over the years and thank him for sparing neither his time nor the red ink on my project.

I would like to thank Glenn F. Williams at the U.S. Army Center of Military History for encouraging my work, and for introducing me to my editor and publisher, Bruce H. Franklin, who has provided much useful commentary and valuable advice. I would also like to thank my copy editor, Ron Silverman, for making the manuscript a better product than I ever could have on my own and Trudi Gershenov for her striking jacket design.

Several other individuals were instrumental in the preparation of this manuscript. At Independence National Historical Park, Bob Giannini took time out from his busy schedule to show me two items that took my research in a new direction. The first, a 1774 report, recorded Robert Jewell's tragic accident while firing a cannon. The second item was a set of excavated Associator buttons that had inexplicably found their way to the bottom of a Philadelphia privy pit. Bob's colleague, Jed Levin, kindly photographed those buttons, which are some of the few surviving personal artifacts that can be traced back to the Associators. What had begun as a search for their existence gradually morphed into a quest to discover what motivated the Associators to do what they did.

Bruce Bazelon, Rex Kessler, Eric Manders, and Peter Schmidt, gave enormously of their expertise and knowledge on Pennsylvania military culture. Norris V. Claytor and Dennis Boylan provided vital moral support and wisdom, as well as insight into Philadelphia's social networks. Jennifer A. Nichols read numerous drafts and patiently endured endless monologues on the Associators, as did Mark Reardon. Jim Mullins, Tom McGuire, and Rebecca Raines were invaluable supporters and contributors to this project.

I salute the members of the Corps of the 1st Regiment and the First Troop Philadelphia City Cavalry for their service and fellowship, the latter in particular for letting me ride as one of them in their ranks. To James Wharton go my thanks for his timely and invaluable technical assistance. Finally, I would like to thank my family, especially my parents, David and Anna Seymour, for filling my childhood home with books and countless visits to old houses, ships, and forts that inspired an early and enduring interest in things past. And my wife, Johanna, for her unflagging patience, love, and support.

Index

University of Pennsylvania, 112
Updegraff, Herman, 67

Vanderspiegle, William, 83, 86, 102
Vernon, Edward, 32-33, 32
Voltaire, 142
von Knyphausen, Wilhelm
    Freiherr, 160-161

Wade, Francis, 130
Walking Purchase (1737), 100
Ward, Edward, 62
Ward, Henry, 93
War of Austrian Succession, 40,
    56-57, 122, 182
War of Jenkins' Ear, 25-26, 32
Wars of the Three Kingdoms, 2
Washington, George
    army's headquarters at
        Newtown and, 164
    Associator Artillery and, 180
    Battle of Trenton and, 169
    building fort at Great Meadows
        and, 63
    casualties and, 174
    competent boat handlers and,
        165-166
    crossing the Delaware River and,
        163
    defense of ports and, 158
    Edward Hand and, 186
    flanking movement around
        Cornwallis's main force
        and, 172
    Flying Camp rotations and, 157
    founding of Continental Army
        and, xxi
    Lancelot Théodore Turpin de
        Crissé and, 149
    Matthias Alexis de Roche de
        Fermoy and, 171
    Nathanael Greene and, 159
    Philadelphia Light Horse and,
        175
    rejection of Dinwiddie's terms
        and, 62
    review of Philadelphia
        Associator commands and,
        181, 202

Robert Hunter Morris and, 68
specialist troops and, 182
strength of army and, 170
supply of cannon and, 152
Thompson's battalion of rifle-
    men and, 156
victories at Trenton and
    Princeton, 178
Watkins, Jane, 119
Watkins, Joseph, 30, 119
Watson, John Fanning, xviii, 177-
    178, 187
Wayne, Anthony, 185-186
Weiser, Conrad, 14, 19, 24, 70-71,
    75, 195
Welsh Quakers, 103
Westmoreland County
    Association, 132
Wharton, Thomas, 128, 131, 147,
    164, 200
Whigs, 119, 122, 126, 141, 183
Whitefield, George, 44, 46, 119-
    120
Willet, Austin, 142
Williams, William, 142
Willing, Thomas, 114, 196
Will, William, 130
Wilson, James, 132, 150, 202
Windmill Island, 26, 51
Wolfe, James, 97
Wolf, Michael, 132
Wood, John, 18
Worrel, James, 63-64
Wright, Aaron, 142, 156
Wright, Richard, 98
Wright, Thomas, 95

York Associators, 86, 132, 145-146
York Blues, 124-125
York County Associators, 95, 147,
    152, 159
York County Committee of Safety,
    132
York Rangers, 187
York Rifles, 186
Youghiogheny River, 100
Young, James, 76

Ziegler, David, 188